THE JACK-ROLLER

THE JACK-ROLLER

A DELINQUENT BOY'S
OWN STORY

by CLIFFORD R. SHAW

with a new introduction by
Howard S. Becker

Phoenix Books

THE UNIVERSITY OF CHICAGO PRESS   CHICAGO & LONDON

THE UNIVERSITY OF CHICAGO PRESS, CHICAGO 60637
The University of Chicago Press, Ltd., London

Originally published 1930 · First Phoenix Edition 1966 · Seventh Impression 1974

Printed in the United States of America

International Standard Book Number: 0-226-75126-0
Library of Congress Catalog Card Number: 66-23698

INTRODUCTION

HOWARD S. BECKER

The Jack-Roller was first published in 1930 and has enjoyed a continuing and well-deserved popularity ever since. It was not the first published sociological life history. That honor goes to the documents published by Thomas and Znaniecki in *The Polish Peasant*.[1] But it was the first of a series to be published by Clifford Shaw and his associates, and was followed by *The Natural History of a Delinquent Career* and *Brothers in Crime*. During the same period, Edwin Sutherland published the still popular *Professional Thief*. And similar documents have been published occasionally since, most recently *The Fantastic Lodge* and *Hustler*.[2]

The life history is not conventional social science "data," although it has some of the features of that kind of fact, being an attempt to gather material useful in the formulation of general sociological theory. Nor is it a conventional autobiography, although it shares with autobiography its narrative form, its first-person point of view and its frankly subjective stance. It is certainly not fiction, although the best life history documents have a sensitivity and pace, a dramatic urgency, that any novelist would be glad to achieve.

I wish to thank Blanche Geer, Morris Janowitz, Henry McKay, and Stanton Wheeler for their comments on an earlier version of this introduction. In addition, I am grateful to my colleagues in the Sociology Department of Northwestern University, who devoted a faculty seminar to discussion of an earlier draft.

[1] W. I. Thomas and Florian Znaniecki, *The Polish Peasant in Europe and America* (2d ed., New York, 1927), II, 1931–2244.

[2] Clifford R. Shaw, *The Natural History of a Delinquent Career* (Chicago, 1931), and *Brothers in Crime* (Chicago, 1936); Chic Conwell and Edwin H. Sutherland, *The Professional Thief* (Chicago, 1937); Helen MacGill Hughes (ed.), *The Fantastic Lodge* (Boston, 1961); Henry Williamson, *Hustler*, edited by R. Lincoln Keiser (Garden City, N.Y., 1965).

The differences between these forms lie both in the perspective from which the work is undertaken and in the methods used. The writer of fiction is not, of course, concerned with fact at all, but rather with dramatic and emotional impact, with form and imagery, with the creation of a symbolic and artistically unified world. Fidelity to the world as it exists is only one of many problems for him, and for many authors it is of little importance.

The autobiographer proposes to explain his life to us and thus commits himself to maintaining a close connection between the story he tells and what an objective investigation might discover. When we read autobiography, however, we are always aware that the author is telling us only part of the story, that he has selected his material so as to present us with the picture of himself he would prefer us to have and that he may have ignored what would be trivial or distasteful to him, though of great interest to us.

As opposed to these more imaginative and humanistic forms, the life history is more down to earth, more devoted to our purposes than those of the author, less concerned with artistic values than with a faithful rendering of the subject's experience and interpretation of the world he lives in. The sociologist who gathers a life history takes steps to ensure that it covers everything we want to know, that no important fact or event is slighted, that what purports to be factual squares with other available evidence and that the subject's interpretations are honestly given. The sociologist keeps the subject oriented to the questions sociology is interested in, asks him about events that require amplification, tries to make the story told jibe with matters of official record and with material furnished by others familiar with the person, event, or place being described. He keeps the game honest for us.

In so doing, he pursues the job from his own perspective, a perspective which emphasizes the value of the person's "own story." This perspective differs from that of some other social scientists in assigning major importance to the interpretations people place on their experience as an explanation for behavior. To understand why someone behaves as he does you must understand how it looked to him, what he thought he had to contend with, what alternatives he saw open to him; you can only understand the effects of opportunity structures, delinquent subcultures, social norms, and other commonly invoked explanations of behavior by seeing them from the actor's point of view.

The University of Chicago sociology department promoted this perspective vigorously during the 1920's. Almost every study made some use of personal documents. Theoretically grounded in Mead's social psychology, its practicality in research attested by *The Polish Peasant,* and its use persuasively urged by Ernest W. Burgess, the life history enjoyed great popularity. It was one of the many research devices that found a place in the overall research scheme of the department.

The research scheme did not grow out of a well-developed axiomatic theory, but rather from a vision of the character of cities and city life which permeated much of the research done at Chicago in the exciting period after the arrival of Robert E. Park in 1916. *The Ghetto, The Gold Coast and the Slum, The Gang*[3]—all these were part of the research scheme. And so were the ecological studies of the succession of ethnic groups in Chicago and of the distribution of juvenile delinquency, mental illness, and other forms of pathology. Park enunciated the general scheme, as it developed, in occasional papers on the nature of the city and the role of communication in social life, and in introductions to the books his students produced. Everything was material for the developing theory. And studies of all kinds, done by a variety of methods, contributed to its development.[4] The contribution of any study could thus be evaluated in the context of the total enterprise, not as though it stood alone.

When I first went to San Francisco several years ago and

[3] Louis Wirth, *The Ghetto* (Chicago, 1928); Harvey W. Zorbaugh, *The Gold Coast and the Slum: A Sociological Study of Chicago's Near North Side* (Chicago, 1929); Frederic M. Thrasher, *The Gang: A Study of 1,313 Gangs in Chicago* (Chicago, 1928).

[4] See Everett C. Hughes' account of this "great movement of social investigation" in "Robert Park," *New Society* (December 31, 1964), 18–19; and Robert E. Park, *Human Communities* (Glencoe, Ill., 1952).

began to think about doing research there, I automatically began looking for the Local Community Fact Book, the demographic studies, the analyses of neighborhoods and institutions, and all the other kinds of background material I had come to take for granted when I worked in Chicago. But they were not there; no one had done them. Perhaps it is because no one group of researchers had ever existed there as well organized as the group that got its start under Park during the twenties. That group saw connections between all the various problems they were working on. Above all, they saw that the things they were studying had close and intimate connections with the city, considered in the abstract, and with Chicago itself, the particular city they were working in. For the Chicago group, whatever the particular subject matter under study, the researcher assumed that it took its character in part from the unique character and form of the city it occurred in. He relied, implicitly and explicitly, on the knowledge that had already been gathered, as he contributed his own small piece to the mosaic of the theory of the city and knowledge of Chicago that Park was building.

The image of the mosaic is useful in thinking about such a scientific enterprise. Each piece added to a mosaic adds a little to our understanding of the total picture. When many pieces have been placed we can see, more or less clearly, the objects and the people in the picture and their relation to one another. Different pieces contribute different things to our understanding: some are useful because of their color, others because they make clear the outline of an object. No one piece has any great job to do; if we do not have its contribution, there are still other ways to come to an understanding of the whole.

Individual studies can be like pieces of mosaic and were so in Park's day. Since the picture in the mosaic was Chicago, the research had an ethnographic, "case history" flavor, even though Chicago itself was seen as somehow representative of all cities. Whether its data were census figures or interviews, questionnaire results or life histories, the research took into account local peculiarities, exploring those things that were distinctively true of Chicago in the 1920's. In so doing, they partially completed a mosaic of great complexity and detail, with the city itself the subject, a "case" which could be used to test a great variety of theories and in which the interconnections of a host of seemingly unrelated phenomena could be seen, however imperfectly.

Our attention today is turned away from local ethnography, from the massing of knowledge about a single place, its parts, and their connections. We emphasize abstract theory-building more than we used to. The national survey is frequently used as a basic mode of data collection. Above all, researchers are increasingly mobile, moving from city to city and university to university every few years, building no fund of specialized local knowledge and passing none on to their students. The trend is away from the community study—there will be no more elaborate programs of coordinated study such as those that produced the *Yankee City Series*[5] or *Black Metropolis*.[6] And a great loss it will be.

In any case, the scientific contribution of *The Jack-Roller* can be assessed properly only by seeing it in relation to all the studies done under Park's direction, for it drew on and depended on all of them, just as all the later studies of that Golden Age of Chicago sociology depended, a little, on it. Much of the background that any single study would either have to provide in itself or, even worse, about which it would have to make unchecked assumptions, was already at hand for the reader of *The Jack-Roller*. When Stanley speaks of the boyish games of stealing he and his pals engaged in, we know that we can find an extensive and penetrating description of that phenomenon in Thrasher's *The Gang*. And when he speaks of the time he spent on West Madison Street, we know that we can turn to Nels Anderson's *The Hobo*[7] for an understanding of the milieu Stanley then found himself in. If we are concerned about the representativeness of Stanley's case, we have only to turn to the ecological studies carried on by Shaw and McKay[8] to see the

[5] Published in several volumes by W. Lloyd Warner and his collaborators.

[6] St. Clair Drake and Horace Cayton, *Black Metropolis* (New York, 1945).

[7] Nels Anderson, *The Hobo* (Chicago, 1923).

[8] Clifford R. Shaw and Henry D. McKay, *Juvenile Delinquency and Urban Areas* (Chicago, 1942).

same story told on a grand scale in mass statistics. And, similarly, if one wanted to understand the maps and correlations
contained in ecological studies of delinquency, one could then
turn to *The Jack-Roller* and similar documents for that understanding.

I am not sure what the criteria are by which one judges the
contribution of a piece of scientific work considered in its total
context, but I know that they are not such currently fashionable
criteria as are implied by the model of the controlled experiment.
We do not expect, in a large and differentiated program of
research, that any one piece of work will give us all the answers
or, indeed, all of any one answer. What must be judged is the
entire research enterprise in all its parts. (One can, of course,
assess *The Jack-Roller* by the criteria appropriate to life histories, perhaps those suggested by Kluckhohn, Angell and
Dollard.)[9] Criteria have yet to be established for determining
how much one piece of a mosaic contributes to the conclusions
that are warranted by consideration of the whole, but these are
just the kind of criteria that are needed. In their place, we can
temporarily install a sympathetic appreciation of some of the
functions performed by the kind of work represented by *The
Jack-Roller*.

What are some of the functions that can be usefully performed by a life history document? In the first place, *The Jack-
Roller* can serve as a touchstone with which to evaluate theories
that purport to deal with phenomena like those of Stanley's
delinquent career. Whether it is a theory of the psychological
origins of delinquent behavior, a theory of the roots of delinquency in juvenile gangs, or an attempt to explain the distribution of delinquency throughout a city, any theory of
delinquency must, if it is to be considered valid, explain or at
least be consistent with the facts of Stanley's case as they are
reported here. Thus, even though the life history does not in

[9] Clyde Kluckhohn, "The Personal Document in Anthropological Science," in
Louis Gottschalk *et al., The Use of Personal Documents in History, Anthropology,
and Sociology* (New York, 1945), pp. 79–173; Robert Angell, "A Critical Review
of the Development of the Personal Document Method in Sociology 1920–1940,"
ibid., pp. 177–232; John Dollard, *Criteria for the Life History* (New Haven, 1932).

itself provide definitive proof of a proposition, it can be a negative case that forces us to decide a proposed theory is inadequate.

To say this is to take an approach to scientific generalization that deserves some comment. We may decide to accept a theory if it explains, let us say, 95 per cent of the cases that fall in its jurisdiction. Many reputable scientists do. In contrast, one can argue that any theory that does not explain all cases is inadequate, that other factors than those the theory specifies must be operating to produce the result we want to explain. It is primarily a question of strategy. If we assume that exceptions to any rule are a normal occurrence, we will perhaps not search as hard for further explanatory factors as we otherwise might. But if we regard exceptions as potential negations of our theory, we will be spurred to search for them.[10]

More importantly, the negative case will respond to careful analysis by suggesting the direction the search should take.[11] Inspection of its features will reveal attributes which differ from those of otherwise similar cases, or processes at work whose steps have not all been fully understood. If we know the case in some detail, as a life history document allows us to know it, our search is more likely to be successful; it is in this sense that the life history is a useful theoretical touchstone.

The life history also helps us in areas of research that touch on it only tangentially. Every piece of research crosses frontiers into new terrain it does not explore thoroughly, areas important to its main concern in which it proceeds more by assumption than investigation.[12] A study of a college, for instance, may make assumptions (indeed, must make them) about the char-

[10] See, for instance, George H. Mead, "Scientific Method and Individual Thinker," in John Dewey, et al., Creative Intelligence (New York, 1917), pp. 176–227, and Alfred Lindesmith, Opiate Addiction (Bloomington, 1947), pp. 5–20. Lindesmith turns the strategy into a systematic method of inquiry usually referred to as analytic induction.

[11] See, for a similar view growing out of the tradition of survey research, Patricia L. Kendall and Katherine M. Wolf, "The Analysis of Deviant Cases in Communications Research," in Paul F. Lazarsfeld and Frank Stanton (eds.), Communications Research 1948–1949 (New York, 1949), pp. 152–79.

[12] See Max Gluckman (ed.), Closed Systems and Open Minds (Chicago, 1964).

acter of the city, state, and region it is located in, about the social class background and experience of its students, and about a host of other matters likely to influence the operation of the school and the way it affects students. A study of a mental hospital or prison will make similarly unchecked assumptions about the character of the families whose members end up in the institution. A life history—although it is not the only kind of information that can do this—provides a basis on which those assumptions can be realistically made, a rough approximation of the direction in which the truth lies.

In addition to these matters of neighboring fact, so to speak, the life history can be particularly useful in giving us insight into the subjective side of much-studied institutional processes, about which unverified assumptions are also often made. Sociologists have lately been concerned with processes of adult socialization and, to take an instance to which Stanley's case is directly relevant, with the processes of degradation and "stripping" associated with socialization into rehabilitative institutions such as prisons and mental hospitals.[13] Although the theories concern themselves with institutional action rather than individual experience, they either assume something about the way people experience such processes or at least raise a question about the nature of that experience. Although Stanley's prison experiences do not, of course, provide fully warranted knowledge of these matters, they give us some basis for making a judgment.

The life history, by virtue again of its wealth of detail, can be important at those times when an area of study has grown stagnant, has pursued the investigation of a few variables with ever-increasing precision but has received dwindling increments of knowledge from the pursuit. When this occurs, investigators might well proceed by gathering personal documents which suggest new variables, new questions, and new processes, using the rich though unsystematic data to provide a needed reorientation of the field.

[13] Harold Garfinkel, "Conditions of Successful Degradation Ceremonies," *American Journal of Sociology,* 61 (1956): 420–24; and Erving Goffman, *Asylums* (Garden City, N.Y., 1961), pp. 127–69.

Beneath these specific contributions which the life history is capable of making lies one more fundamental. The life history, more than any other technique except perhaps participant observation, can give meaning to the overworked notion of *process*. Sociologists like to speak of "ongoing processes" and the like, but their methods usually prevent them from seeing the processes they talk about so glibly.

George Herbert Mead, if we take him seriously, tells us that the reality of social life is a conversation of significant symbols, in the course of which people make tentative moves and then adjust and reorient their activity in the light of the responses (real and imagined) others make to those moves. The formation of the individual act is a process in which conduct is continually reshaped to take account of the expectations of others, as these are expressed in the immediate situation and as the actor supposes they may come to be expressed. Collective activity, of the kind pointed to by concepts like "organization" or "social structure," arises out of a continuous process of mutual adjustment of the actions of all the actors involved. Social process, then, is not an imagined interplay of invisible forces or a vector made up of the interaction of multiple social factors, but an observable process of symbolically mediated interaction.[14]

Observable, yes; but not easily observable, at least not for scientific purposes. To observe social process as Mead described it takes a great deal of time. It poses knotty problems of comparability and objectivity in data gathering. It requires an intimate understanding of the lives of others. So social scientists have, most often, settled for less demanding techniques such as the interview and the questionnaire.

These techniques can, I think, tell us much, but only as we are able to relate them to a vision of the underlying Meadian social process we would know had we more adequate data. We can, for instance, give people a questionnaire at two periods

---

[14] See George Herbert Mead, *Mind, Self, and Society* (Chicago, 1934); Herbert Blumer, "Society as Symbolic Interaction," in Arnold Rose (ed.), *Human Behavior and Social Processes* (Boston, 1962), pp. 179–92; and Anselm L. Strauss *et al., Psychiatric Ideologies and Institutions* (New York, 1964), pp. 292–315.

in their life and infer an underlying process of change from the differences in their answers. But our interpretation has significance only if our imagery of the underlying process is accurate. And this accuracy of imagery—this congruence of theoretically posited process with what we could observe if we took the necessary time and trouble—can be partially achieved by the use of life history documents. For the life history, if it is done well, will give us the details of that process whose character we would otherwise only be able to speculate about, the process to which our data must ultimately be referred if they are to have theoretical and not just an operational and predictive significance. It will describe those crucial interactive episodes in which new lines of individual and collective activity are forged, in which new aspects of the self are brought into being. It is by thus giving a realistic basis to our imagery of the underlying process that the life history serves the purposes of checking assumptions, illuminating organization, and reorienting stagnant fields.

But perhaps the most important service performed for sociology by a document like *The Jack-Roller* is one that it also performs for those who are not sociologists. David Riesman has described social science as, in part, a "conversation between the classes."[15] It describes to people the way of life of segments of their society with which they would never otherwise come in contact. The life history, because it is the actor's "own story," is a live and vibrant message from "down there," telling us what it means to be a kind of person we have never met face to face. The United States is fortunate in having fewer barriers, in the form of closed social circles and rules against interaction outside of them, than most societies. Nevertheless, the distances between social classes, between ethnic groups, and between age groups are such that it is hard for most sociologists (let alone others whose work does not push them toward this knowledge) to comprehend what it means to live the life of a Negro junkie or a Polish delinquent.

Johan Galtung suggests the function of this kind of knowledge in the scientific process in his discussion of the causes of the ex-

[15] David Riesman, *Abundance for What* (Garden City, 1965), pp. 493–4.

cessive abstractness and formality of Latin American sociology. He argues that Latin American society is more rigidly stratified, both horizontally and vertically, than the societies of northern Europe and North America. This means that the Latin American, when he comes to sociology, will never have had the informal interaction with members of other classes and social segments that young people in other societies gain through travel, through summer employment, and in similar ways. As a result, Galtung says, preconceived ideas of the character of other members of the society are never put to the test of direct confrontation with social reality:

Sociologists who would never accept the idea that the only thing which has motivated them has been the desire to make money have no difficulty in perceiving the capitalist as interested only in the most money for the least work, or the worker as motivated in a similar manner. A more intimate knowledge of them would invariably reveal shadings, greater identification, greater variety in motives, but the paucity of interaction protects the sociologist from this knowledge. From this comes the great interest in the alienation of the lower classes: without denying its reality, a factor which maintains the image of the alienation of the working class is the alienation of the intellectual himself, with respect to his society in general and certainly with respect to the working class.[16]

By providing this kind of voice from a culture and situation that are ordinarily not known to intellectuals generally, and to sociologists in particular, *The Jack-Roller* enables us to improve our theories at the most profound level: by putting ourselves in Stanley's skin, we can feel and become aware of the deep biases about such people that ordinarily permeate our thinking and shape the kinds of problems we investigate. By truly entering into Stanley's life, we can begin to see what we take for granted (and ought not to) in designing our research—what kinds of assumptions about delinquents, slums, and Poles are embedded in the way we set the questions we study. Stanley's story allows us, if we want to take advantage of it, to begin to ask questions about delinquency from the point of view of the delinquent. If we take Stanley seriously, as his story must impel us to do, we

[16] Johan Galtung, "Los factores socioculturales y el desarrollo de la sociología en América latina," *Revista Latinoamericana de Sociología,* 1 (March, 1965): 87.

might well raise a series of questions that have been relatively little studied—questions about the people who deal with delinquents, the tactics they use, their suppositions about the world, and the constraints and pressures they are subject to. Such studies are only now beginning to be done. Close study of *The Jack-Roller* might provide us with a wide range of questions to put as we begin to look at the dealings of policemen, judges, and jailers with delinquents.

Given the variety of scientific uses to which the life history may be put, one must wonder at the relative neglect into which it has fallen. Sociologists, it is true, have never given it up altogether. But neither have they made it one of their standard research tools. They read the documents available and assign them for their students to read. But they do not ordinarily think of gathering life history documents themselves or of making the technique part of their research approach.

A number of simultaneous changes probably contributed to the increasing disuse of the life history method. Sociologists became more concerned with the development of abstract theory and correspondingly less interested in full and detailed accounts of specific organizations and communities. They wanted data formulated in the abstract categories of their own theories rather than in the categories that seemed most relevant to the people they studied. The life history was well suited to the latter task, but of little immediately apparent use in the former.

At the same time, sociologists began to separate the field of social psychology from that of sociology proper, creating two specialties in place of two emphases within one field, and focused more on "structural" variables and synchronic functional analyses than on those factors that manifested themselves in the life and experience of the person. Again, the life history made a clear contribution to the latter task but seemed unrelated to studies that emphasized group attributes and their interconnections.

But perhaps the major reason for the relatively infrequent use of the technique is that it does not produce the kind of "findings" that sociologists now expect research to produce. As sociology increasingly rigidifies and "professionalizes," more and more emphasis has come to be placed on what we may, for simplicity's sake, call the *single study*. I use the term to refer to research projects that are conceived of as self-sufficient and self-contained, which provide all the evidence one needs to accept or reject the conclusions they proffer, whose findings are to be used as another brick in the growing wall of science—a metaphor quite different than that of the mosaic. The single study is integrated with the main body of knowledge in the following way: it derives its hypotheses from an inspection of what is already known; then, after the research is completed, if those hypotheses have been demonstrated, they are added to the wall of what is already scientifically known and used as the basis for further studies. The important point is that the researcher's hypothesis is either proved or disproved on the basis of what he has discovered in doing that one piece of research.

The customs, traditions, and organizational practices of contemporary sociology conspire to make us take this view of research. The journal article of standard length, the most common means of scientific communication, is made to order for the presentation of findings that confirm or refute hypotheses. The Ph.D. thesis virtually demands that its author have a set of findings, warranted by his own operations, which yield conclusions he can defend before a faculty committee. The research grant proposal, another ubiquitous sociological literary form, pushes its author to state what his project will have proved when the money has been spent.

If we take the single study as the model of scientific work, we will then use, when we judge research and make decisions about how to organize our research, criteria designed to assure us that the findings of our single study do indeed provide a sound basis on which to accept or reject hypotheses. The canons of inference and proof now in vogue reflect this emphasis. Such methodologists as Stouffer, and others who followed him, developed techniques for assessing hypotheses based on the model of the controlled experiment.[17] Compare two groups, those who have been exposed to the effects of a variable and those who have not, before and after the exposure. The multiple comparisons made possible by this technique allow you to test not only your original hypothesis, but also some of the likely alternative explanations of the same results, should they be what you have predicted. This is the approved model. If we cannot achieve it, our study is deficient unless we can devise workable substitutes. If we do achieve it, we can say with assurance that we have produced scientific findings strong enough to bear the weight of still further studies.

Criteria drawn from the experimental model and used to evaluate single studies in isolation, however useful they may be in a variety of contexts, have had one bad by-product. They have led people to ignore the other functions of research and, particularly, to ignore the contribution made by one study to an overall research enterprise even when the study, considered in isolation, produced no definitive results of its own. Since, by these criteria, the life history did not produce definitive results, people have been at a loss to make anything of it and by and large have declined to invest the time and effort necessary to acquire life history documents.

We can perhaps hope that a fuller understanding of the complexity of the scientific enterprise will restore sociologists' sense of the versatility and worth of the life history. A new series of personal documents, like those produced by the Chicago School more than a generation ago, might help us in all the ways I have earlier suggested and in ways, too, that we do not now anticipate.

[17] See the very influential paper by Samuel A. Stouffer, "Some Observations on Study Design," *American Journal of Sociology,* 55 (January, 1950): 355–61, and any of a large number of books and articles on method which take essentially the same position.

CONTENTS

CHAPTER I

VALUE OF DELINQUENT BOY'S OWN STORY

The subject matter of this volume is limited to the case-study of the career of a young male delinquent, to whom we will refer as Stanley. The case is one of a series of two hundred similar studies of repeated male offenders under seventeen years of age, all of whom were on parole from correctional institutions when the studies were made. The author's contact with Stanley has extended over a period of six years, the initial contact having been made when Stanley was sixteen years of age. During this period it has been possible to make a rather intensive study of his behavior and social background and to carry out a somewhat intensive program of social treatment. The case is published to illustrate the value of the "own story" in the study and treatment of the delinquent child. As a preparation for the interpretation of Stanley's life-history, which comprises the major portion of this volume, a brief description of the more general uses of "own story" material, along with illustrations from a number of different cases, is presented in this chapter.

The life-history record is a comparatively new device of sociological research in the field of criminology, although considerable use has been made of such material in other fields. The life-record itself is the delinquent's own account of his experiences, written as an autobiography, as a diary, or presented in the course of a series of interviews. The unique feature of such documents is that they are recorded in the first person, in the boy's own words, and not translated into the language of the person investigating the case. While the use of the life-record requires considerable refinement, it has already demonstrated its value, not only for research into the factors contributing to delinquent conduct, but also for the more practical purposes of social treatment.

Healy and Bronner[1] were among the first students of the prob-

[1] William Healy and Augusta Bronner, *Judge Baker Foundation Case Studies*, Series 1, Cases 1–20.

lem of delinquency to stress the importance of life-history material. In their case studies the child's "own story" is secured as part of the routine investigation, and has proved to be of great value both in the analysis and treatment of their cases. Since the publication of Healy's original studies, Drucker and Hexter, authors of *Children Astray*, have made extensive use of this sort of material, particularly with reference to diagnosis and treatment. W. I. Thomas, in his study of delinquency among girls, has also made considerable use of life-history material. Although the autobiographical excerpts which he presents in *The Unadjusted Girl* are somewhat fragmentary, they are by far the most illuminating materials in the volume.

During recent years a number of interesting and illuminating autobiographies of delinquents have been published.[2] The value of these documents, however, is greatly diminished because of the absence of supplementary case material which might serve as a check on the authenticity of the story and afford a basis for a more reliable interpretation of the experiences and situations described in the documents. As a safeguard against erroneous interpretations of such material, it is extremely desirable to develop the "own story" as an integral part of the total case history. Thus each case study should include, along with the life-history document, the usual family history, the medical, psychiatric, and psychological findings, the official record of arrest, offenses, and commitments, the description of the play-group relationships, and any other verifiable material which may throw light upon the personality and actual experiences of the delinquent in question. In the light of such supplementary material, it is possible to evaluate and interpret more accurately the personal document. It is probable that in the absence of such additional case material any interpretation of the life-history is somewhat questionable.

It should be pointed out, also, that the validity and value of the personal document are not dependent upon its objectivity or veracity. It is not expected that the delinquent will necessarily

[2] Among the more interesting of these autobiographies are: (1) *You Can't Win*, by Jack Black; (2) *Stealing through Life* and (3) *My Life in Prison*, by Ernest Booth; (4) *Lock Step and Corridor*, by Charles L. Clark; and (5) *In the Clutch of Circumstance*, anonymous.

describe his life-situations objectively. On the contrary, it is desired that his story will reflect his own personal attitudes and interpretations, for it is just these personal factors which are so important in the study and treatment of the case. Thus, rationalizations, fabrications, prejudices, exaggerations are quite as valuable as objective descriptions, provided, of course, that these reactions be properly identified and classified. W. I. Thomas states this point very clearly in the following quotation:

There may be, and is, doubt as to the objectivity and veracity of the record, but even the highly subjective record has a value for behavior study. A document prepared by one compensating for a feeling of inferiority or elaborating a delusion of persecution is as far as possible from objective reality, but the subject's view of the situation, how he regards it, may be the most important element for interpretation. For his immediate behavior is closely related to his definition of the situation, which may be in terms of objective reality, or in terms of a subjective appreciation—"as if" it were so. Very often it is the wide discrepancy between the situation as it seems to others and the situation as it seems to the individual that brings about the overt behavior difficulty. To take an extreme example, the warden of Dannemora Prison recently refused to honor the order of the Court to send an inmate outside the prison walls for some specific purpose. He excused himself on the ground that the man was too dangerous. He had killed several persons who had the unfortunate habit of talking to themselves on the street. From the movement of their lips he imagined that they were calling him vile names and he behaved as if this were true. If men define situations as real, they are real in their consequences.[3]

WHAT THE DELINQUENT'S "OWN STORY" REVEALS

In our study and treatment of delinquent boys in Chicago, we have found that the "own story" reveals useful information concerning at least three important aspects of delinquent conduct: (1) the point of view of the delinquent; (2) the social and cultural situation to which the delinquent is responsive; and (3) the sequence of past experiences and situations in the life of the delinquent.

THE DELINQUENT BOY'S POINT OF VIEW

The boy's "own story" is of primary importance as a device for ascertaining the personal attitudes, feelings, and interests of the child; in other words, it shows how he conceives his rôle in rela-

[3] W. I. Thomas and Dorothy Swaine Thomas, *The Child in America* (New York: Alfred A. Knopf, 1928), pp. 571-72.

tion to other persons and the interpretations which he makes of the situations in which he lives. It is in the personal document that the child reveals his feelings of inferiority and superiority, his fears and worries, his ideals and philosophy of life, his antagonisms and mental conflicts, his prejudices and rationalizations. As Burgess has already indicated, "In the life-history is revealed, as in no other way, the inner life of the person, his moral struggles, his successes and failures in securing control of his destiny in a world too often at variance with his hopes and ideals."[4]

Healy has already emphasized the importance of understanding the emotional attitudes, mental conflicts, and the ideational life of the delinquent child. The importance which he attaches to the life-history record in the study of these subjective aspects of delinquent conduct is suggested in the following quotation:

No study of delinquents that is either scientific or practical from the standpoint of treatment can be undertaken without getting at the facts which can only be obtained through the individual's own story well guided by sympathetic questioning. It requires more technical understanding and training than perhaps any other part of the study.

The "own story" affords the only means of acquiring knowledge of many facts concerning outside situations as well as factors in the mental life which may be active elements in producing that which we are studying, namely, the tendency to delinquency. There is a much richer psychology concerned with inner mental life, memories, ideations, imageries, etc., with their emotional backgrounds than is dreamed of during an ordinary examination of a delinquent young person. And this is not material of theoretical or academic interest; it is most useful in its practical bearing upon what ought to be done in the case.

Some of this material is so deeply buried that it requires considerable skill on the part of the inquirer to overcome inhibitions and forgetfulnesses so that underlying fundamental truths of the situation may be brought to the surface.[5]

In order to illustrate the value of the "own story" in the study of the feelings and attitudes of the delinquent, a limited number of excerpts from the life-records of delinquent boys are presented. Case 1 is that of a fourteen-year-old boy who was brought to

[4] E. W. Burgess, "The Family and the Person," *Personality and the Social Group* (Chicago: University of Chicago Press), p. 133.

[5] William Healy and Augusta F. Bronner, *Judge Baker Foundation Case Studies,* Case No. 1, pp. 29a–31a.

the juvenile court repeatedly on charges of habitual truancy from home, picking pockets, and shoplifting. His career in delinquency began at an early age in the form of truancy. While truanting from home he became a member of a gang of older boys who were engaged in shoplifting and picking pockets. In the light of the total case history it appeared that the early truancy from home was directly related to the family situation. As revealed in the following excerpt from the boy's "own story," one important aspect of the situation was the intense emotional attitude of hostility which developed in relation to the stepfather.

Case No. 1.—When I was eight years of age all my troubles started. My father died and I cried and was lonesome for a long time. He was my best friend and stood by me and I could not sleep for thinking about him. I worked with him in the store after school and he gave me things to eat and money and lots of things. I didn't have any brother or sister so he gave me everything.

About five months after he died my mother married another fellow. This fellow came in and started to run my father's store. This fellow had three kids and he brought these kids to my father's house to live. Two of his kids was boys and one was a girl. The boys was three years older than me and the girl was the same age as me.

This fellow told me I was too little to work in the store and his boys would take my place. That made me sore and I went to my mother and she said for me not to say anything. I started to have fights with this fellow and his kids. It made me sore when this fellow let his kids have everything and me nothing.

Everything changed and I started to be sad and unhappy. My mother always took this fellow's part against me. She liked me, but she didn't want to make any trouble with him. I had a fight every day with this fellow and his kids because they got candy in the store and I couldn't get anything.

One day after school I went to the store and started to wait on a customer. This fellow said, "You let Bill [one of his own kids] do that and you get out of here." That made me boil inside and I cussed them, and this fellow chased me and I ran away. I stayed out of the house all night and slept under a neighbor's doorstep. It rained in the night and I got wet and cold. The next morning I didn't go home but went to school and my mother came there to get me. I told her I didn't like anything at home and wouldn't go back. Finally she took me home and this fellow bawled me out and I cussed him again, and then he beat me with a strap for cussing him and running away. Then trouble started for sure.

I wanted to run away but they tied me to the bed. Then this fellow's kids would come along and laugh at me and point their fingers at me. That made me red hot and I started to kick and curse them. This fellow came running into the room from the store and slapped me. Then I began to get afraid of him. He was big and strong and I became so afraid of him that I wouldn't say a word. I started to be lonesome and spend my time away from home. All the time I thought about my father and how things was at home before he died. I hated everything and felt like killing this fellow and his kids. Every day I thought how I could kill them. I couldn't get the idea out of my head. I thought about it at night and all the time when I was by myself. . . . .

Things got worse and I started to stay away from home most of the time. The first time I stayed away one night, then two or three nights and finally a whole month.

When I stayed away a month the police found me and took me to court, but I was sent home. But I couldn't stand it there. Everything made me mad and I felt like killing this fellow, so I ran away many times and was finally sent to the Chicago Parental School. . . . .

I was paroled from the school after five months and was to live at home. I hated them more than ever when I came back. They was the cause of all of my trouble and now they thought I was a criminal. This fellow thought his kids had it all over me. When I saw them in my father's store and eating candy, it made me want to kill somebody. I can't tell you how mad I got at them. I couldn't hold my feelings back. I felt they didn't have any right to have my father's things.

At the end of the first week I had a fight. I refused to sweep out the store when this fellow told me to, and he bawled me out. I couldn't do anything for him because of the way I felt about him, and he made me do the dirtiest work. When I wouldn't clean the store he got sore and started to grab me, but I ducked and ran away. This time I was gone for three months. I didn't want to ever go back. When I was away this time I got in with two guys downtown and they started me in to picking pockets and making the stores (shoplifting) in the Loop. . . . .

The following case is presented to further illustrate the value of the "own story" in the study of personal attitudes. This short excerpt reveals the boy's attitudes toward his own delinquent experiences. From his own point of view his delinquencies assume the character of a very stimulating and fascinating game.

Case No. 2.—Every morning the bunch would come past my home about school time. We left home at this time to make our parents think we were going to school. It was easy for me for my mother was working and didn't know much about me. We would sneak a ride on the elevated railway, climbing up the structure to the station, to the Loop. After getting downtown, we would make the round of the big stores. If we couldn't steal enough candy and canned goods for lunch, we would go without lunch. I do not know of anything else that interested me enough to go without a meal but "making the big stores" did. I do not know whether a good thrashing would have cured me or not, as I never received one for stealing, just the one my father gave me when he was mad. But anyway the shoplifting experiences were alluring, exciting, and thrilling. But underneath I kind of knew that I was sort of a social outcast when I stole. But yet I was in the grip of the bunch and led on by the enticing pleasure which we had together. There was no way out. The feeling of guilt which I had could not overbalance the strong appeal of my chums and shoplifting. At first I did not steal for gain nor out of necessity for food. I stole because it was the most fascinating thing I could do. It was a way to pass the time, for I think I had a keener adventurous spirit than the other boys of my age, sort of more mentally alert. I didn't want to play tame games nor be confined in a schoolroom. I wanted something more exciting. I liked the dare-devil spirit. I would walk down between the third rails on the elevated lines in the same daring spirit that I stole. It gave me a thrill, and thrilled my chums in turn. We were all alike, daring and glad to take a chance.

When we were shoplifting we always made a game of it. For example, we might gamble on who could steal the most caps in a day, or who could steal caps from the largest number of stores in a day, or could steal in the presence of a detective and then get away. We were always daring each other that way and thinking up new schemes. This was the best part of the game. I would go into a store to steal a cap, be trying one on, and when the clerk was not watching walk out of the store, leaving the old cap. With the new cap on my head I would go into another store, do the same thing as in the other store, getting a new hat and leave the one I had taken from the other place. I might do this all day and have one hat at night. It was the fun I wanted, not the hat. I kept this up for months and then began to sell the things to a man on the West Side. It was at this time that I began to steal for gain.

THE DELINQUENT'S SOCIAL WORLD

A second aspect of the problem of delinquency which may be studied by means of the "own story" is the social and cultural world in which the delinquent lives. It is undoubtedly true that the delinquent behavior of the child cannot be understood and explained apart from the cultural and social context in which it occurred. By means of personal documents it is possible to study not only the traditions, customs, and moral standards of neighborhoods, institutions, families, gangs, and play groups, but the manner in which these cultural factors become incorporated into the behavior trends of the child. The life-record discloses also the more intimate, personal situations in which the child is living; that is, the attitudes, gestures, and activities of the persons with whom he has intimate contact. With reference to this point, Thomas states:

Perhaps the greatest importance of the behavior document is the opportunity it affords to observe the attitudes of other persons as behavior-forming influences, since the most important situations in the development of personality are the attitudes and values of other persons.[6]

The following case is presented to illustrate the use of the boy's "own story" in the study of behavior problems in their relation to the social relationships within the family group. Although this excerpt constitutes only a small part of the total case history, it reveals important aspects of the family situation. Since it is not possible to present the complete case-study, it may be stated that the boy's "own story" is confirmed by verifiable material obtained from independent sources. This fourteen-year-old boy was referred to a child-study clinic because of much petty stealing in the neighborhood, sex practices, repeated truancy from home, indifference to schoolwork, and frequent conflicts with his father. Investigation of the case revealed an intense emotional conflict between the father and mother. This conflict, which was probably directly related to the behavior problems in the case, is vividly described in the following short excerpt from the boy's "own story."

Case No. 3.—There has always been trouble in our family as long as I can remember. My father and mother quarrel and find fault with each other over almost everything. Most of the time my father nags and finds fault with my mother. He nags about her friends, what she reads, her religious ideas and opinions, the way she dresses and talks, just about everything that she does. He says to her, "Why do you go out with such and such a person, she's dumb," "Why do you read novels and newspapers and cheap trash instead of fundamental books like Wells, *Outline of History*, and the *Book of Knowledge*," "You wear too flashy clothes," "Your ideas are dumb and show you are not well read," "You're too sentimental and emotional about things, be more rational," etc. When he says these things it starts a quarrel. After the quarrel my mother cries and begs his pardon and everything is all right for a while. I can't remember any time that they didn't have quarrels like these. . . . .

[6] W. I. Thomas and Dorothy Swaine Thomas, *The Child in America* (New York: Alfred A. Knopf), p. 571.

My dad is very peculiar and not like any other man I have ever known. He is one-sided in his opinions and very dogmatic. He always insists that he is right although he is proved wrong. He is proud of himself, but he is very critical of people and always finds fault with what they say or do. But if any-one should criticize him there is trouble, he doesn't like it. He wants you to do everything just as he says, and sets himself up as a model. He is precise and particular about how he talks and the way he dresses. Once when I started to wash in warm water after he had told me to use cold water, he got mad and grabbed me by the throat with one hand, and started to hit me with the other but my mother took my part and then he got mad at her and told her to mind her own affairs. . . . .

I can't figure him out, so I just accept him at face value and let it go at that. He is sarcastic and belittles me in every way. He calls me "a giddy goat," "a silly ass," "a bad egg," and makes remarks about my dumness and says I have a "child's mind." And the looks he can give you! He makes you feel miserable by just his peculiar, synical expression. He doesn't approve of anything I do. My friends are all "bad characters and thieves," I read "trashy books," I'm not "dependable or truthful," I'm "vulgar," go to "cheap shows," "have too much interest in girls," "can't grasp fundamental things," "have wrong ideas about religion and everything." He thinks everything about me is wrong.

Everything will be nice in the house until my dad comes home from work, then the atmosphere changes. It soon feels like a morgue. He's cold and synical and turns up his nose at everything. If I say a word about something that happened at school or read in the newspaper, he'll look at me as if to say, "Oh, is that all you've got to talk about? Why don't you get interested in something worth while?" So soon the whole atmosphere is changed and we just sit at the table without saying a word. If there is conversation it's always an argument and dad has to be right or there's trouble. . . . .

My mother is altogether different from my dad. She is sympathetic and patient. If I do a wrong she scolds like most mothers, but in a nice way. She confides in me and even talks to me about her trouble with dad. She takes my part against him. I usually go out to shows with my mother. The whole family doesn't do things together very often. Usually my dad works or reads, my brother works in his shop and mother and I go out together. She tells me that she has always had trouble with dad and that when my brother and me get out of school we will leave him. The trouble with the situation is that neither side ever gets together. My mother is religious and wants to go to church, but my dad objects and won't let her go. He thinks he is too intelligent to be religious. She likes movies and novels but he refuses to let her enjoy these things. . . . .

Now to discuss the last but not least member of the family, my brother. He is altogether different from me not only in looks but in disposition. He generally sides with both my father and my mother so as to be safe. I have learned through painful expirance that this is a wise thing to do. Our tastes do not agree with each other except in the picking of girls. He doesn't like to work very well except at the work bench where he can work with tools. He is very clever with his hands when it comes to making things. He doesn't seem to be disturbed about the family situation. He cusses at my dad behind his back, and sympathizes with my mother when my dad is not around. We hardly ever play together like brothers.

So our family is not like any other family; it is like dog eat dog, every fellow for himself. We never enjoy ourselves together or do things like other families. My mother has her own ideas and my dad has his, and they never agree. They never get together. I side with my mother, and that makes my dad sore, then he thinks I am a double-crosser. My brother plays up to both of them and they both think he is a double-crosser. . . . .

There is sufficient material already available to indicate rather clearly that the spontaneous play group and the more highly organized gang are important factors in the problem of delinquency. In a study of six thousand stealing cases coming before the Juvenile Court of Cook County, it was found that in 90.4 per cent of the cases two or more boys were involved in the act. In many of these groups delinquency becomes a traditional form of behavior and is transmitted from the older to the younger members of the group. The following short excerpt will serve as an illustration of the value of the "own story" in securing a description of the traditions, activities, and moral standards in the delinquent's gang and play groups.

Case No. 4.—When I started to play in the alleys around my home I first heard about a bunch of older boys called the "Pirates." My oldest brother was in this gang and so I went around with them. There were about ten boys in this gang and the youngest one was eleven and the oldest one was about fifteen. . . . .

Tony, Sollie, and my brother John were the big guys in the gang. Tony was fifteen and was short and heavy. He was a good fighter and the young guys were afraid of him because he hit them and beat them up. Sollie was a little guy about twelve years of age. He couldn't fight, but he was a smart guy and told stories and made plans for the gang. He was the brains of the gang. My brother was fifteen and was bigger than Tony and was a good fighter. He could beat any guy in the gang by fighting, so he was a good leader and everybody looked up to him as a big guy. I looked up to him as a big guy and was proud to be his brother. . . . .

When I started to hang out with the Pirates I first learned about robbin. The guys would talk about robbin and stealing and went out on "jobs" every night. When I was eight I started to go out robbin with my brother's gang.

We first robbed junk from a junk yard and sometimes from the peddlar. Sometimes we robbed stores. We would go to a store, and while one guy asked to buy something the other guys would rob anything like candy and cigarettes and then run. We did this every day. Sollie always made the plans and Tony and John would carry out the plans. . . . .

The gang had a hangout in an alley and we would meet there every night and smoke and tell stories and plan for robbin. I was little and so I only listened. The big guys talked about going robbin and told stories about girls and sex things. The guys always thought about robbin and bummin from school and sometimes from home. . . . .

Besides robbin, the gang went bummin downtown and to ball parks and swimming. On these trips we always robbed everything we could get. . . . .

When I was ten the gang started to robbin stores and homes. We would jimmy the door or window and rob the place. I always stayed outside and gave jiggers. The big guys went in and raided the place. They showed me how to pick locks, jimmy doors, cut glass, and use skeleton keys and everything to get into stores and houses. Every guy had to keep everything a secret and not tell anybody or he would be beat up and razzed. The police were enemies and not to be trusted. When we would get caught by the police we had to keep mum and not tell a word even in the third degree.

I looked up to my brother and the other big guys because of their courage and nerve and the way they could rob. They would tell me never to say a word to anybody about our robbin. My mother didn't even know it. Some kids couldn't be in the gang because they would tell everything and some didn't have the nerve to go robbin. The guys with a record were looked up to and admired by the young guys. A stool-pigeon was looked down on and razzed and could not stay in the gang. . . . .

The guys stuck together and helped each other out of trouble. They were real good pals and would stick up for each other. They were always planning new crimes and new ways to get by without being caught. Everyone hated the police and looked upon them as enemies. Anybody who was friendly to the police was not trusted. The plans for stealing were always secret and anybody who talked about them to fellows outside of the gang or to the police was not trusted and became an enemy of the Pirates. . . . .

Unfortunately very little effort has been made to secure reliable data concerning the social processes which go on within detention homes, correctional schools, and penal institutions, and the influence of these processes upon the attitudes, personality, and philosophy of life of the inmates. Most studies of such institutions have been concerned primarily with the physical equipment and the formal administrative organization. The value of an approach from the standpoint of the actual experience and emotional reactions of the inmates is suggested in the following cases.

Case No. 5.—While in the Detention Home, I felt scared inwardly, and did not want to talk to any of the boys there. It seemed that all the boys but me felt at home there. That was the lonesomest time I ever spent. The boys at the Detention Home talked, as all young delinquents and criminals do, of what they had done on the outside and really what they tell you, if in any part true, is about one hundred times worse than any paper could print it. According to them, they have committed more crimes than there are on the calendar, and to them the Ten Commandments are better known as the ten suggestions. I didn't understand the thing at first. I thought that as compared to them, I was only an infant in crime, although on the outside I had thought myself an expert shoplifter. I felt much below them at first until I learned that most of the things they told were fake stories. Most of the conversation was about crime; everybody talked and thought about things in crime. It was crime, crime, and more crime.

In a place like the Detention Home and every place where delinquents are committed, anybody who feels sorry out loud for what he has done is openly jeered by his fellow-inmates. You may feel sorry to yourself, but you dare not make it known. They try to make you think that there is honor among crooks when it is really a case of "dog eat dog." A fellow will save himself first and his fellow-inmates later. I've lied, and, using the prison vernacular, double-crossed everyone who has tried to help me. Why I have, I cannot say. I was on the wrong side of the wall from the start and could not get on the right side. From the very start, I learned about crime, liked it, and didn't know anything else. And when I was put in the Detention Home and later in schools, jails, and prisons, I never heard anything but crime and more crime.

Case No. 6.—In the Detention Home, and in every institution where criminals are confined, the inmates always talk about their experiences in crime. That is the main topic of conversation. Their minds always run to things in the racket. Every fellow tries to impress upon everybody else what a great criminal he is and how many big deals in crime he has pulled off. Anything in the underworld like scandals, murders, robberies is interesting and talked about. Every fellow tries to tell the biggest exploit and make the other fellows look up to him as a big shot and a daring gunman.

They talk about the outside and how they're going to get by the next time. They talk against the police, and the older guys tell the young fellows how to get by in the racket and not get caught. The fellow who is timid and cries is razzed and made fun of. If there's anything that makes a young crook miserable it's to be razzed by a big shot for being a coward.

Case No. 7.—When a fellow arrives in the jail he is a little shy and has little to say. But this soon wears off and he considers himself "an old timer," a "big shot." When I was first assigned to my cell, I was asked, "What cell you got, Sonny?" I replied, "Five twenty-three." Then a fellow in the cell said, "Well, you're my buddie, then." I turned and saw a nice-looking young fellow about twenty years old reclining against the cell door. He said, "Yes, crying out loud, that makes four in our cell now. You'll have to sleep on the floor." "That's all right," I said, not wanting to show him that I felt sore or that I couldn't rough it.

This fellow was Italian and in jail on a robbery charge and being held for Joliet. He was a fine fellow and had a good racket but had a bum rap and was now going to the Pen. for a long term. He asked about my racket and I told him. We spent many long hours talking about our experiences in the racket. . . . . A little later the other buddies came into the cell. . . . .

The main topic of conversation would always be about stealing. One guy would tell about the burglaries he had done or other dangerous robberies he had succeeded in doing, or the big jobs he put over on the law. There were men in jail arrested for burglary, robbery, confidence game, and everything. One cell buddy, Stub, a short guy, was in for petty larceny. He was the laughing-stock of the crowd. . . . .

The old timers would enjoy giving advice to the newcomers about how to plead or what to say. They were good story-tellers. One old timer by the name of Slim was a great story-teller. All of his stories were of big burglaries, bank robberies, and crimes. We all listened and was thrilled. In two days we were all good chums. I tried to be just like the old timers, especially Slim. He rolled his own cigarettes so I rolled mine, even though I had money for tailor-made ones. I was afraid he might get the idea that I was trying to show him up. . . . .

SEQUENCE OF EVENTS IN THE LIFE OF THE DELINQUENT

There can be little doubt that behavior trends, and perhaps the total personality as well, are greatly influenced by the situational pressures and experiences which occur in the life of the individual. Therefore, any specific act of the individual becomes comprehensible only in the light of its relation to the sequence of past experiences in the life of the individual. As Thomas indicates:

It appears that behavior traits and their totality as represented by the personality are the outcome of a series of definitions of situations with the resulting reactions and their fixation in a body of attitudes or psychological sets. Obviously, the institutions of a society, beginning with the family, form the character of its members almost as the daily nutrition forms their bodies, but this is for everybody, and the unique attitudes of the individual and his unique personality are closely connected with certain incidents or critical experiences particular to himself, defining the situation, giving a psychological set, and often determining the whole life-direction.[7]

The study of case histories has indicated that very frequently the delinquent behavior of older offenders may be traced back to experiences and influences which have occurred very early in life. In many of these cases it is possible to describe the continuous process involved in the formation and fixation of the delinquent-behavior trend. In the search for factors contributing to delinquency in a given case, it is desirable, therefore, to secure as complete a picture of the successive events in the life of the offenders as possible. Here again, the "own story" has proved to be of great value. To quote Thomas again:

The behavior document (case study, life-record, psychoanalytic confession) represents a continuity of experience in life situations. In a good record of this kind we are able to view the behavior reactions in various situations, the emergence of personality traits, the determination of concrete acts and the formation of life policies in their evolution.[8]

The value of the life-history document in the study of the sequence of events in the life of the delinquent, and the manner in which this sequence has contributed to the development of a delinquent-behavior trend, is well illustrated in the detailed life-history presented in the subsequent chapters of this volume. Nevertheless two short excerpts will be presented at this time to illustrate the way in which the "own story" reveals crucial or critical experiences in the life of the delinquent. The experiences described in these excerpts marked the beginning of two long careers in very serious juvenile delinquency and adult crime. Under the continued influence of a delinquent-group situation, the behavior tendencies originating in these initial experiences in delinquency gradually became crystallized into well-defined criminal behavior patterns. At the present time the authors of these documents are serving long sentences in adult penal institutions.

[7] W. I. Thomas, "Personality in the Urban Environment," *The Urban Community* (Chicago: University of Chicago Press), p. 39.

[8] W. I. Thomas and Dorothy Swaine Thomas, *The Child in America* (1928), p. 571.

Case No. 8.—The first time I ever stole anything I didn't realize I was stealing; I just thought it was an interesting game. It happened when I was seven years old. I remember that quite clearly, as I had just started to school a few days before and I was in the second grade, having started to school the year before. On this day, a Saturday in late September, I was playing in front of my home with a boy by the name of William. He was five years older than me and lived in the same block that I did. He asked me to go along with him and he would show me something. I liked this fellow quite a bit. He was in tune to something in my heart. We had become good friends a few days before, so I went along with him. He had initiative, was full of ideas and full of fun. We lived on the northwest corner of L and W Streets, a few blocks west of the Loop. William took me to a fruit store that was located about a block from my home. This fruit store had baskets, barrels, and boxes containing fruit and vegetables setting out in front of it, as the weather was still warm. He, that is William, started to walk past the fruit store, and as he came to a box of fruit he took some fruit and walked on. He motioned for me to do the same thing. I waited a second, being afraid and nervous, but William motioned for me to hurry, and as I didn't want to be a coward, I followed and did the same thing. We each went by the store once more taking some fruit. After we ate the fruit in the alley, he took me home again. I though this quite an adventure and enjoyed taking the fruit very much. . . . .

During the next few days I mingled with William and his chums and we stole from many fruit stores in the neighborhood. William had a lot of chums; most of them were older than me, and we stole some little things every day, usually fruit from the stands, and sometimes we stole things from the stores.

When I began to hang out with this bunch of boys I began to stay out of school. None of the boys in the bunch went to school and so I didn't go. William usually led the way. He, by the way, is now dead. He was shot a few years ago by the gang he was traveling with, for telling their secrets to the police. He was an interesting chum and knew lots about stealing. One day he came over to my house and took me down to Roosevelt Road, a few blocks away from my home. We bummed all day, going to shows and wandering around the streets. At night we went to a poolroom on Roosevelt Road that had a part of a window missing. He crawled in first and I followed. He emptied the cash register and gave me two dollars and a lot of nickels and dimes. That was my first burglary, but as I look back now it seemed natural and I didn't have much fear or think it was wrong. I just went with William and his bunch and we did everything together. William knew how to steal, and it seemed natural for me to go with him. I liked him a lot and he liked to have me with him. We didn't do much else but steal and play hookey from school. Most of the boys around there stole a little, like fruit and junk, played hookey from school, and most of the older boys stole big things like cars and broke into stores. . . . .

Finally I had my first visit to the department stores in the Loop. William and two other boys had been shoplifting things in the Loop and making lots of money. They talked a lot about it, but had never asked me to accompany them. This day when they asked me to go to the Loop I was happy and knew what we were going to do. They took me through most of the big department stores and the five and ten cent stores. I was greatly impressed by the sights I saw—the crowds and big stores. My chums stole from the counters, but it was new to me, so I didn't try. There followed many more visits to the Loop, and finally I began to steal little trinkets from the counters under my escort's tutoring. He knew the house detectives and spotted them for me, and showed me how to slip things into my hat or put my hat on the thing I wanted to steal and then take it with my hat. We operated in different stores so the detectives would not spot us or get acquainted with us, so to speak. Within a few weeks I became an expert shoplifter. I lost interest in the companions of former days. I liked the new game of stealing I had learned, and it really was a game and I played it with much zest and relish. I wanted to learn more about this new game and to indulge in it wholeheartedly, and I did this to the exclusion of all else. I forgot about school almost entirely. Compared to stealing and playing in the Loop, school life was monotonous and uninteresting.

Case No. 9.—When I was eight years old I did my first job in the racket. This job was the biggest thrill I ever got in my life. It happened along in April. That day I was hanging around with my oldest brother and his gang. They had been playing baseball all afternoon and I was watching them.

When it got too dark to play ball we all went into the alley to have a smoke and tell stories. The big guys got to talking about stealing and my brother said he had a good place spotted where we would get some easy "dough" (money). The place was a butcher-shop in Thirty-first Street. The big guys planned everything and I only listened. These guys were seven or eight years older than me and had pulled off a lot of big jobs before. They would never let me go with them on big jobs, but this night I went along and they didn't say a word. We all went to the butcher-shop about 11:30 o'clock. It was very dark and everything was quiet and I was nervous and stayed close to my brother. We all slipped around into the alley behind the butcher-shop and my brother and another big guy went up to the building to see if the doors were unlocked. My brother had been in the place a few days before to see how to get in and where the cash register was, and so he led the way. I and two other guys waited close to the alley between two buildings. We were going to give "jiggers."

In a little while my brother came back and said everything was locked tight. The owner lived up over the butcher-shop, so we couldn't make much noise by breaking the glass or jimmie the door. We all went up to the back door and then my brother got a box and stood on it, and tried the transom and it opened. It was too little for my brother or the other guys to get through. Then I was thrilled when they said I'd have to crawl through the transom. That was the kick of my whole life.

I was only eight and always was very little so I could get through the transom easy. I was scared but made up my mind to go through anyway. I was too thrilled to say no.

My brother lifted me up on his shoulders and I crawled through the transom. I hung down on the inside and stood on an ice-box and then crawled down on the floor. The door was locked with a padlock and chain, but I was able to unlock the window and let the big guys in that way. The big guys looked for money first and found twenty-two dollars. Then we all got everything we wanted to eat and seven cartons of cigarettes and ditched the place.

When we got out, my brother divvied up everything and I got four dollars and a lot of cigarettes. I felt like a "big shot" after that night and the big guys said I could go with them every time they went robbin. Almost every night we went robbin and many times I had to crawl through transoms and one time through an ice-box hole. That's why the big guys called me the "baby bandit."

As illustrated in the foregoing cases, the "own story" reveals the essentially human aspects of the problem of delinquency. For in such documents one gains a sympathetic appreciation of the child's own personal problems and the sort of world in which he lives.

USE OF DELINQUENT BOY'S "OWN STORY"

Having illustrated in the foregoing pages the sort of material revealed in the boy's "own story," it is desirable at this time to indicate briefly the use of such data. In the first place, the child's "own story" is of particular importance in the diagnosis and treatment of cases of delinquency. The attitudes and intimate situations revealed in the life-story not only throw light upon the fundamental nature of the behavior difficulty, but, along with the other case material, afford a basis for devising a plan of treatment adapted to the attitudes, interests, and personality of the child.

An intensive study of the detailed life-histories of more than two hundred young repeated offenders on parole from the St. Charles School for Boys indicates rather clearly the great importance of dealing with the intimate personal aspects of the delinquent's situation. The large amount of failure in probation and parole work is not at all surprising, since the worker is forced, under the pressure of a heavy case load, to deal primarily with the more formal and external aspects of his cases. An essential preliminary step in the effective treatment of any case of delinquency is to secure a knowledge of the delinquent's personal attitudes and intimate situations as revealed in his "own story." In many cases this knowledge is to be secured only after painstaking study and prolonged contact with the delinquent. In the absence of such knowledge, the worker's relation to his case is necessarily more or less formal, and the treatment consists chiefly of attempts to gain control and effect adjustment through threats of arrest and punishment.

Many of the St. Charles delinquents whom we studied had been placed in foster-homes prior to their commitment to this institution. Judging from their life-histories, many of the failures of the foster-home placements, particularly in the cases of the older delinquents, were due to the fact that the foster-homes were selected with too little regard for the attitudes, interests, and social values of the child. Apparently, in many cases, the foster-home had been selected solely upon the basis of its superior economic, educational, and cultural status. The discrepancy between the child's cultural background and that of the foster-home seriously complicated the problem of adjustment.

Take, for instance, the case of Stanley, whose history is presented in the following chapters. At the age of fourteen years he was placed in the home of a wealthy and childless couple. They became so interested in him that they proposed to adopt him and make him their heir. Judged by outside standards, this home offered every advantage. Yet, from the standpoint of the boy, the situation was so strange, formal, and uninteresting that adjustment was not possible. The social distance was too great. To quote from his "own story":

The surroundings in my new home and neighborhood took my breath away. My first day at the foster-home was like a sweet dream. The new luxury seemed to dazzle and blind me. My new father rode with me to work every morning and home in the evening. We had nice lunches together at noon. He talked nice to me, gave me spending money and good clothes, but

I missed my old pals and the gay life we had lived. Here I did not have any boy chums, but had to spend my time playing the victrola. My foster parents didn't have much life, but spent their time reading and playing a tame game of cards. They had lots of company of snobbish people, and they looked down on me. Even if they were nice, it was because of pity and charity. There was something missing. Eating at the table I was ill at ease. I couldn't do the things just right, and my foster-mother looked at my blunders through the corner of her eye. I compared everything with my sister's common fare and poor surroundings, and finally longed to go back to my friends and pals. Back home I wasn't dressed up all the time, and could play and romp and gamble and swear. But here I was not free to move and talk as I was in the habit of doing before. Everything was different—strange and stiff. I felt out of place—a city waif dependent upon charity. I had been in jail half a lifetime, but now I was suddenly placed in luxury after living in a dirty hovel. My adventurous spirit rebelled against this dry life, and it soon won out. That is one of life's cynical jokes, how I felt. I said to myself, What's the use of having riches, if you can't enjoy life?

Life-history data have theoretical as well as therapeutic value. They not only serve as a means of making preliminary explorations and orientations in relation to specific problems in the field of criminological research but afford a basis for the formulation of hypotheses with reference to the causal factors involved in the development of delinquent-behavior patterns. The validity of these hypotheses may in turn be tested by the comparative study of other detailed case histories and by formal methods of statistical analysis.

The most extensive scientific use of personal documents in the general sociological field is that of Thomas and Znaniecki in their study of contemporary Polish peasant culture in Europe and America. This elaborate and illuminating study was based largely upon the analysis of personal letters and autobiographical documents. By the use of such material it was possible to analyze the behavior of the Polish peasant in its relation to Polish peasant culture in Europe and to describe the personal disorganization which occurs among the Polish peasant immigrants as a result of the disintegration of their culture in the large urban communities in America. Since it may be assumed that the personal document is equally valuable in the study of the problem of delinquent behavior and in the study of human conduct in general, the conclusions of Thomas and Znaniecki in regard to the scientific value of such documents are especially significant in the present discussion:

Whether we draw our materials for sociological analysis from detailed life-records of concrete individuals or from the observation of mass-phenomena, the problems of sociological analysis are the same. But even when we are searching for abstract laws life-records of concrete personalities have a marked superiority over any other kind of materials. We are safe in saying that personal life-records, as complete as possible, constitute the *perfect* type of sociological material, and that if social science has to use other materials at all it is only because of the practical difficulty of obtaining at the moment a sufficient number of such records to cover the totality of sociological problems, and of the enormous amount of work demanded for an adequate analysis of all the personal materials necessary to characterize the life of a social group. If we are forced to use mass-phenomena as material, or any kind of happenings taken without regard to the life-histories of the individuals who participate in them, it is a defect, not an advantage, of our present sociological method.

Indeed it is clear that even for the characterization of single social data— attitudes and values—personal life-records give us the most exact approach. An attitude as manifested in an isolated act is always subject to misinterpretation, but this danger diminishes in the very measure of our ability to connect this act with past acts of the same individual. A social institution can be fully understood only if we do not limit ourselves to the abstract study of its formal organization, but analyze the way in which it appears in the personal experience of various members of the group and follow the influence which it has upon their lives. And the superiority of life-records over every other kind of material for the purposes of sociological analysis appears with particular force when we pass from the characterization of single data to the determination of facts, for there is no safer and more efficient way of finding among the innumerable antecedents of a social happening the real causes of this happening than to analyze the past of the individuals through whose agency this happening occurred. The development of sociological investigation during the past fifteen or twenty years, particularly the growing emphasis, which, under the pressure of practical needs, is being put upon special and actual empirical problems as opposed to the general speculations of the preceding period, leads to the growing realization that we must collect more complete sociological documents than we possess. And the more complete a sociological document becomes the more it approaches a full personal life-record.[9]

⁹ William I. Thomas and Florian Znaniecki, *The Polish Peasant in Europe and America*, II, 1832–34.

There are those who, while granting the importance of the personal document for diagnosis and treatment, seriously question its value for the purpose of scientific generalization because of its subjective and non-quantitative character. While this is indeed a limitation, nevertheless it seems to be true that there are many aspects of delinquency which are not, for the present at least, susceptible to treatment by formal statistical methods. While quantitative methods are applicable to a wide range of the more formal aspects of delinquent conduct, some more discerning, though perhaps less exact, method is necessary to disclose the underlying processes involved in the formation of delinquent-behavior trends. Perhaps with the further refinement of such techniques as the questionnaire and personality rating scales, many aspects of delinquent behavior which we now study by means of personal documents will be subject to more objective analysis.

— SECURING DELINQUENT BOY'S "OWN STORY"

We have employed various techniques to secure "own-story" material in our case-studies of delinquents. Our immediate purpose in every case has been to procure a revealing and useful document, and to employ any method which the exigencies of the case demanded. Marked differences between delinquents in regard to attitudes, personality, education, and special abilities have made it necessary to vary our techniques in different cases. It was felt that the story should be as spontaneous as possible and always follow the natural sequence of events in the life of the delinquent. By enabling the offender to tell or write his story according to this natural sequence, we hoped to be able to describe more accurately the natural process involved in the development of his delinquent-behavior trend and to develop a more empirical method for the study of delinquent careers.

The technique which we have most frequently employed to secure the delinquent's "own story" is that of the personal interview. The task of securing complete and useful documents by this technique usually necessitates a series of interviews, which in some cases extend over a relatively long period of time. In most of our cases a stenographic record of the interview is made, so that the story is recorded in the exact language of the interviewee. Thus the record of the interview is not only complete, but its objectivity is preserved. A translation of the story into the language of the interviewer would, in most cases, greatly alter the original meaning.

It has been possible to secure in many of our cases rather detailed and revealing written documents, particularly in the cases of older juvenile delinquents. Usually these documents present a more coherent and connected picture of the boy's life than could be secured through a series of personal interviews. As indicated previously, these documents are always developed as an integral part of the total case history, so that, in the light of the information secured through personal interviews, official records, and clinical findings, the verbal responses of the boy might be properly identified and interpreted.

The initial step in securing the written document has been to obtain, usually by means of personal interviews, a list of the boy's behavior problems, delinquencies, arrests, court appearances, and commitments. These experiences were then arranged in the order of their occurrence and presented to the boy to be used as a guide in writing his "own story." He was always instructed to give a complete and detailed description of each experience, the situation in which it occurred, and the impression which it made upon him.

If the initial document was relatively meager, the boy was urged to make further elaboration. This process of elaboration was continued until the story was made as complete as possible.

In many cases it was necessary to illustrate the kind of material desired in the life-story. These illustrations, however, were drawn from the boy's own life, having been previously obtained through the initial personal interview. By this method the document was secured with a minimum of guidance and control on the part of the investigator, and the story necessarily followed the natural sequence of events in the life of the boy.

This technique may be concretely illustrated by a brief description of the steps involved in securing the rather detailed life-history of Stanley, whose "own story" is presented in the subsequent chapters of this volume. Our first interview with Stanley occurred when he was sixteen years and eight months of age. Through that interview we secured a list of his behavior difficulties, delinquencies, and commitments. These were arranged in chronological order and returned to him to be used as a guide in writing his "own story." He was instructed to give a detailed description of each event, the situation in which it occurred, and his personal reactions to the experience. His first document was a brief account of his experiences up to that time.[10]

Our study of this case was interrupted by the boy's commitment to the Chicago House of Correction. At the end of this commitment the study of the case was continued. On resuming the study, our first interest was to secure a more complete written document. We pointed out to him that his first story was an excellent summary of his life, but lacked detailed descriptive material. In response to our suggestion that he write a more detailed story, the original document was increased to its present length, which is approximately two hundred and fifty typewritten pages. All of the suggestions and illustrations used to indicate the sort of material desired were drawn from his own experiences.

[10] This original document is presented in Appendix II.

CHAPTER II

HISTORY OF STANLEY'S BEHAVIOR DIFFICULTIES

An important initial step in the study of a delinquent child is to procure a rather complete and accurate description of his delinquencies and other behavior difficulties. Among other things, this description should show the specific offenses in the order of their occurrence, the chronological age of the child at the time of each offense, the immediate circumstances in which each offense occurred, and the number of persons involved. It is especially important to know also the age of the child at the time of the onset of the delinquent career and the immediate circumstances surrounding the initial experience in delinquency. It is not infrequent that knowledge of the specific act of delinquency and the particular situation in which it has occurred will give valuable clues for the further investigation of significant aspects of the case.

In the present chapter materials are presented to give an objective picture of Stanley's behavior difficulties. Stanley, whose career in delinquency began at the age of six and a half years, was of average intelligence and normal physical condition.[1] He was studied very thoroughly by Dr. William Healy[2] at the age of seven years and ten months. Although the major portion of Healy's study will be presented in subsequent chapters, a few of his observations are recorded at this time, to throw light upon the boy's behavior problems and the situations existing at the very beginning of his delinquent career. Quoting from Dr. Healy's record:

This little boy is in the Detention Home again. He has been here five or six times. He runs away from home every time he is sent back. He tells us to-day that his father is a hard drinking man, drunk every pay-day and sometimes breaks windows. Says that he does not want to go back home. His

[1] For a summary of the clinical findings, see Appendix I.

[2] At the time he studied this case, Dr. Healy was director of the Juvenile Psychopathic Institute, which is now the Institute for Juvenile Research.

older step-brother and another older boy have made him steal. They steal vegetables and break into freight cars. These same boys long ago taught him bad sex habits. Says that these older boys do bad things to him in the public baths; that they look at the girls there and say bad things about them. These boys got him into this bad habit (masturbation), which he has done much. . . . .

We find this boy very interesting on account of his repeated truancies, although he is very bright, rather ahead of his age. He is undernourished and has exceedingly carious teeth. Home conditions are very bad. Strong dislike for his step-mother. Strongly influenced by bad companions. The whole situation very bad and unlikely to be any better. Boy should be placed in an entirely new situation. There is little hope for improvement in the present home environment. He does not wish to return home. We have told the judge that it was impossible for the boy to make good in the present situation. It would be well for him to go to the Polish Manual Training School, but he will have to wait a little time.

OFFICIAL RECORD OF ARRESTS AND COMMITMENTS

This section includes the official account of Stanley's arrests and commitments, which was compiled from the records of the police, juvenile court, correctional institutions, social agencies, and behavior clinics. This record shows clearly the sequence of behavior problems, proceeding from the minor difficulties of truancy and petty stealing, at the early age of six years, to the more serious delinquency of "jack-rolling" and burglary, in the adolescent period.

1. Six years, six months of age:
   Found sleeping under a doorstep late at night several blocks away from his home. He was in the company of an older boy, and had been away from home two days. Returned to his home by the police.
2. Six years, six months:
   Picked up by the police as a runaway and released to the father. Boy was in the company of the same companion, and had been away from home three days.
3. Six years, seven months:
   Picked up as a lost boy and placed in the police station. Parents were notified and the boy was released to them. Had been away four days.
4. Six years, seven months:
   Picked up by the police and placed in the Detention Home. Released to parents. Had been away from home one week.
5. Six years, nine months:
   Found sleeping in an alley four blocks away from his home. Had been

away from home five days. Was in the company of an older companion. Complained that his stepmother beat him. Placed in Detention Home and later released to the father.

6. Six years, nine months:
Picked up as a runaway and placed in the Juvenile Detention Home. Held one day and released to the father.

7. Six years, eleven months:
Police found the boy begging food at a bakery near Halsted and Madison Streets, four miles away from home. He had been away three weeks. Told police he "didn't like it at home." Said stepmother beat him up. Released to father at police station.

8. Seven years, three months:
Found sleeping in an alley several blocks from his home. Had been away three weeks. Placed in the Detention Home and later released to the father.

9. Seven years, seven months:
Picked up as a truant from home and school. Had been away one day. Released to the father at the police station.

10. Seven years, ten months:
Found eating food from a garbage can in an alley near Desplaines and Halsted streets. Had been away from home four weeks. Told the police his parents were dead and that he had no home. Taken to police station and then to the Detention Home, where he was identified and sent home.

11. Eight years, two months:
Arrested while shoplifting in a five and ten cent store on Forty-seventh Street. He was in the company of his stepbrother, William, and an older companion. Returned to his stepmother by the police and promised to attend school and remain at home.

12. Eight years, two months:
Picked up as a runaway and released to the father at the police station.

13. Eight years, seven months:
Arrested while stealing vegetables at the Randolph Street Market. He was in the company of four other children, one of whom was his stepbrother, William. Placed in police station and released to stepmother.

14. Eight years, nine months:
Picked up as a truant from home. Said he had no home. Placed in Detention Home, where he was identified and released to father.

15. Eight years, ten months:
Picked up on West Madison Street (four miles from home) for begging, petty stealing, and truanting from home. Placed in Detention Home, where he was identified and taken home by a probation officer.

16. Eight years, ten months:
Picked up in a car barn, after having been away from home two days. Placed in the Detention Home, where he remained until brought into

court. In presenting the case to the court, the officer stated: "This boy is an habitual runaway and his father is unable to control him." The father responded by saying: "About a year ago I was here with him [Stanley] the first time, and been five or six times in the station since then. He told boys in neighborhood he wanted a free ride and he takes free rides to the station and I fast ride him back home." Father asks to take boy home and the latter promises the court that he will be good. Boy released to father, under supervision of a probation officer.

17. Eight years, ten months:
Arrested while playing truant from home and placed in the Detention Home. Admonished by probation officer and released to live at home.

18. Eight years, eleven months:
Arrested while playing truant and placed in the Detention Home. Had been away from home five days. Brought to court on a dependent petition a few days later. The following is an excerpt from the record of the court hearing:

"A dependent petition for the above child was filed when he was in Court the last time. The boy was paroled to live at home. He remained one day and ran away and was again picked up by the police. Taken to the Detention Home. He was released and sent home with the understanding that if he was again brought into Court on a like charge, he would be committed to an institution. He remained just one hour and was again picked up by the police and taken to the Detention Home. Father is unable to manage the boy and petitioner respectfully asks that he be committed to an institution."

Court: Ask the father what is the matter with the boy?
Father: Boy don't want to stay at home.
Court: How old is he?
Father: He is eight going on nine.
Court: Where is your wife?
Father: She is dead.
Officer: He now has his *third* wife; he has been married three times. This is the third woman.
Court: Can't you manage this little boy?
Father: His stepmother treats him all right; she lets him go out on the back porch and he will run away.
Court: Does he go to school?
Officer: No, sir.
Court: Why can't he go to Parental School?
Officer: They refused to take him. The representative of the Parental School said that the boy was not a parental school case, because he is not enrolled in school.
Judge: Take him home and start him in school tomorrow; get him entered in school; have him registered; if he stays out three days, we

can send him to the Parental School. If he "skips" bring him in and we will send him to the Parental School.

The case was continued for three months.

After being enrolled in school, the boy was released to the father under supervision of the probation officer.

19. Eight years, eleven months:

Arrested on a charge of truancy and stealing from railroads. Had been away from home and school two weeks. Placed in Detention Home. Released two weeks later to live at home.

20. Nine years, one month:

Arrested and brought to court. Boy told the court: "Do not want to live at home. Stepmother hollers on me and beats me. I want to live with the Irish woman and her kids." Boy released to live at home pending investigation of the home of the Irish lady, where he was living at time of arrest. Ran away from home same day.

21. Nine years, one month:

Voluntarily went to the Detention Home to seek shelter, having been away from home one week.

22. Nine years, one month:

Committed to Chicago Parental School.

23. Nine years, seven months:

Paroled from the Chicago Parental School to live at home.

24. Nine years, seven months:

Found sleeping in an alley near Halsted and Madison streets. Had been away from home four days. Released to father at police station.

25. Nine years, eight months:

Picked up by police as a runaway. Placed in Detention Home and later brought to court. In court the officer stated: "This boy has been before the court many times for absenting himself from home without cause. He ran away about two weeks ago. Stepmother asks that he be committed to an institution." In responding to the court, the boy stated: "I want to live in the Detention Home and never go back home." Placed on probation to live at home.

26. Nine years, nine months:

Arrested and brought to court charged with truancy and stealing. Was with another boy. It was stated in court that "this boy is an habitual runaway. He has been given many opportunities at home but does not appreciate them." Committed to the St. Charles School for Boys.

27. Eleven years:

Paroled from St. Charles to live at home.

28. Eleven years, one month:

Picked up by police at Desplaines and Madison streets (six miles from home). He was eating stolen buns and garbage in the alley when the officer found him. Boy said parents were dead. Taken to the Detention Home, where he was identified and sent home.

29. Eleven years, one month:
Went to Hull-House Social Settlement seeking food and shelter. Placed in the hands of the police and returned to the St. Charles School for Boys.

30. Eleven years, eleven months:
Paroled to live in a farm near Batavia, Illinois.

31. Twelve years, two months:
Ran away from farm.

32. Twelve years, two months:
Arrested on West Madison Street as a vagrant. Placed in Detention Home and later paroled to father.

33. Twelve years, seven months:
Arrested in the Y.M.C.A. Hotel. Had been away from home five months. Placed in Detention Home and returned to St. Charles.

34. Fourteen years:
Paroled to stepmother.

35. Fifteen years:
Arrested on West Madison Street, charged with burglary and "jack-rolling." Had been away from home eight months. Placed in the county jail. Case came up in the Boy's Court, and boy committed to the Illinois State Reformatory at Pontiac for a definite term of one year.

36. Sixteen years, one month:
Released from the Reformatory.

37. Sixteen years, nine months:
Arrested on West Madison Street, charged with burglary and "jack-rolling." Had been away from home seven months. Placed in the county jail and a few days later committed to the Chicago House of Correction for a definite sentence of one year.

38. Seventeen years, eight months:
Released from the House of Correction.

WORK AND SCHOOL RECORD

Stanley's work record, which began when he was twelve years of age, is presented at this time because it throws light upon certain significant aspects of his behavior problems. It indicates clearly the absence of a definite vocational interest and suggests the great difficulties that he encountered in making satisfactory adjustment to other persons. The list of jobs is incomplete, since only those which could be verified through official records and other reliable sources have been listed. In many instances, the boy's own reason for leaving the job is inserted in quotation marks. These statements are especially indicative of his typical attitudes and personality.

1. Errand boy in a business concern near the Loop. Worked three weeks. "I was laid off because I came late to work two or three times, and the boss got cocky with me."
2. Errand boy in a printing department. Worked two weeks. "I was fired because I played around with the girls in the office too much."
3. Worked on a farm. "I got tired of the lonesome farm life and ran away and came back to Chicago."
4. Errand boy in a manufacturing establishment. Worked about three months. "I quit this job to go with a fellow who lived on West Madison Street. The work was too monotonous."
5. Machine operator in a spring factory. Worked about a week. Fired for smoking in toilet.
6. Errand boy in a drug manufacturing establishment. Worked less than one week. Dismissed because he distracted the other employees.
7. Errand boy in a printing shop. Worked two days. Had difficulty with people where he lived, so gave up job to return to West Madison Street.
8. Errand boy for an engraving company. Worked four weeks. Gave up position when he ran away from the city.
9. Piecework in a factory. Worked about ten days. Had difficulty at home and refused to work.
10. Messenger boy for Western Union. Worked one week.
11. Stockroom worker in a mail order house. Worked six weeks. Gave up position when he left the city.
12. Machine operator in factory. Worked two weeks and was fired when a girl reported to the employer that boy cursed her. "I didn't get along well with this girl. I got into a hot argument after I failed to bring back the kind of cookies she wanted for lunch. I would not be browbeaten by her."
13. Machine operator in Western Union. Fired after two months when he refused to obey his superior, who reprimanded him for not doing the work according to instructions. "I didn't want the boss to have the satisfaction of getting the best of me, so I quit the job."
14. Machine operator in factory. Worked two months and quit when he was laid off one week while inventory was being taken.
15. Temporary work in a department store. Worked three days.
16. Stockroom worker in printing shop. Worked three weeks and quit to take a better job.
17. Laboratory assistant in hospital. Worked four months. Dismissed for engaging in a fight with a pharmacist. "I had a quarrel with this fellow

[pharmacist] because he tried to order me around. I would not let him run over me."

18. Stockroom worker in a department store. Worked two weeks, and quit because "the work was too dirty."

19. Complaint adjuster in department store. Worked three months and quit because he did not get a raise in salary.

20. Complaint adjuster in department store. Worked one month and quit because he "didn't like inside work during the spring of the year."

21. Painting. Outside work. Worked two weeks. Gave up job because "fellow bossed me too much."

22. Filling orders in grocery store. Quit after two weeks because he was irritated by the man who gave him orders. "The Greek who had charge of me got eggy with me. I wouldn't let him run over me. I told him I would work as I wanted to."

23. Clerk in a factory. Worked two months and quit because his employer reprimanded him for being late on two or three occasions.

24. Filling orders in the same grocery store where he was previously employed (see No. 22). Worked two days and quit when he was told to sweep the floor, which he did not consider part of his work.

25. Stockroom worker in a department store. Was laid off at the end of the rush season after working six weeks.

26. Employed in a tailor shop. Fired after two weeks for fighting. "One night a wise guy bawled me out and I socked him, and they gave me the air."

27. Blacksmith helper at packing-house. Worked two weeks and was dismissed for being late to work.

28. Stockroom worker in publishing house. Laid off during slack season after working three months.

29. Packer in publishing house. Laid off after two weeks.

30. Stockroom worker in rubber company. Worked two weeks. Quit because "the work was too dirty."

31. Employed in chewing-gum factory. Laid off during slack season after working four weeks.

32. Stockroom clerk for wholesale coffee company. Worked five weeks. Quit because "work was monotonous."

33. For two years now has been employed as a salesman, and has apparently made a fairly satisfactory adjustment in this field.

As indicated in the foregoing official record of arrests and commitments, Stanley was habitually truant from school. He entered public school at the age of six years. Despite his frequent truancies, he was graduated at the age of thirteen and a half, while in the St. Charles School for Boys.

The foregoing materials give a rather detailed picture of the more formal aspects of Stanley's behavior problems. The subjective and personal aspects of these problems (without which the picture is necessarily incomplete) are revealed in the boy's "own story" which follows in subsequent chapters.

CHAPTER III

STANLEY'S SOCIAL AND CULTURAL BACKGROUND

As indicated previously (p. 8), it is always important to study the delinquent behavior of the child in its relation to the social and cultural setting in which it occurs. What, for instance, are the traditions,.moral standards, activities, and sentiments prevailing in the community? What are the typical attitudes with reference to delinquency and crime? Is the community sufficiently integrated to be conscious of its social problems and to act collectively with reference to them? What are the traditions, attitudes, and relationships within the family group? Are there conflicts and emotional discords which directly or indirectly involve the child? To what extent does the family constitute a social unit capable of exercising consistent control over its members? What is the nature of the family's relationship to the larger social community? What contacts does the child have outside of the family? Does he belong to any spontaneous play groups or organized gangs? If so, what are the traditions, moral codes, and typical activities of these social groups? Guided by such questions, the following material concerning Stanley's social background was secured.

THE COMMUNITY BACKGROUND

Stanley, who is at present approximately twenty-two years of age, has lived for comparatively long periods of time in three different areas of the city. The location and boundaries of these areas (A, B, and C) are indicated on Map I. During the first seventeen and a half years of his life, which was the period in which his delinquencies and commitments occurred, he lived in Areas A and B. Since his release from the House of Correction four and a half years ago, he has lived in Area C. A brief description of these different areas will be presented at this time.

This area, which includes the large packing plants, stock yards, and a portion of the central manufacturing district, is bounded by Halsted Street on the east, Western Avenue on the west, Thirty-ninth Street on the north, and Forty-seventh Street on the south. During his early childhood Stanley lived in the large Polish neighborhood which occupies the western portion of this area, between Ashland and Western avenues. It was while he lived in this neighborhood, which is known locally as "Back of the Yards," that his career in delinquency began.

The neighborhood back of the yards is a part of the large industrial community which has developed around the Union Stock Yards and central manufacturing district during the last half-century. It is one of the grimiest and most unattractive neighborhoods in the city, being almost completely surrounded by packing plants, stock yards, railroads, factories, and waste lands. The life in the neighborhood is largely dominated by, and economically dependent upon, the larger industrial community of which it is a part. The population is composed largely of families of unskilled laborers, most of whom depend upon the stock yards and local industries for employment. The air in the neighborhood is smoky and always filled with a disagreeable odor from the stock yards. In describing the physical aspects of the neighborhood, Howard E. Wilson states:

The houses, built close to the walk, monotonously two stories high and alike in faded architecture, were not old but were cheaply and poorly constructed, and all colored to one drabness by the smoke and dirt. A visitor to the neighborhood wrote, "Anyone who spends even a few brief hours in that part of the city known as 'back of the yards' is impressed by the want of color. Grey streets, grey houses, and smoke-laden air combine to give a background of unrelieved monotony. This gloomy aspect, accentuated by the absence of trees, grass, or shrubbery, has come to be accepted by the people living in the community as a thing inevitable."[1]

The proximity of the neighborhood to industry has greatly diminished its desirability for residential purposes. There has been a marked tendency on the part of families and individuals who have prospered to escape from the neighborhood into the

[1] Howard E. Wilson, *Mary McDowell, Neighbor*, pp. 26–27.

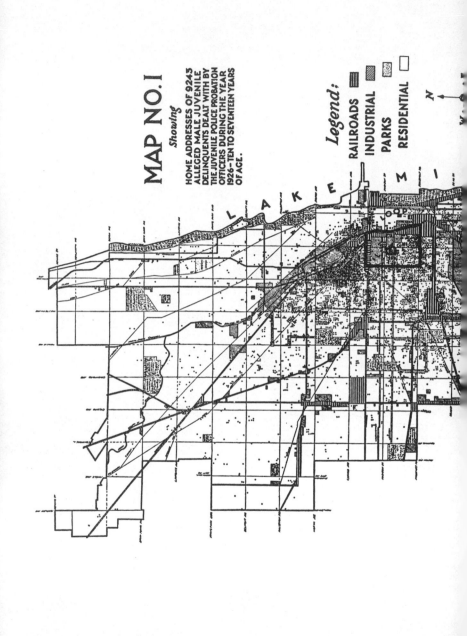

MAP NO. I

Showing

HOME ADDRESSES OF 9243
ALLEGED MALE JUVENILE
DELINQUENTS DEALT WITH BY
THE JUVENILE POLICE PROBATION
OFFICERS DURING THE YEAR
1926–TEN TO SEVENTEEN YEARS
OF AGE.

Legend:

RAILROADS
INDUSTRIAL
PARKS
RESIDENTIAL

N

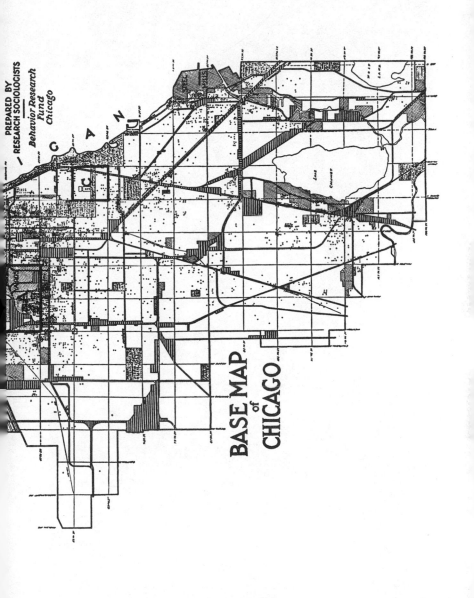

BASE MAP
of
CHICAGO

more desirable communities farther removed from the dirt and odor of the stock yards and factories. Thus, the composition of the population has undergone marked changes since the time of the first settlement. The original settlers, who moved into the area to work in the stock yards, were predominantly Irish, German, and Scandinavian; while the present population is largely Polish, Russian, and Lithuanian. In 1900 the population was 33.5 per cent Irish; 20.4 per cent Czechoslovakian; 14.6 per cent German; 9.2 per cent Scandinavian; 7.8 per cent Polish; 4.7 per cent Lithuanian. By 1920 45.2 per cent was Polish; 28.5 per cent Russian; 11.9 per cent Lithuanian; only 5.6 per cent Czechoslovakian, 1.5 per cent Irish, 1.7 per cent German; and there were practically no Scandinavians. Such marked changes in the cultural composition of the neighborhood has undoubtedly entailed considerable disorganization and confusion of moral standards.

In the present Polish neighborhood back of the yards, with a population in 1920 of 52.1 per cent foreign-born, there is a definite break between the foreign-born parents and their native-born children. In many of the families the relation between the child and parent assumes the character of an emotional conflict, which definitely complicates the problem of parental control and greatly interferes with the incorporation of the child into the social milieu of his parents. In his study of the reaction of the Polish culture to the urban community in our large American cities, Thomas describes very clearly the breakdown of parental control which occurs under the pressure of the new situation. The situation he describes is essentially characteristic of the process which is now going on in the Polish neighborhood back of the yards. For this reason some of his observations are included at this point:

If we contrast now the conditions at home with those which the emigrants meet in America, we see that a loss of control over the child is inevitable if the parents do not develop new means as substitutes for the old ones. First, there is in America no family in the traditional sense; the married couple and the children are almost completely isolated, and the parental authority has no background. (In a few cases, where many members of the family have settled in the same locality, the control is much stronger.) Again, if there is something equivalent to the community of the old country, i.e., the parish, it is much less closed and concentrated and can hardly have the same influence. Its composition is new, accidental, and changing; moreover, it is composed of various elements, influenced each separately and each somewhat differently by the new environment, and has consequently a rather poor stock of common traditions. Further, the members of the new generation, brought up in this new environment, are more likely to show a solidarity with one another as against the parents than a solidarity with the parents as against the younger members of the family. Finally, economic independence comes much earlier than in the old country and makes a revolt always materially easy. On the other hand, the parents' authority ceases also to be controlled, except by the state in the relatively rare cases of a far-going abuse. The traditional measure of its exertion is lost; the parents have no standard of education, since the old standard is no longer valid and no new one has been appropriated. The natural result is a free play given to individual caprice, excessive indulgence alternating with unreasonable severity. Thus the moral character of parental authority in the eyes of the children is lost.[2]

Although there is comparatively little crime among the adults living in Area A, juvenile delinquency is particularly prevalent. During the three-year period between 1924 and 1926, 28 per cent of the young men from seventeen to twenty-one years of age were arrested and arraigned in the Boys' Court on charges of serious crime. No other area in the city had a higher rate during that period. Map I, which shows the home addresses of 9,243 alleged delinquent boys (from ten to seventeen years of age) handled by the juvenile police probation officers of the city during 1926, indicates a marked concentration of cases in this area. No less than 17.6 per cent of the boys in this age group were dealt with by the police as alleged delinquents during that year. Only 7 per cent of the 113 areas of the city had a higher rate. In view of this high rate of delinquency, contact between the young child and the older delinquent is almost inevitable. It is known also that this area has been characterized by a high rate of delinquency for almost thirty years. During this period delinquency has become a more or less permanent aspect of the social life among the boys in the area. Stealing from railroads, pilfering, burglary,

[2] William I. Thomas and Florian Znaniecki, *The Polish Peasant in Europe and America* (New York: Alfred A. Knopf), I, 710-11.

and larceny of automobiles are among the more prevalent types of offenses.

In the light of the disorganized community situation back of the yards, the persistence of a high rate of delinquency is not at all surprising. With the marked changes in the composition of population, diffusion of divergent cultural standards, and the rapid disorganization of the alien culture, the continuity of community traditions and cultural institutions is broken. Thus the effectiveness of the community in the control and education of the child is greatly diminished. In this situation "it is perfectly natural," to quote from Thomas, "for the boy to steal, burglarize or rob, since respect for property is not a matter of instinct, but a long and complex social education."[3]

AREA B

As previously indicated in the official records of arrests and commitments, Stanley very early became involved in the underworld life of the large rooming-house district west of the Loop, Chicago's central business district. After his parole from the St. Charles School for Boys, he was temporarily placed in institutions in this district, and later lived for several months in rooming-houses along Madison Street. According to official records, it was while he lived in this district that his first experiences in "jack-rolling" and burglary occurred.

Roughly speaking, the rooming-house district west of the Loop is bounded on the north by Randolph Street, Jackson Boulevard on the south, Racine Avenue on the west, and the Chicago River on the east. This district is characterized by physical deterioration, a mobile and transient population composed largely of homeless adult males, and an absence of community organization. Here are to be found also the rescue missions, the flophouses, the cheap hotels, pawnshops and secondhand stores, houses of prostitution, closed dance halls, and the hangout of the criminal.

Nels Anderson, author of *The Hobo,* described this district, its institutions, and population as follows:

[3] *Ibid.,* I, 1796.

West Madison, being a port of homeless men, has its own characteristic institutions and professions. The bootlegger is at home here; the dope peddler hunts and finds his victims; here the professional gambler plies his trade, and the "jack-roller," as he is commonly called, the man who robs his fellows, while they are drunk or asleep; these and others of their kind find in the anonymity of this changing population the freedom and security that only the crowded city offers.

The street has its share also of peddlers, beggars, cripples, and old, broken men; men worn out with the adventure and vicissitudes of life on the road. One of the most striking characteristics is the almost complete absence of women and children; it is the most completely womanless and childless of all the city areas. It it quite definitely a man's street.

West Madison Street, near the river has always been a stronghold of the casual laborer. At one time it was a rendezvous for the seamen, but of late these have made South Chicago their haven. Even before the coming of the factories, before family life had wholly departed, this was an area of the homeless man. It will continue to be so, no doubt, until big business or a new union depot crowds the hobo out. Then he will move farther out into that area of deteriorated property that inevitably grows up just outside the business center of the city, where property, which has been abandoned for residences, has not yet been taken over by business, and where land values are high but rents are low.[4]

Map II, which shows the home addresses of 7,541 adult male offenders, indicates a marked concentration of cases in this rooming-house district. The freedom and anonymity of the situation offer an environment in which the adult offender may live in relative obscurity and with a minimum of interference from the police. Although most of the criminals living in the district commit their crimes in the more well-to-do sections of the city, cases of "jack-rolling" and homosexual practice are especially common in, or adjacent to, the rooming-house district.

The area extending north and south from the rooming-house district is one of Chicago's most disorganized and deteriorated sections. In this area our study shows the greatest concentration of cases of poverty, family disintegration, bad housing, and juvenile delinquency. In the area between Lake Street on the north and Twelfth Street on the south, and extending from the Loop to Racine Avenue (see Area B, Map I), as many as 26.5 per cent

[4] Nels Anderson, *The Hobo* (Chicago: University of Chicago Press, 1923), pp. 5–6.

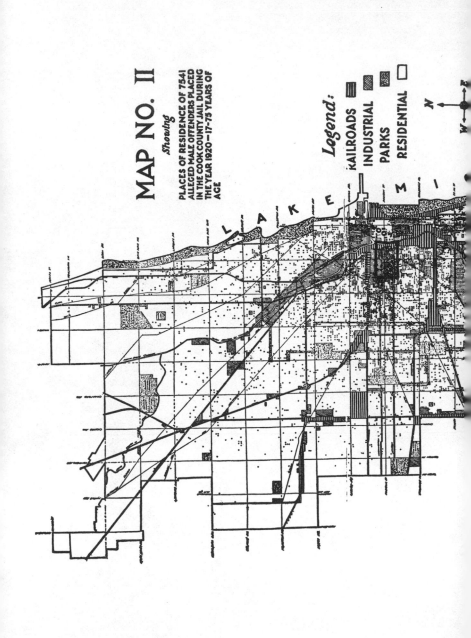

MAP NO. II

Showing

PLACES OF RESIDENCE OF 7541
ALLEGED MALE OFFENDERS PLACED
IN THE COOK COUNTY JAIL DURING
THE YEAR 1920—17–75 YEARS OF
AGE

Legend:

RAILROADS

INDUSTRIAL

PARKS

RESIDENTIAL

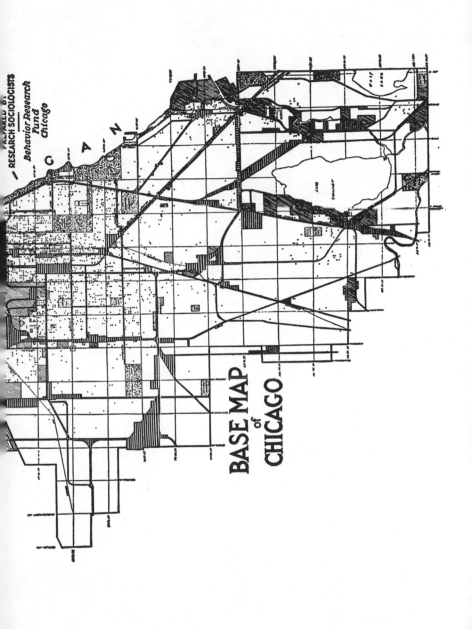

BASE MAP
of
CHICAGO

PREPARED BY
RESEARCH SOCIOLOGISTS
Behavior Research
Fund
Chicago

LAKE MICHIGAN

of the young men between seventeen and twenty-one years of age appeared in the Boys' Court on felony charges during the three-year period 1924–26. The only area having a higher rate was Area A. In the year 1926, 22.0 per cent of the boys between ten and seventeen years of age were dealt with by the juvenile police probation officers as alleged delinquents. Only 3.0 per cent of the 113 areas of the city had a higher rate. The rate of juvenile delinquency in this area has been consistently high for at least thirty years, which is as far back as records of delinquency are available.

AREA C

At the time of his release from the House of Correction Stanley was placed with a family living in Area C (see Map I). This area, which includes portions of the communities of Woodlawn and Hyde Park, stands in marked contrast to the areas described in the foregoing pages. The population is composed chiefly of middle-class native-born Americans, business men, clerks, sales-men, and professional people. Only 15.9 per cent of the population was foreign-born in 1920. Although once an area of single homes, it is rapidly becoming an area of apartment houses and residential hotels. Despite the fact that there is considerable mobility, from the standpoint of cultural standards, the population is essentially homogeneous. There is sufficient community tradition, public opinion, and common interest to afford a basis for effective collective action with reference to local and city-wide social problems.

In this area cases of poverty, bad housing, adult crime, physical deterioration, and juvenile delinquency are comparatively infrequent. The rate of delinquency among the young men between seventeen and twenty-one years of age for the period 1924 to 1926 was only 3.6 per cent as compared to 28.0 per cent in Area A, and 26.5 per cent in the area west of the Loop. Of the total number of boys from ten to seventeen years of age, only 1.7 per cent were dealt with by the juvenile police probation officers as alleged delinquents in 1926; while in Area A, the rate was 17.6 per cent, and in the area west of the Loop 22.0 per cent.

Some of the more important indices of the social life in these three areas are summarized in Table I. It is especially important to compare the indices for Area C with those of the other two areas.

TABLE I

	Area A	Area B	Area C
Percentage of boys 10–17 years of age who were arrested as alleged delinquents during the year 1926.......	17.6	22.0	1.7
Percentage of males 17–21 years of age arraigned in Boys' Court on felony charges during 1924–26............	28.0	26.5	3.6
Percentage of adult males incarcerated in Cook County Jail in 1920........	1.12	3.36	0.68
Percentage of families dependent upon charity in 1926....................	2.09	7.76	0.23
Percentage of foreign-born, for year 1920	52.1	51.1	15.9

THE FAMILY BACKGROUND

The family situation in which Stanley lived during his early childhood presents a rather complicated picture of human relationships. The situation was one in which family disorganization, emotional tensions, and marked confusion of moral standards were outstanding features. The significance of these conditions is probably reflected in the ineffectiveness of the family in the discipline and control of its members.

Stanley's father was born in a rural community in Poland. His genealogy indicates several generations of Polish peasant ancestry. His formal education was very meager. He worked on his father's farm until he was twenty. At that age he married, and a few months later came to America. He established a home in the Polish community near the stock yards in Chicago, where he lived until his death thirty-seven years later. He was of large stature, quiet, and industrious. Official records indicate that he was an excessive drinker and often abusive to his family. He was an unskilled laborer and worked twenty years for a public utilities company, earning from twelve to twenty dollars a week. His first wife, whom he married in Poland, bore him five children. She died in Chicago fifteen years after their marriage. Soon after her death the father married the young woman who became Stanley's mother. She, too, was born in Poland of Polish peasant parentage, and had emigrated to the United States with her family when she was a small child. Stanley was her second child, a brother being older and a sister younger. When Stanley was four years old, his mother died of tuberculosis. Unfortunately, it is nowhere recorded whether she and the father were compatible; nor do we have any description of her personality. A few months after her death his father married a widow who had seven children from two previous marriages. She, too, had been born in Poland of peasant ancestry.

Children.—From father's first marriage: Male, thirty-six. Married. Has family. No official record of delinquency. Female, thirty-five. Married. Has family. No official record of delinquency. Male, thirty-four. Married. Has family. No official record of delinquency. Female, thirty-one. Married. Has family. No official record of delinquency. Male, twenty-nine. Married. Has family. No official record of delinquency.

From the father's second marriage: Male, twenty-five. Truant from home and school repeatedly. Stole from railroads, and was involved in other petty stealing in the community; had difficulty with stepmother. Committed to the Chicago Parental School for truancy from home and school. Stanley, twenty-two. Subject of present case-study. Female, twenty. Truant from home, difficulties with stepmother, petty stealing from home and neighbors. Appeared in juvenile court and placed under supervision of guardian. Now married and has family.

From the stepmother's two previous marriages: Female, thirty-five. Married. Has family. No official record of delinquency. Female, thirty-two. Married. Has family. No official record of delinquency. Female, thirty. Married. Has family. No official record of delinquency. Female, twenty-nine. Married. Has family. No official record of delinquency. Male, twenty-six. Married. This is the stepbrother with whom Stanley was involved in his initial delinquencies. Although arrested and taken to the police station, he never appeared in the juvenile court. Female, twenty-one. Single. No official record of delinquency. Female, nineteen. Single. No official record of delinquency.

After the father's third marriage intense emotional conflicts developed within the family group. The stepmother complained repeatedly that the father was a heavy drinker and abusive. When Stanley was seven years old, she had the father arrested on a charge of excessive drinking and cruelty. He was arraigned

in the Court of Domestic Relations and placed on adult probation. In addition to the difficulties between the father and stepmother, conflicts developed between the different sets of children.
The stepmother favored her own children and discriminated
against Stanley and his brother and sister. The father's children
from his first marriage were not directly involved in this conflict
since they were old enough to escape from the situation. The
following reports, which were made by the probation officer at
the time Stanley was about nine years of age, are indicative of
the conflicts which obtained in the family at that time:

Called at the home to-day, and talked with Stanley's step-mother. She
said that her husband beat her every time he gets drunk. He hits her with
anything he gets hold of. She said that she couldn't do anything with Stanley
and his brother, and that they both steal and run away from home. She
wants him committed to an institution. Says she is afraid to have them in
the house with her own children who are good and obedient. I feel that she
wants to get rid of the husband's three children. Says that she has to beat
them to make them mind, but her own children are very good. Stanley and
his brother and little sister say that the step-mother beats them, but she is
nice to her own children.

One month later:

Called at the home to-day, and talked with Stanley's step-mother. She
said that he was away from home, and that she couldn't do anything with
him. She thinks he is a very bad influence in the home. The home was clean
and orderly, but poorly furnished. Father is still drinking heavily and is
abusive. Stanley's little sister, Marie, was there. She looks very puny and
undernourished. She was surly and defiant. She has run away from home
many times, and tells the police she has no home. When identified at the
police station she refuses to go home. Says that the step-mother abuses her.
Little girl seemed afraid and cried. Could not tell why she lies and steals
money from her home. Step-mother said that her own little girl, about
Marie's age, is very nice and causes no trouble at all.

The following letter, which was written by Stanley's little
eight-year-old sister and sent to him while he was in St. Charles,
reveals clearly the conflicts which obtained in the family situation during the early period:

Dear Stanley I am writing you a letter. Ma is not going to buy you a box
of candy because pa did not give ma the pay. Pa hit ma and ma went to the
St. Anthonys hospital. ma had a cracked rib the doctor said. The other week

he hit ma fast. He said that he is going to kill ma and he hit rosie when she came he grabed her by the hair and chased her out. Pa comes drunk every day he cals ma names he curses at ma. Ma did not say a word to him ma has to close herself up in the dinning room.

From Marie
Good by.

Another important aspect of the family situation was the fact that the stepmother condoned Stanley's petty stealing. There is considerable evidence to indicate that she not only received stolen property, but actually encouraged him to steal from markets and freight cars. That this fact was known to the court is indicated in the following excerpt from the report of the probation officer on the case:

Visited at the home of Mrs. K. (Stanley's step-mother) to-day, to warn her against letting the children steal. Told her that complaints had come to our attention about her children stealing from the freight cars. She acknowledged the charge, and only said she could not help it. Said Stanley went with older boys, who stole and that he should be sent away to an institution. She acknowledged that she used the stolen goods, and didn't seem to be greatly concerned about the thefts. . . . .

In his study of Stanley's early behavior difficulties that Healy attached considerable importance to the family situation is suggested in the following extracts from his record (report made at the time Stanley was seven years and ten months of age):

The home conditions in this case are very bad. Father heavy drinker. Boy poorly nourished and neglected. Dislikes step-mother. Says she beats him and sends him out to steal. Boy very unhappy at home. Wants to live in Detention Home. Should be placed in congenial foster home. Not likely to be any improvement if he remains in his own home.

One year later, quoting from Healy's record:

This little boy is in the Detention Home again. Home conditions still very bad. Father gets drunk. Boy says that he doesn't want to go home. Still associating with same old companions. During past year nothing constructive has been done in the case. Boy's teeth have not been attended to. Step-brother makes him steal all the time, strawberries and other things. Same old bad companions, same father; the whole thing very bad but unlikely to be any better.

Unfortunately, Healy's recommendation to place Stanley in a foster-home was not followed, and his career in delinquency continued.

CONTACT WITH DELINQUENT GROUPS

According to official records, Stanley's first contacts with delinquents occurred when he was about seven years of age. At that time he became a member of a gang of older delinquent boys, among whom was his older stepbrother. This gang had a long tradition of petty stealing, burglary, and sex practices. Many of the members had records in the Juvenile Court and a few were already on parole from correctional institutions. It was while in the company of members of this group that Stanley's first experiences in pilfering, stealing from railroads and markets, and sex experiences occurred (see quotation from Healy's record, p. 24).

This gang is more or less typical of the numerous delinquent groups which develop in the delinquency areas of the city. It consisted of about twelve members, who ranged in age from six to seventeen years. The major activities and moral code were essentially delinquent in character. It is from such groups that professional criminals are largely recruited.

Stanley's contact with adult criminals in the rooming-house district west of the Loop and in the correctional institutions to which he was successively committed are sufficiently described in his own life-history.

Before concluding our description of Stanley's cultural background, it should be noted that he was a prodigious reader. The list of books which he has read covers a surprisingly wide range of subject matter. His preference for such books as those of Horatio Alger, James Oliver Curwood, and Zane Grey was obvious during the St. Charles period. Later, however, he showed a decided preference for books pertaining to crime and underworld life. His extensive reading is perhaps reflected in the rather superior literary quality of his own autobiography.

STANLEY'S OWN STORY

CHAPTER IV

STARTING DOWN GRADE[1]

To start out in life, everyone has his chances—some good and some very bad. Some are born with fortunes, beautiful homes, good and educated parents; while others are born in ignorance, poverty, and crime. In other words, Fate begins to guide our lives even before we are born and continues to do so throughout life. My start was handicapped by a no-good, ignorant, and selfish stepmother, who thought only of herself and her own children.[2]

As far back as I can remember, my life was filled with sorrow and misery. The cause was my stepmother, who nagged me, beat me, insulted me, and drove me out of my own home. My mother died when I was four years old, so I never knew a real mother's affection. My father remarried when I was five years of age. The stepmother who was to take the place of my real mother was a rawboned woman, devoid of features as well as emotions. She

[1] This is the first chapter of Stanley's "own story" of his experiences in truancy and delinquency. Aside from a number of corrections in punctuation, the story is presented precisely as it was written by the boy. He is also entirely responsible for the organization of the material into chapters, and suggested all of the chapter headings with the exception of that of chapter x. The sincerity of the story cannot be questioned. Through our numerous personal contacts with Stanley during the last five years we are convinced that the story reveals his fundamental attitudes and typical reactions to the various situations in which he has lived. Furthermore, the events described in the story are confirmed throughout by official records and by information secured directly from persons who had contact with Stanley during the period in which his delinquencies occurred. The story should be read with a view to getting insight into the boy's attitudes, typical reactions, and the social and moral world in which he lived. From this standpoint, as previously indicated, rationalizations, prejudices, exaggerations are quite as valuable as objective desciption.

[2] This introductory paragraph is typical of Stanley's self-justificatory attitude toward his own problems and situations. In this paragraph and throughout the entire document, he makes a rather definite attempt to place the responsibility for his misconduct upon fate, circumstances, and other persons, particularly his stepmother. Regardless of the justifiability of this attitude, it reflects a fundamental aspect of his personality.

was of Polish stock, and had the habits and customs of the people of the Old World. She came to America when about thirty years old; was married at the time, and had seven children. Her husband was in ill health and he died soon after arriving in Chicago. After burying her husband, she found herself without financial resources for herself and children. Realizing her predicament and the necessity of immediate action, she ventured out to find a husband, a man to support herself and her seven children; literally to slave and labor and bring home the bacon. Her venture was not so successful at first. Men were not wont to fall for her precious few charms. And, besides, did she not have seven children as an added burden?

My father was in a similar predicament, my mother having died and left three children. His thoughts went in quest of a woman to be his wife and a mother to his children. So it happened that Fate brought about a meeting of the two. A hasty courtship ensued, and in a short time they were married. My father worked for the Gas Company, and my stepmother proceeded to establish a home.

To this day I wonder how my father could have picked out such a woman for a wife. My conclusion is that she, in her desperation, used all her charm and coercion to get a man—any man who was able and inclined to work. My father, being fond of his whiskey and beer, and being in need of a mistress, became intoxicated and, thus blinded to her nature and circumstances, yielded to her coercion.[3]

She brought her seven children to our home. With us three children, my brother, my sister, and myself, there were twelve to feed and clothe. We all lived in four rooms in a basement. My father did not whimper. All he asked for was his regular meals, a bed to sleep in, and his daily can of beer and whisky. His mind was like a motor, always on one course. He didn't think of his children as boys and girls to be loved. He thought of us as just "kids," who had to be provided for, and he was the good provider. There his parental duties ended. Never did he show any

[3] Even if this account of the circumstances attendant upon the father's marriage to the stepmother were entirely fictitious, it would be none the less indicative of the boy's attitude toward his stepmother.

love or kindness. We "kids" were worth boarding and tolerating because sometime we would be financial assets.

For six months things went rather smoothly. Then my troubles began. My father and stepmother began to argue and quarrel about us children. I didn't know much about it at first, for I was more interested in playing with the cat behind the stove. But I soon felt the change. From a quiet woman, the stepmother changed to a hell-cat full of venom and spite. The first time she struck me was when I was in my favorite nook behind the stove, playing with the cat. She pulled me out and beat me, striking me in the face and on the back with her hard and bony hand. That was the first time that I ever knew fear. After many beatings I became more and more afraid, and I crouched behind the stove in fear. Well do I remember my first fears and horrors of her. I became unhappy and did not caper and play with my brother and sister as I had been wont to do. My father gave me no comfort. He spent his time at work, at the saloon, and in bed. Never did he pet or cheer me.

The stepmother favored her own children in every way. They received what luxuries were to be had, while my brother and sister and I had crumbs to pick off the table. She let her children eat at the table, and made us wait. Whenever one of her children would do a wrong they would tell her that I did it, and then I, instead of the culprit, would get the beating. My father couldn't interfere, because if he did the stepmother would threaten to leave. That would have been the best thing for his children, but of course he didn't want her to go.

Things went on this way. We fought with her because she favored her children at meals and beat us for their misdemeanors. Hard indeed it was for me to get enough to eat. Often when I would go to the store to buy food for the family, I would take a little biscuit or anything I could without my stepmother knowing it. So that much was I ahead when I got my portion at mealtime. My father worked steady and received good wages, so there was no good reason why we could not have enough to eat. But the stepmother was saving and fed her own children and let us go starved and half-naked on the street.

The stepmother also made us (brother, sister, and myself) do all the hard work in the house. And then she would beat us if we complained. That is what embittered me against her and her children. I developed a hatred against her that still lasts; a hatred that was so burning that when she would look into my eyes she would read it there, and in that way she knew my feeling. The Lord knows I tried to love her, but my nature could not stand her caresses in one of those sympathetic moods which she seldom had. Occasionally she would seem to feel sorry for her abuses and cruelty, and would ask me to kiss her; but my feelings protested. My fear and hatred made me avoid her and resent her caresses. Then she would get angry and beat me.[4]

So I grew old enough to go out on the street. The life in the streets and alleys became fascinating and enticing. I had two close companions that I looked up to with childish admiration and awe. One was William, my stepbrother. The other one was Tony, a dear friend of my stepbrother, William. They were close friends, four years older than me and well versed in the art of stealing.[5]

[4] Family situations of this kind are not at all uncommon in the cases of truant and delinquent children. It is probable that such situations not only play an important part in the formation of delinquent behavior trends, but greatly influence the development of attitudes and personality. Presumably Stanley's attitudes of persecution and suspicion originated in the antagonistic family relationship described in this paragraph. Among the more important factors in the situation is the stepmother's attitude of partiality toward her own children and her discrimination against Stanley and his brother and sister.

[5] As indicated in Healy's case-study, Stanley's initial stealing and sex experience occurred while he was in the company of William and Tony. It may be assumed that Stanley's initial experience in delinquency was an aspect of the play activity of his gang and neighborhood. Cutting lead pipes from vacant buildings, stealing pennies from newspaper stands, making raids on local fruit stores and groceries, and breaking into freight cars were as much a part of the established and accepted play life of the gang and neighborhood as crap-shooting, fighting, stealing rides on trucks and street cars, gathering and selling junk, and playing such games as ball, tag, and cops and robbers. From his point of view, it is probable that his early experiences in stealing had no more moral significance than the non-delinquent practices in which he engaged, and like the latter were acquired through his participation in the social life about him. The study of life-histories indicates that careers in delinquency very frequently originate in the type of social situation described in this paragraph (see Cases 8 and 9, pp. 15–17).

To my child-seeing eyes, I visioned Tony as a great leader in the neighborhood, and he directed his gang around with much bravado. He and William were always stealing and talking about stealing and I fell in with them as soon as I began to play around in the neighborhood.

Tony was a squatty boy, rough features, closely set eyes, and a body that bespoke strength and ruggedness. With his strength and fighting ability, he maintained leadership over his gang. He was also daring and courageous. I remember vividly how awed I was by his daring in stealing and fighting. These things made him a guy to be looked up to and respected in the neighborhood.

Tony liked his whiskey and in our neighborhood one could find as many as four or five saloons in one block in those days. He would dare me to drink and I would, although it burned my throat. I was what they call "game" and I just swallowed it without a word, to maintain that high distinction which I was openly proud of.

Tony had two sisters who always played with us and went on our stealing adventures. They could steal as good as any boy. Also they had sex relations openly with all the boys in the neighborhood. I remember how the boys boasted that they had had sex relations with each of them. All the boys talked about it and the girls didn't care; they seemed to be proud of it and expect it. The funny thing about it was that Tony knew all about his sisters and their behavior and only made merry about it.

The boys in the gang teased me about Tony's sisters, asking me how many times I had had sex relations with them. Even the girls would talk to me about sex things, put their arms around me, and touch my body. At first I was too young to know what it all meant, but I soon learned and developed many sex habits, like masturbation and playing with girls.

Tony didn't work, but made his money by stealing, and he made lots of it for a boy of his age.

My stepmother sent me out with William (my stepbrother) to pick rags and bottles in the alleys. She said that would pay for my board and make me more useful than fretting and sulking at home. I did not mind that in the least. In fact, I enjoyed it, because I was at least out of the old lady's reach. I began to have a great time exploring the whole neighborhood—romping and playing in the alleys and "prairies," gathering rags, bones, and iron, and selling them to the rag peddlers. This romping and roaming became fascinating and appealed to my curiosity, because it was freedom and adventure. We played "Indian" and other games in the alleys, running through the old sheds and vacant houses. Then we gathered cigarette "buttses" along the street and took them to the shed, where we smoked and planned adventure.[6] I was little and young, but I fell in with the older guys. Outside, in the neighborhood, life was full of pleasure and excitement, but at home it was dull and drab and full of nagging, quarreling, and beating, and stuffy and crowded besides.

On the trips with William, I found him to be a rather chummy companion. I regarded him, not as a brother, but rather as a boy friend from another home. He was five years my senior. He sort of showed it in his obvious superiority. But I didn't seem to notice that fault. He was a "mamma's boy" at home, but oh, Lord, how he changed on our trips! He taught me how to be mischievous; how to cheat the rag peddler when he weighed up our rags. He would distract the peddler's attention while I would steal a bag of rags off the wagon. We would sell the rags back to the victimized peddler. He also took me to the five and ten cent store on Forty-seventh Street, and would direct me to steal from the counter while he waited at the door. I usually was successful, as I was little and inconspicuous. How I loved to do these things! They thrilled me. I learned to smile and to laugh again. It was an honor, I thought, to do such things with William. Was he not the leader and I his brother? Did I not look up to him? I was ready to do anything William said, not because of fear, but because he was my companion. We were always together, and between us sprang up a natural understanding, so to speak.

One day my stepmother told William to take me to the railroad

[6] Stanley's description of his experiences with William and Tony illustrates the value of the "own story" in the study of the attitudes and social values prevailing in the community and social group of which the delinquent is a member.

yard to break into box-cars.[7] William always led the way and made the plans. He would open the cars, and I would crawl in and hand out the merchandise. In the cars were foodstuffs, exactly the things my stepmother wanted. We filled our cart, which we had made for this purpose, and proceeded toward home. After we arrived home with our ill-gotten goods, my stepmother would meet us and pat me on the back and say that I was a good boy and that I would be rewarded. Rewarded, bah! Rewarded with kicks and cuffs.

After a year of breaking into box-cars and stealing from stores, my stepmother realized that she could send me to the market to steal vegetables for her. My stealing had proved to be very profitable to her, so why not make it even more profitable? I knew it was for my own good to do what she wanted me to do. I was so afraid of her that I couldn't do anything but obey. Anyway, I didn't mind stealing, because William always went with me, and that made me feel proud of myself, and it gave me a chance to get away from home.

Every Saturday morning we would get up about three o'clock and prepare for the venture. William, Tony, and his two sisters and I would always go. We would board a street car, and the people on the car would always stare at us and wonder where such little kids were going so early in the morning. I liked to attract the attention of people and have them look down upon me with curiosity. The idea of my riding in a street car at that early hour appealed to my adventurous spirit and keyed me up to stealing. In the street car, William would give me orders on what to steal and how to go about it. I listened to him with interest and always carried out his orders. He had me in the palm of his hand, so to speak. He got the satisfaction of ordering me, and I got the thrill of doing the stealing. He instructed me on how to evade peddlers and merchants if they gazed at me while I was stealing. After arriving at the market, William would lay out the plan of action and stand guard while I did the stealing. He knew

[7] There are many areas in the city in which stealing from freight cars is a very prevalent practice. It is not unusual to find cases in which the entire family participates in this type of delinquency.

what the stepmother wanted, and he always filled her orders to overflowing. All in all, I was a rather conceited little boy who thought himself superior to the other boys of his age; and I didn't miss impressing that little thing upon their minds. I was so little that the peddlers were not suspicious of me, and it didn't take long to fill our baskets and be ready for the journey home. All spring, summer, and fall did we go to the market, and never did I get caught and never did we go home with empty baskets.

Stealing in the neighborhood was a common practice among the children and approved by the parents. Whenever the boys got together they talked about robbing and made more plans for stealing. I hardly knew any boys who did not go robbing. The little fellows went in for petty stealing, breaking into freight cars, and stealing junk. The older guys did big jobs like stick-up, burglary, and stealing autos. The little fellows admired the "big shots" and longed for the day when they could get into the big racket. Fellows who had "done time" were big shots and looked up to and gave the little fellows tips on how to get by and pull off big jobs.

In spite of all my stealing for her, the stepmother continued to favor her own children, and to beat me. She wouldn't give me any spending money nor any decent clothes. She continued to beat me, and my hatred for her kept getting stronger. I was selling papers in the winter and was barefoot. The stepmother said that I wasn't her "kid," and that she wouldn't spend her money to buy clothes for me. She told me to go out and beg and steal to get spending money.

Things became so bad that my brother and sister ran away just to get out of the stepmother's reach. They put them in jail just for running away. That left only me at home, but I was just about ready to go. Fate had decided against me and my brother and sister. Were my brother and sister not already suffering for the crimes of someone else? Were they not in jail simply because life was intolerable with the stepmother and her brood of culprits? I learned all the meanness of my childhood from my stepbrother William, but never once was he whipped or arrested. Fate was in his favor. I became unhappy, and fear and hatred took possession of me. One day a policeman came to our house and told my stepmother that he saw William and me stealing in a store. After he left, the stepmother accused me of leading William astray, and she proceeded to tie me to a chair for the customary beating. Fear possessed me and gave me added courage and strength. I tore myself loose from her and ran away.

For the first time in my life I was out of the hole I called home, away from my stepmother. But where would I go? A boy of six years and four months. I didn't lose much time, but went back to our old home in Bridgeport. I met my old chums there and told them that I was bumming from home. We played together all day, but at night I got afraid and lonesome. I thought about home and the beating that was waiting for me. Fear kept me from returning home. I roamed the street until late at night, and then found a dry spot under a doorstep, where I curled up and slept till morning. Thus I roamed and begged and stole food until four days later, when I was arrested. The policeman took me to the station, and the desk sergeant ordered some bread and milk put before me. I thought that, compared with the place I called home, the jail seemed more like a haven of rest. I told them about my stepmother and my stepbrother, but they said, "You will have to go back home." My adventurous spirit sank to zero. They called my father, who came to take me back home. As we got near home, I was growing nervous because I knew I was due a beating as soon as my father went to work. My stepmother smiled when we got home, but when my father left she took a stick, and I got the beating of my life. After she got through, she said, "Run away again, I don't care; I don't want you around here, you'll lead all my boys to be criminals."[8]

[8] In a recent conversation with Stanley (December, 1929), he made the following significant statement with regard to his stepmother: "I don't believe that I exaggerated the faults of my stepmother, but if I did, I certainly didn't exaggerate my feelings toward her." This statement illustrates one of the primary assumptions of this volume, namely, that in the study and treatment of the delinquent child it is essential to deal with his personal attitudes, his definition of the situation, although these may be exaggerations or even misinterpretations of the objective situation. Even if it were true that Stanley's interpretation of the family situation were somewhat exaggerated, it cannot be doubted that he acted "as if" these interpretations were true (in this connection see the statement of W. I. Thomas, p. 3).

Once away from home, the other times were easy. That was the easiest way to get out of my stepmother's reach, and, besides, it made a strong appeal to my young and adventurous spirit. I ran away so many times that my father grew weary of going to the station to get me. He told the stepmother to keep me at home or he would get somebody who would. From then on, I was tied to the bed, but I continued to loosen myself and run out again. My feelings were to roam without a care on my mind, to be away from home, where I always got the clouts. And roam I did. I would romp back to our old home and neighborhood, and then on down to West Madison Street and the Loop. I would gaze at the movie houses, restaurants, poolrooms, and at the human wreckage that made its uncertain and guideless way along West Madison Street. Their conversations and carefree personalities appealed to my childish imagination. A score of times or more did I thus roam from home to West Madison when I was eight and nine years old.

Freedom now possessed me. I felt that I could get along some way on my own hook. But I soon learned that Fate was still master of my destiny. I was supposed to go to school, but it never appealed to me. To sit in a schoolroom all day was like being confined in prison. I would sit in school and think of traveling and roaming without a care. I always wanted to play hookey, so finally I was arrested and taken to the Juvenile Detention Home, where I learned the first law of nature—self-preservation.

CHAPTER V

THE BABY BANDHOUSE[1]

The Detention Home at first seemed like a palace to me. It was clean and in order. The very first night I took a nice bath (the first one I ever had), had a change of clothes, and a good meal. I felt like I'd never want to go back to that "old hole" (home) with my stepmother. I went to bed in a clean little white bed, and I thought, "Well, is this jail? Who ever thought it was so nice?"

Inside the Detention Home I found a motley crowd of aspiring young crooks—young aspirants to the "hall of fame of crookdom." In their own minds they had already achieved fame in the world of crime, and proceeded to impress that fact upon the other boys. The whole thing seemed to be a contest, among young crooks, to see who was the biggest and bravest crook. They loiter about the place, congregating in small groups, talking about their achievements and ambitions in their common vocation, crime. The older crooks are gods and stand around telling about their exploits. Much of it is bunk, but they succeed in making the other boys, especially the younger ones of more tender feelings and not so wise to the world, believe it. I listened eagerly to the stories and fell into the web myself. I was really awed by the bravery and wisdom of the older crooks. Their stories of adventures fascinated my childish imagination, and I felt drawn to them. My timid spirit (you remember I was only eight) wanted to go out and achieve some of the glories for myself.

Well do I remember how Pat Maloney impressed my childish mind. He was seven years my senior, a big husky Irish lad, and a "master bandit." He was in for stealing automobiles, burglary,

[1] This chapter is a description of Stanley's experiences and contacts in the Juvenile Detention Home and the Chicago Parental School. The former institution is designed for the detention of dependent and delinquent children, pending the disposition of their cases in the Juvenile Court. The Parental School receives commitments of children charged with truancy from school and other behavior difficulties arising in relation to the school situation.

and "bumming" from home and school. To him the last-mentioned offenses were only minor infractions of the law. The young guys, me included, looked up to him. He paraded among us like a king on dress parade. My feelings of pride swelled to the breaking point when he picked me out and took a liking to me. He must have pitied me, for I was little and frail and timid. I listened eagerly to his stories of how he ran away from home because of his stepfather (like myself), and how he learned to open locks and break into houses and stores, and how he used to go to the White Sox ball park to watch cars for people, and then pick out a good one and drive it away. He was a wise crook, but he had a kind and tender heart. He sympathized with me and said he knowed why I couldn't live at home with my stepmother, and that I didn't need to, because it wouldn't be hard to make a go of it on my own hook when I got a little wiser and knowed a little more about stealing. He said fellows like us, who didn't have any home, had to steal to make a go of it. He was a good pal of mine, and I felt real sorry when he was taken to court and sentenced to St. Charles. He didn't whimper when the sentence of two years was imposed, and I respected him for his courage and grit. It made me feel shame because I cried about my predicament, but he simply smiled and showed a determined face.

During the times I was in the home I met crooks of every creed and color. They were there for every crime, running away from home, bumming from school, taking automobiles, stealing from parents, shoplifting, breaking into houses and stores, petty stealing, and sex perversions. It was a novelty to learn that there were so many crimes and ways of stealing that I had never heard about. I was green at first, and the boys pitied and petted me, but I was well on the way to Crookdom at the end of my stay in that place.[2]

After a while a policeman came to me and said that I was going home. He warned me about running away again and said that

[2] Our case histories indicate rather clearly that the social contacts established in institutional situations are a medium through which delinquent codes and techniques are transmitted from one boy to another. This social process is well illustrated by Stanley's experiences in the Detention Home and the institutions to which he was subsequently committed (see also Cases 5, 6, and 7, pp. 12–14).

I would be sent away till I was twenty-one if I didn't stay at home. I accepted his advice and started home. As I was on the car I thought of Patty and how brave he was, and made up my mind that I could take care of myself; so I got off the car and started to wander down toward the Loop. I got to West Madison Street and begged money to go to a show. I made up my mind never to go back home, where I always got nagged and beat up. I roamed for two days, and got so hungry that I had to get food out of garbage cans. A policeman saw me picking up garbage in an alley at Madison and Halsted streets, and arrested me and took me to the Detention Home. I was glad to get back to the Home and have a bath, good food, and a clean bed. The next day I was taken home by a woman from the court; I guess they had decided not to trust me to go home alone. On the way home she told me to be a good boy and go to school and not run away from home any more.

The stepmother met us and was all smiles till the lady from the court left, and then she sprang into me with fury, but I escaped her and ran into the alley. I saw the lady from the court waiting for a car at the corner, so I hid in the alley until she left, and then proceeded to get the hell out of the neighborhood. Where would I go, a mere kid, without a home and no friends to help me? My legs naturally carried me to West Madison Street, where I slipped into a show. I fell asleep and was awakened by a policeman, who requested me to accompany him. He took me to the station and then to the Detention Home. I was rather glad to get back, because I was used to the place, and it was far better than being home with my stepmother. I was told that I was becoming a "habitual runaway" and a "bad actor," but they sent me back home again that same day. It was no use, for I had the roaming instinct, and during the next few months I was put in the Detention Home eight more times for running away from my stepmother. Everybody knew me at the Detention Home, and they were always looking for me to come back. They saw that I was hopeless, so they booked me for hearing. Everybody thought there was something wrong with me. They had my head examined to see if I was a "dummie," and I guess they found that I was, for they said that I'd have to be "committed." I was becoming a dangerous character, for the teachers at school said I was "a menace to society." Now that was strange, for I was only a harmless little boy of eight years who had a roaming instinct because I couldn't live with a selfish and hell-bent stepmother. But the day of my trial arrived. I was led into the courtroom by a big policeman, who told the judge that I was a bad actor and would not stay at home. The judge said, "Sonny, you are not very large to be away from home. You need to be at home with your parents. They love you, and you must stay with them. I'll give you a chance to go back home and make good. But remember, I'll send you away where you'll have to be good if you come here again." I was too scared to say a word. I was taken back home that day, but found the stepmother as cruel as ever. She started to whip me again, and I slipped through the back door into the alley and was free again.

I wandered away from home and "hitched" a ride on a truck, which carried me several blocks from home. My questless journey led me to a group of boys who were playing games around a church. They saw me and invited me to join them in the game, which I did. It got dark and the other boys were called in by their parents. That left me alone, so I crawled into a corner of the church entrance and soon went to sleep. I was soon awakened by people coming to the church. An Irish woman with a decided Irish brogue saw me and took pity on me. She asked me where I lived. I told her that I had no home. Then she asked me to go home with her and have something to eat.

I followed her to her home, which was on the top floor of an old frame building. She immediately placed a meal before me and I ate with great relish. The home was poorly furnished, but it was warm and cozy. Her many children began to play with me, and soon I was part of the family.

In this family I was happy and contented. I had lots of good things to eat and fun. We played games in the attic. There we played telephone, using the clothesline as the telephone wire. One fellow would be lineman, another switchboard operator, etc. The mother would give us bread, butter, and jam, and cookies between meals. My! but it was a great life and I could have lived there forever.[3]

My stay in this happy home came to an end suddenly after four or five weeks. The end came unexpectedly. The Irish lady had given me some pennies to buy candy with. On my way to the store, two detectives stopped me, who ordered me to go with them, which I did. They took me back to the Juvenile Detention Home and to court, where I was released to live with my stepmother.

I wandered away the same day and stayed on the streets all day, and at night, being hungry and cold, stopped at a settlement house on Halsted Street. A kind lady talked to me and asked me about my parents. I said that my parents were dead and that I didn't have any home. She called the police, and in a few minutes I found myself in the Detention Home again. They knew me at the Home, and said, "Didn't you just leave here this morning?" and I said, "Yes, I can't live at home with my stepmother." They said, "You can stay here tonight, and we will let the judge settle your case."

The next day I was summoned to court. I had to be dragged away from the blocks I was playing with in the playroom. I never had them at home, so you can imagine how interested I was in them. I wasn't a bit interested in my case, for I was busy gazing around and satisfying my curiosity. The judge asked my stepmother if she wanted me back home. She refused to take me and told the interpreter that I was incorrigible and leading her children astray, and that a few years in the reform school would de me some good. The judge accepted her suggestion and commit- ted me to the Chicago Parental School for three months. That was when I was about nine years old.

My first night at the Parental School was the first time I ex perienced real sorrow and homesickness.[4] The institution was

[3] Stanley's favorable reaction to this family situation suggests that perhaps placement in a congenial and sympathetic foster-home should have been attempted at that time. As previously indicated, Healy had already repeatedly recommended such a plan of treatment.

[4] It should be pointed out that Stanley's description of the Chicago Parental School is not indicative of the present situation in this institution. Subsequent to

surrounded by acres of tilled soil. To a common observer it was a beautiful scene to gaze upon, but to me, a timid boy of nine years, it was something new and lonely. I had never been out of the city before, and the quiet and peaceful surroundings made me very lonesome and sad. It all seemed like a foreign town to me, and it took me several weeks to get used to it. I couldn't sleep the first night, and the first day seemed like an age. The first thing in their procedure was to clip off the hair close to the scalp. We were then given the rules of the institution, which we had to adhere to strictly. If not—punishment was the sure result.

The institution had too much discipline. I was very scared and frightened, and put into submission from the first till I was released. Physically I was a slave, but mentally I was free, and I took advantage of this freedom and dreamed. I dreamed boyish dreams of the outside world, of my home and friends in the city. Many times I would be rudely awakened from my dreams during the day, and would realize that I was in a realistic world that was full of sorrow for me. Other boys had mothers to visit them and take candy and cookies to them, but I had none, only a selfish stepmother. She visited me once and tried to kiss me, but my soul could not take the caress, even though I tried. That angered her, and she didn't come down any more. Indeed, I did not miss her, for the less I saw of her the better I felt.

During the five months' imprisonment I worked as an errand boy part-time, and went to school. Discipline was so strict throughout the institution that a boy could not even talk, and there wasn't any interesting recreation or diversion. The boys all hated the place, the guards were hard boiled, and severe punishment was inflicted for the least infraction of the rules. For each misdemeanor a boy received a mark against his conduct, and it is removed by strenuous exercise, and if you were slack you would be anointed with cowhide, and they weren't any too

---

his commitment, a special investigation of the methods of discipline in the institution was made (1922). As a result of the findings of that investigation, the institution was placed under new management. Mr. O. J. Milliken became superintendent, and under his very excellent management the conditions described in Stanley's story have been eliminated.

gentle about laying it on. The most common kinds of punishment were muscle grinders, squats, benders, standing in corner, whipping, confinement in "the cage," chewing soap, being deprived of food and sleep, strenuous labor, and making the sentence longer. Many times I experienced these forms of torture. Being just a child without friends, I cringed in fear and developed a childish revenge against the cruel institution. Why was I in such a place, and why was I punished, just because fate was against me? I was just a mere child, too weak to strike back or defend myself. My only pleasure was in my childish dreams, which carried me away into the free world outside. I dreamed of my chums, our stealing and roaming in the city, of my pals at the Detention Home, especially Patty Maloney, whose stories of adventure I could not get out of my mind. Some day I'd be big and brave like him, and then I wouldn't worry and have fear of these cruel officials. Other boys had nice mothers and friends to bring boxes of goodies to them, and stood by them in this cold world, but I had only a disgusting stepmother. I got lonely and sullen and full of fear, but my dreams kept me alive, and I dreamed every day. There I started to be a dreamer of dreams. That is one of life's cynical jokes—how I could dream such beautiful dreams in such a hole of strict discipline and drabness. So I dreamed and existed five months and I was paroled to live at home.

When I was on the street again I felt like a tied-up colt that runs and kicks and raises hell in general. Two days after I was out I was abused again. The stepmother treated me like a prince for two days, but then she began to make up for lost time. I began to feel like going a million miles away, just to keep out of her reach. That is how I got the roaming instinct. Now I had more courage and more experience in the world, and knew I could get along some way, so I made up my mind not to take much insult from my stepmother. Other boys could make it on their own hooks, and so could I. Besides, I had a lot of "education" during the last six months. So I left home after a quarrel the third day, and met another kid and we sallied out to forage for ourselves. He was a little green, but I told him about the adventures we could have, and then he was glad to go. I hesitated just a minute, thinking of my trip to the Parental School, but I thought I could get along. We traveled to the Loop, and then to Halsted and Madison—my old haunt. We bummed our way into shows, and having a gnawing at our stomach we "lifted" some fruit off a stand and satisfied our hunger. That night we looked for a place to sleep, and found a spacious front porch that we could hide under and sleep. During the night I was awakened by a tug at my leg. Looking up I saw my old friend, a policeman, standing there, and he bade us to go with him. We were taken to the Detention Home, this being the thirteenth time I had entered its pearly gates. I was an "old timer" there at the early age of ten, and being a kid, felt it was an honor to be so well known. Besides, I was a "habitual or professional runaway" and considered a bad actor. In the home the kids all knew I'd done time and sort'a looked up to me for my wide experience in the world.

After a month I was summoned to court. The policeman said, "Your honor, this is a professional runaway. He will not stay at home and will not attend school. Also, he has a record in the Parental School." Looking at me, the judge said, "Young man, what is the trouble with you? Why don't you stay at home? Don't you remember what I told you when you were here before?" I was too scared to reply. He asked the stepmother if she wanted me, and she said she did not, so the judge said, "I'll enter a St. Charles order; he'll have to stay there." I was elated. I was going out on a train ride, and it would be the first one in my life. My companion was let free because it was his first offense, and his mother cried to take him back home. I thought I was better off than him, then. But I soon got down to earth when I was entered in the St. Charles School for Boys.

CHAPTER VI

GETTING EDUCATED

I was awed by the sight of the St. Charles School for Boys,[1] for it is a beautiful landscape to gaze upon from the outside. But it is quite a different place on the inside, as I learned during fifty months of incarceration there. My formal entry consisted of a few questions regarding my birth, age, nationality, religion, and so on. At the receiving cottage I was directed to remove my clothes, which consisted of a pair of pants and a blouse—no shoes, underwear, or cap did I wear. I was so scared that I couldn't remove my scant attire, but a little help from the rough hands of a boy guard caused me to get them off in a hurry. After a bath, I received my prison suit of overalls, blouse, hard shoes, and white cap.

[1] As indicated previously, Stanley was committed to the St. Charles School for Boys a few months prior to his tenth birthday. His attitude toward the school was one of resistance and antagonism. He was especially resistive to the military system, boy captains, the formal punishments, and the restrictions against conversation in the cottages. These attitudes were quite consistent with his usual reaction to formal authority and discipline. Case histories of this type suggest the desirability of developing a more informal and diversified institutional program adaptable to the different types of personality. In view of Stanley's personality, we would scarcely anticipate a favorable reaction to the formal régime in St. Charles. Mr. M. H. Cone, who has been a St. Charles parole officer in the Chicago district for many years and who was responsible for the supervision of Stanley, gives the following description of the institution:

"The institution at the present time covers a tract of land of twelve hundred acres in Kane County in the Fox River Valley, one of the most picturesque regions in Illinois, being located thirty-eight miles west of Chicago on the Lincoln Highway. It is nationally known for its perfection of beauty in arrangement and equipment, being one of the show spots of the State, having a property valuation of $1,250,000.00.

"The State gives a most careful study to all beneficial factors which may enter into the moral, physical and intellectual betterment of the youth, whose attitude, in the opinion of the Court, is beyond the normal restraint of parental control. Most all forms of healthy outdoor exercise are allowed and encouraged. School and industrial training form the important part of the daily routine. The closest possible kindly supervision by night as well as by day, controls the life in every cottage. The result of this effect is shown in the co-operative activity throughout

The institution is built or designed *à la* military style,[2] so that strict observance of the rules was necessary or punishment was due as sure as rain. Of course I knew I was in a reform school and expected discipline, having been in Chicago Parental School. But the discipline was so strict that inwardly I harbored rebellion.

For making even a little noise or even talking out loud, you would get a beating. The first night I thought I could never stand it. I got so lonesome for the city and my old pals that I couldn't sleep and cried most of the night. Everything was under pressure and forbidden.

The boys were not allowed to talk in the cottage, either at the table or in the reading room.[3] So they slipped around in their soft house-slippers, quietly and weirdly. They reminded me of dumb mutes. This everlasting quietness, without any talking from my fellow-prisoners, gave me a creepy, clammy feeling and almost drove me crazy for a few weeks.

It was soon impressed upon my mind that life in this institution was a matter of survival of the fittest, and it was hard enough for the fittest. Secretly, most of the boys stuck together against

the School on the part of all interested in it or connected with it through commitment.

"In this institution Stanley served three terms, covering periods altogether of some fifty months, before he was sixteen years old. At the close of his first term, because of unsuitable conditions for a successful parole in his own home, he was given a trial on an outside farm. Here he remained but a few days. As the only recourse left, he was given a chance with his step-mother. But after a brief stay with her, he reported to me in rags, saying: 'She give me de gate.' He claimed, with good reason, 'that even the street was better than living with one who was always hollerin.' "

[2] Quoting again from Mr. Cone: "The two outstanding features at the St. Charles School are order and obedience. Because it teaches obedience and promotes discipline, military training is a necessity, being carried on to a high point of efficiency. With this training goes an appeal to all that is best in the future citizen. He is taught reverence and respect for the flag of his country so that his conduct may be in accord with its ideals."

[3] Quoting again from Mr. Cone's record: "In order to avoid unnecessary noise and confusion in a cottage, where as many as fifty or sixty boys are housed, conversation is prohibited. Also this restriction is a means of establishing habits of obedience and order in the boys who are so much in need of proper discipline and restraint."

the official and against the boy captain and other boy officers. The boys had a code which is found throughout the criminal world; it is, "To squawk on a fellow-prisoner is an unpardonable sin and only the lowest characters will squawk." But there were boys who would squawk and they would usually become boy officers, so we did not trust them but harbored hatred toward them. They were not fit to be associated with decent boys. The boys had to have a secret code there to protect themselves from the guards, boy captains, and other officials. A squawker is usually a goodie-good boy and finds life miserable, for he is maligned by the other boys until he turns to their desires or he gets protection from the house father and becomes a boy officer.

In each cottage is a house father, house mother, and a boy captain.[4] The father and mother live in the cottage. Most of the fathers that I had were pretty good, but the captains were terrible. They are boys and are selected by the house father. Usually they are bullies, conceited and domineering, and like to lord it over, showing their authority. They also are squawkers, and deceitful and favor some boys and take out their grudge on others. In many cases they are the worst boys in the cottage, but they get by because of their position and they stand in with the father. In our disputes between the captain and other boys, the father will always favor the captain, even if he is in the wrong. So there grows up under the surface a lot of revenge and hate among the boys who feel that they are not getting a fair break.

I fell in the web without any experience, but soon got onto the ropes. My feeling was for the code and against the officials. Don't trust anybody except tried pals who won't squawk. Nobody trusts you; if they did they wouldn't guard you night and day and always have the cowhide ready for you. Remember the guard or captain is a squawker and your enemy or he wouldn't have his job. He stands in or has a pull with the officials. Harbor revenge, but hold it in leash until the proper time to strike.

[4] Quoting again from Mr. Cone: "The boy captain is a necessary part of the military system. Each cottage has a boy captain who is selected by the house father because of his ability in handling the other boys. He is largely responsible for the conduct of the boys in the cottage and is required to report instances of misconduct to the house father."

The institution has too much discipline. Every time you turn around you break a rule. So you are always in fear of doing something wrong, of breaking a rule and then getting a bawling out or some form of punishment. I was punished many times, often for trivial things, and many times because I wouldn't squawk, and there grew up in me a hatred against these enemies; a hatred that still burns. I still remember the times that I was kicked and cuffed, and these memories shall always live with me.

The different forms of punishment were beatings, bawling out, being deprived of food and sleep, muscle grinders, squats, haunches, benders, etc. In muscle grinders the victim gets down, stretches out his toes and hands, and then goes up and down for an hour. It soon tires one out. In squats you put your hands behind the neck, then raise and lower yourself, bending the knees. An hour of this will leave anyone exhausted. In haunches, you stand on tiptoes, arms outstretched, and raise and lower the body. Ten minutes of this and you'll do anything to be relieved. In benders you touch the floor with the tips of fingers, without bending knees. One hour of this will cure any disease. Polishing the floor for hours while you are resting the weight of the body on the tips of the toes is another form of punishment. All of these are often accompanied with clouts and general razzing.

The strict discipline, hard punishment, no recreation, fear, and unfair breaks made life miserable. Besides, life was monotonous. While I yearned for freedom, I never received a letter of consolation or a visit from a friend or relative to brighten me. I became lonely, alone, never liked to be near people. Life held not a single charm for me. I learned to read books and to dream, and these took me out of my miserable surroundings into a new world full of novelty. I read all of Alger's books, some of them many times, and other books of adventure, and dreamed of becoming a success in the business world, like Alger's heroes. I wanted a chance to make good, for I had the ambition, but who would monkey with a little mite like me? I was cast by the wayside and forgotten, kept in St. Charles because that was the easiest way to get rid of me. After years of incarceration (five in all in St. Charles) I lost my ambition and became indolent, carefree, and "drifty." I whiled and dreamed my life away without any concern for the future. My only interest was to get along any easy way, and the easiest way I knew was to beg and steal.

I was finally transferred to Cottage K with five of the youngest boys, and it is the worst cottage in the whole joint. The forenoons were spent in school, and the afternoons in the garden. I got along fairly well in my studies, but I was judged a bad character for my age by the teacher, so I received some marks against my conduct which were not true. But I didn't care how bad they thought I was, anyway. If I would explain I would only get a trimming in exchange.

One Saturday afternoon all of us were playing on the drill field, and the first lieutenant (a boy) asked me to go to the cottage and bring his harmonica. While I was in the cottage I saw two other boys who had sneaked into the cottage, and they were stealing something. I took the harmonica to the lieutenant and ten minutes later I was accused of stealing some cigars from the basement. I denied the charge, and could have cleared myself by telling on the two boys, but I wouldn't squawk and break the code; consequently I was given a good beating and forced to do "haunches" another hour. Many times did I suffer because I wouldn't squawk, but I'd die before I'd turn on a fellow prisoner.

There was lots of sex perversions in the form of masturbation and sodomy committed in one of the cottages. The bullies would attack the younger boys in the dormitories and force them to have relations. Some of the boys caught venereal diseases and had to be treated. That was very easy in a place like that, where there were a lot of boys living together in close quarters, especially where the older boys mingle with the younger ones. The younger ones get all the bad habits of the older boys, and sex habits are very common in every institution where boys or men are confined. I've seen lots of it. I knew little boys who had sex relations with four or five older boys every night. It was easy in the dormitory to slip into another boy's bunk.[5] They sepa-

[5] Every effort is made to cope with the problem of sex perversion among the boys. At present an officer is placed on guard in the dormitory each night.

rate the boys by their weight,[6] and that puts young fellows in with oldtimers, who are little but well educated in crime. The oldtimer stands as a hero and impresses his superiority on the younger boys, who are always ready to admire a brave crook. As a child in St. Charles, I looked up to the fellows who had done deeds of daring in a criminal line. I wanted to go out and do something worthy of commendation too. While in my cottage I met young crooks and old crooks, and began to think I was a pretty wise crook and began to tell lies about my exploits to make a good impression on my fellow-prisoners.

On entering the school the prisoners are given the general razz and forced into submission from the start. The officers tell you to "get used to it, it's too late now to sob about your crimes." They do get used to it by getting on to the ropes and harboring revenge and other feelings in secret.

We had lots of military drilling after the day's work. This was to prepare for the dress parade which we had every Sunday. Most of the boys, including myself, disliked this, because the least little mistake was a cause for razzing by the captain. Woe betide the boy who made a mistake on dress parade, for the captain would give him notice to report to him at the cottage, and then the boy would repay tenfold for his mistake. So the drilling was spoiled by the boy captains, who liked to show their authority. Whipping was not allowed by the superintendent, but it was tolerated by many of the house fathers and done by the captains. Drilling could have been done to the good of the boys, because we were interested in "copping" first prize for having the best company in the regiment. But the boy captains spoiled the whole thing.

We had ball games out on the field in the summer and in the gymnasium in the winter, but this was spoiled because the boy captains and their special friends and the bullies always played the games while us little fellows had to sit on the bleachers and only long to be in the game. It was the case of "The Fox and the Grapes," just another chance for the boy officers to show their

[6] In order to facilitate organization of the boys into military units, classifications are made upon the basis of weight.

authority to the younger boys, who harbor a grudge against them and get a bad disposition.

Everything was regular and had a fixed routine and monotonous. We always knew what to expect at every meal, for they had a fixed bill of fare for each day through the week, throughout the whole year. On Sunday we had a piece of gingerbread, which broke the monotony a little bit.

All in all, the institution put fear in me and held me back from romping and playing and enjoying myself like a boy ought to. I always felt under ban and not free to be interested in life. I was little and pitied myself and couldn't defend myself against the bullies that lorded it over me. Life was lonesome, dull, and full of childish fears. Everything in the institution had its drawbacks for a frail child like me, because there was too much discipline and the boy captains didn't give me a fair break.

In October, I was paroled to live with my stepmother, after doing time sixteen months. My! but it felt good to get out of prison with its shackles and discipline, out into freedom again. But home was just like it always was, and I was many times worse. I felt a little cocky and rebellius. I started to school in the fifth grade, but I was too restless to settle down to such monotonous work. I dreamed of the movies, of roaming, and of playing hookie, and thought, here I am free again, so why not enjoy myself. So I bummed from school and was having a happy time when the teacher reported me to the stepmother. The stepmother had already beat me many times for quarreling with her darling little culprits. Now I got another beating, which were love taps alongside of the ones I got in St. Charles. Then she ordered me out to work, saying that I'd either work or starve.

Becoming disgusted, I left home, without knowing where to go. I roamed a few days and became hungry, dirty, and lonesome. But nothing could force me to go back to the stepmother. I found my way to the Madison Street bridge, and half resolved to throw myself over, but my youth belied the idea. So I roamed the street, finding that better than returning to the "house of hell." I was between two hells. Being on parole, I was supposed to live at home, so if arrested I'd be returned to St. Charles.

One morning, being ravenously hungry, I begged fruit at a little Italian store on South Halsted Street. A little Italian girl there, seeing my rags, took pity on me and fed me, and then took me to the Hull-House, saying the people there would help me. They called the police, and I was loaded into a "patty wagon" and taken to the Detention Home again.

I went back to St. Charles after being out just twenty-four days. Hain't it hell? It was then. Returning to that hole for nothing but breaking my parole. Riding along on the train, looking at the open fields, I felt like I was being forced into an awful prison, without knowing when I'd get out, and being there where I could see this open country and yet held in bondage filled me with sadness and was tormenting to the extreme. I thought how miserable I was, always under pressure and watched and trailed. I was like a wild animal, hunted and pursued, captured and caged, punished and beaten. My life was not my own, to be lived like other boys, free and happy. Always was I persecuted and held down by cruel laws and officials who like to capture me and make my life miserable and lonely. In my torment I made up my mind that I wouldn't stay long in this institution and when I did get out, I'd go so far away they'd never find me again.

When I got back to the institution there was a new superintendent. He cut down on the food, ordered more work, and, being an army officer, demanded rigid discipline. The discipline was worse than it was before, but I knew more about the place and could get along better. I was older now, knew the ropes, and was more satisfied with myself—felt more self-confident and cocky. Crime and imprisonment were becoming more a matter of business, and I didn't worry and feel tender-hearted. I was beginning to be hard-hearted, sarcastic, and resigned to rough treatment. Besides, I was becoming an old timer and the young guys were beginning to look up to me and regard me as a hard-boiled gunman of wide experience. I could tell tales of exploits in a criminal line, and that stood me in well with the guys. A great story-teller was I, and that way I could pass the long hours away. We entered into those forbidden conversations usually in the basement, where the house father could not see us, and there

I told of my early running away, the many times I had been in jail, the easy ways of fooling the police, breaking into box-cars and stores, my life in the parental school, bumming from school, and made up stories about hot rackets I'd been in and big and daring crimes I'd pulled off.

The young crooks in St. Charles were glib-tongued and liked to tell wild stories about crimes and adventures. The young little fellows are given the razz by the bullies and the boy captains and forced to conform to the code. The chances are a million to one against the safety of the boys. Under the strict discipline restrictions and fears, I rebelled and harbored vengeance and hate. The officials thought they could cowhide and beat reform into me. But my thoughts were far away from thoughts of virtue and being good. I thought only of my life with my buddies, our conversations and exploits, my experiences back in Chicago, the far-off day of release, the bad food and strict discipline and the bully boy officers, the misery and sadness of my life, and why everybody was against me and tormenting me. Everybody told me to be good and reform, but how could I do better in such a world in such a hole of discipline and coldness? I wanted to get ahead in a criminal line, instead of being good.

After serving ten more months in this "reform" school of punishment, I was paroled to a farmer at Batavia, Illinois. It was the only thing to do with me, except let me rot in the place, for there wasn't anybody who cared where I was and what became of me. The officials had to do something to get rid of me. On the way to his home, the farmer tried to encourage me to behave myself and be good. I wasn't much interested in myself or anything else. I felt I didn't have anything to say about my life. I was just buffeted from one place to another, just wherever the winds of circumstances and officials took me. The farmer was full of pity for me, for he saw how young and weak and frail I was. He was to pay me seven dollars a month and twenty-five cents a week for spending money and buy my clothes. He had a nice wife, who was very kind, and they took me out to family parties and picnics, gave me extra money, and were in every way nice. But I began to dream about being in the city with the lights shining around me.

While I herded the cows, watching them eating grass and slowly chewing their cud, my thoughts always wandered to the city, with its excitement, movies, and people. My thoughts could not center upon farmwork. Thoughts about the city crowded out thoughts about the lonely, uninteresting, dull farm. I longed and dreamed about the movies and hashhouses, my chums, and the crowds in the city. The quietness of the farm made me blue and finally homesick. The call was inevitable, and I could not fight it off, so I became dreamy and indolent about the work. The farmer bawled me out, and he finally threatened to send me back to St. Charles, so I planned to leave. I left wearing a pair of rubber boots, overalls, and a straw hat, without money.

I walked along the railroad tracks to the nearest town, and slipped into a train to Chicago. What a fine spectacle I was dressed in farmer's clothes! The passengers pitied me and forced money upon me, although I didn't ask for it. I suppose it was because I was young and going to the city like they did when they were kids.

I went to my stepmother's home, for I didn't want to be seen on the streets and taken back to St. Charles. She greeted me and told me I would have to get a job because she was hard up. I got a job the next day as an errand boy near the Loop, for eight dollars a week. But two days later a letter came from the superintendent of the St. Charles School, ordering my father to hold me for arrest and return to the school. Being scared, I ran away, but was arrested that evening and taken to the Juvenile Detention Home.

Mr. Cone came to the Home and did me a good turn by paroling me to my father, so I wouldn't have to go back to St. Charles. I worked and gave my money to the stepmother for a month. Then I thought, What's the use of working and giving everything to her, when I only get kicked in return? So I left and asked Mr. Cone[7] to get me a better place to live.

[7] Quoting again from Mr. Cone's record: "I paroled Stanley to his step-mother, but as usual he remained with her only a few weeks and came to me, asking for assistance. I placed him in the Illinois Eye and Ear Infirmary. Here he worked a few weeks and earned his room and board. Later I placed him with Father Kiley, of the Holy Cross Mission. Father Kiley found a job for him, but he soon disap-

He took me to the Eye and Ear Infirmary[8] at Peoria and Adams streets, near the old-time red-light district and the land of hoboes, where I lived for a month. While here I worked and romped West Madison Street, getting a taste of the life of the hoboes of West Madison Street. I developed a hankering for these crowds of hoboes and spent my evenings in them.

At the end of a month, dressed in a white uniform (a doctor's suit that was many times too large for me, with the trouser legs cut off at the knees) I was taken by Mr. Cone to the Holy Cross Mission (a hoboes' haven of rest) at Desplaines and Randolph streets. Here I was to live with hoboes and the other scum that drifted in from West Madison Street. A priest got me a job as errand boy, and I was getting along fine until I met a young fellow from West Madison Street. He was a bum, away from home. He took me on a touring trip of adventure through the Loop and West Madison. I drew my savings out of the bank, and we spent them in having a good time going to movies, poolrooms, gambling-houses, news alleys, and hashhouses. I was having a great adventure, but one night I stayed out too late and found the doors of the mission locked when I returned. Not knowing where to go, I rode on the elevated train all night. The next morning I was afraid to go back to the mission-house because of the punishment I had coming.

I went out to live with my half-sister, the only person in my family who had loved me and who had always stuck by me. But I dreamed of my experiences of adventure, and also felt that my half-sister was taking all my money for selfish purposes and that I was being cheated. So after three weeks I quit my job and went down to Madison Street. I had ten dollars in my pocket, that being my last pay. It soon ran out, and I began to bum.

I slept in alleys and begged food, and ofttimes ate from garbage cans. I was a waif, dirty, wretched, and ragged. Being afraid to seek assistance, because I'd be returned to St. Charles, I contrived to beg and steal until one day a woman found me

peared again. A few weeks later he was arrested and returned to St. Charles for the third time."

[8] Located on Area B (see Map I, opposite p. 34).

eating stale buns in an alley near Halsted Street. She smiled and said, "Say, kid, what are you doing on Madison Street?" I said, "I'm bumming." She said, "Be a sport and sociable. I'm not going to hurt you. Come up to my flat and have a bite to eat." Noticing her hideous but once beautiful face, I almost shrank back, but her kindly smile and voice drew me to her. So I followed her to her flat, which was beautifully furnished. She bade me sit down while she made a "snack." We ate, and I wondered what her motive could be—thinking that there was something wrong, I was wary. So I eyed her closely as she gathered up the dishes, noticing her coarse and emaciated features as if she had went through some hard experiences.

After washing the dishes, she sat down on a luxurious sofa and invited me to sit with her. I declined, being timid and suspicious of her motive, but her kindness won out. As I sat with her, she put her head on my shoulder and asked me again, "Say, kid, what are you doing on West Madison Street?" This time I was not afraid, but felt a wave of depression and sadness come over me, because a woman was offering me sympathy—something that I'd never received before. "Come on, kid, tell me your troubles," she said, as she gently patted down my hair, almost lovingly. Touched by her feeling toward me, I blurted out all my past life, as I cried like a baby. I even told her about being in jail, and other things that I had never told to anybody. As I told my story, she dried my tears and caressed me gently, and interrupted often by saying, "What a shame!" "Hain't it awful?" "Poor kid, I feel sorry for you." After I finished the story I couldn't stop sobbing, so she held me in her arms and cheered me up and said, "Kid, you'll live with me from now on, and no more will you have to roam on Madison Street to eke out a miserable existence."

During the day she played the piano and caressed me and cooked nice things for me. But many times we were interrupted by men calling at the door, but everyone she turned away by saying she "wasn't well today and that they should call again in a few days." I began to realize her way of making a living (she was a prostitute), but still I couldn't condemn her for it. Had not

I done things just as bad, and was she not kind to me by taking me into her flat? Anyway, she didn't make any advances toward me, only petted me and soothed my troubled soul. I felt peaceful and happy and light-hearted with her.

For a month I lived with her, while she plied her trade with men. They came and went in great numbers. I became afraid that she would be arrested, for she had done time in the Bridewell before, and I would be caught and sent back to St. Charles. I didn't have the heart to tell her that I was going to leave, for she had been very kind to me, so one day while she was out "hustling" I went away. I felt blue after leaving, and missed her kindness, but I was too afraid to go back to her.

I went to the Y.M.C.A. Hotel to get a room. The clerk at the desk said, "Go into that room [pointing to a rear door] to see Mr. ——." In there a "dick" grabbed me and took me to the Detention Home. (It has always been a mystery to me how this dick recognized me, for he called me by name. In my own mind, at that time, I thought I was a very notorious criminal, to be spotted so easily.)

On returning to the Detention Home, I was considered an old timer and a bad character, because of my two terms in St. Charles. I impressed my superiority on the younger crooks, who rather awed me, as Patty Maloney had awed me in the same place five years before. After five days there I was taken to St. Charles I didn't know where I was going, until we reached the Aurora and Elgin station. Then the officer told me I'd do only a few months, this being my third term. That was just a stall to keep me from making a break for freedom. He didn't need to be as cautious as all that, for St. Charles held no fears for me now. I was "on to the ropes," knew how to get by, and, besides, I half-liked being a bad crook, for here I was, a mere kid, with four terms in jail to my credit. A fellow gets over that idea in later life, but it made a strong appeal to my childish mind at that time.

I was placed in Cottage D at the institution and assigned to work at the laundry. This was a good job, because the officer in charge considered my case and treated me good, as he did all of the other guys under him. Life went more smoothly for me now, for I knew the ropes and was not afraid to stand up for my rights. I was more confident and had lost my fears for jail and stealing.

I did eighteen months the third time. As the time for my release came around, I began to conjure up things to do. I had a little ambition to make good and expected some help. But I thought I would not let anybody make a fool out of me, for I had a confident feeling that I could steal and get by with it, so I could turn to that if things didn't go just right, but I was willing to give the right a fair break.

CHAPTER VII

THE LURE OF THE UNDERWORLD[1]

So the day of my parole came around eventually, and dressed up in a suit the stepmother sent to me, I sallied out to seek my fortune, so to speak. With eight dollars in my pocket, which I had coming from the school, I thought I had a fair start, compared with some of Horatio Alger's heroes, whose stories of adventure I had read every one and was surely thrilled with every page, too. By this time I had a confident feeling that I could steal and make a success of it. I knew dozens of other boys who were making a go of it and felt sure that I could do it also. Also, I made up my mind that I wouldn't take any more insults from anybody—I'd stand my ground against the world. I might die doing it, but I wouldn't die a coward.

On arriving in Chicago, my escort, one of the officers of the "School," instructed me to be in bed by nine o'clock, and to keep out of bad company. It was useless to explain that to me, for I had heard it so many times that I knew it by heart and always expected it on such occasions. I left him at the Aurora and Elgin station and strolled out to State and Congress streets.[2]

From the time I used to go to the markets and to West Madison Street with the old gang I had been attracted to throngs of

[1] This chapter is an account of Stanley's experiences in the underworld life of the West Madison Street rooming-house district. It was through his social contacts in this district that he acquired the practice of "jack-rolling." As indicated previously, this section of the city is one of the areas of marked concentration of adult offenders. "Jack-rolling" is one of the most prevalent types of offense committed in the district.

[2] At the time of Stanley's parole, Mr. Cone was the only St. Charles parole officer in the Chicago district and was responsible for the supervision of more than three hundred delinquent boys. At present there are two officers, each of whom has more than two hundred cases. With this large number of cases, the officer's contact with the boy is obviously extremely infrequent and superficial. In the absence of adequate follow-up work, any beneficial influences resulting from the boy's institutional experience are necessarily lost as he returns to the neighborhood situation in which his delinquent experiences occurred.

people, not the Loop throngs, but the West Madison and South State Street throngs. I could not explain this irresistible interest, even if I wanted to. Perhaps it was the telepathy that is from one derelict to another. I do know full well that this human wreckage was always full of interest and mystery to my dreamy mind. Men of all nationalities and races, from the four corners of the earth, were there and brushed shoulders with the crooks and gunmen of the underworld. They were all attracted there, as I was, by the cheap movies, flophouses, cheap hashhouses, and, most of all, by the human derelicts that make West Madison Street what it is. When blue and broken-up I would always find an old pal there to tell my troubles to and receive the sympathy that comes through mutual understanding. All the old bums and human wrecks were my family. We all ate at the same table and enjoyed ourselves at the same theaters. In fact, we consisted of a brotherhood whose object was mutual pity and sympathy. The brotherhood was made up of ordinary "bos," pickpockets, panhandlers, petty thieves, "jack-rollers," and the other wrecks that compose the underworld. Here was my favorite haunt, because my friends made their rendezvous there. It seemed to me that here the lights gleamed brighter, the lures were stronger, and that there were more bums to hide me from the stares of snobbish people.

At State and Congress I stopped to read the billboards of a show and then bought a ticket. Just as I was entering, I met a chum from the St. Charles School for Boys. He had been released about a month, and of course he was now away from home, without any money. He explained that he had a stepfather who beat him up because he couldn't find work. He was only fourteen, and thus under age to work, so firms turned him down for that reason. Here he was, a pitiful sight, ragged, dirty, and out on the streets to shift for himself. The sight touched my feelings. I had eight dollars, so I gave him one, and also the ticket to the show. He was full of gratitude, and said that he'd repay when he'd see me again. I asked him how he lived. He said that he slept in alleys or an empty house or under a porch and begged money for his meals. Now I never thought I would ever be in the same circumstances again, and deep in my heart I felt sorry for him.

LIFE'S "CIRCUMSTANCES"[3]

Like a gale of wind
On a storm-swept sea
Gathering its victims
Into its paw
Swiftly the undercurrent
takes its hold
and surrounds its victim
Down more and more.

Some men are rich
Others are poor
But fate takes a hand
In guiding our lives.
It weaves its web
In a noiseless way;
Be it night or day
It holds full sway.

It follows us through the years and years
And never stops its ceaseless work
We are nothing but straws
In this strife-swept world
And the man with the gold
Is the man with the hold.

I boarded a street car to Paulina Street, where my stepmother lived. I was free, but did not for the life of me know what to do. I felt like a beggar intruding on the stage of life where I was not supposed to be. Really I didn't know where I belonged. There didn't seem to be any place that welcomed me, only jail. On the car I felt the stares of people burning through me. I was humiliated, but yet I was not to blame for my predicament. I felt that my stepmother was the cause of all my trouble, and then I argued with myself about going back to live with her again. If I stayed away I'd surely get back in jail. But as I was a little older now and felt more chesty and confident, I made up my mind to take care of myself and to live with her at the same time.

[3] Stanley's effort to place the responsibility for his misconduct upon external circumstances is clearly indicated in these lines.

So when I reached home (a funny term) my stepmother greeted me with a toothless smile and bade me sit down and eat, which I did. She could only speak her native tongue, which was Polish, and what little I understood meant that she was glad to see me at home again. But she added that I should get a job and go to work, which I intended to do. She said she was sorry that my father died and she wished he was living again. Now that was a funny thing. She only wanted him to live so that she could collect some more money from his labor and starve us (my brother, sister, and I) out. There wasn't any love wasted on my father by her which I know of. He worked like a trooper to support his children, and the stepmother's culprits as well. But his children, his own flesh and blood, got cheated, while the stepmother's culprits got the best of everything. That bit of fraud has always stuck in my mind and embittered me against everything. There is no justice in the world. The worst crooks are never arrested. Justice is getting by with anything. If you've got the upper hand or the high card, you can get justice. It's usually obtained through money, pull, or superior force. In my own case, haven't I been the victim of circumstances because I had no money, no political pull, and was too weak to fight the odds against me? I hate the world, with its shackles and unfair play. I thought why not steal and make a living any easy way, only make sure to get by. If you don't get the other fellow, he'll get you, and no mercy will be extended to you, as my own experience shows. I was not a crook at first, but just a helpless little orphan boy. So why was I punished instead of the right culprits? Well, life is that way—unfair, cruel, and full of injustices.

The first night I met my stepbrother William—my companion in my early stealing expeditions, and the one to whom I was now paroled. He greeted me in a good way, but warned me to go to work immediately, although he wasn't working and didn't intend to. After supper he took me out to a saloon, where his gang had headquarters, and introduced me. There they were playing cards and drinking moonshine and planning thefts. I was impressed by the way I was introduced to these boys, because William mentioned that I'd done time three times in St. Charles. That sort of made me stick out my chest, and I felt that I'd done something worth commendation. They made a place for me immediately, and I told them tales about my experiences. They looked up to me, and like a kid I was proud of it. We all played cards, drank moonshine, exchanged tales about our exploits, and tried to impress upon each other the ways of making easy money. We left for home at eleven o'clock. A nice hour to be in the house the first night on parole.

The next morning William and I went out to look for work. I had five dollars left in my pocket, for I had given the stepmother two. I ventured to tell John that I had the money. He was glad and suggested that we spend it, which we did. I got a job in a dirty spring factory at nine dollars per week. William didn't want to work for that money, but said that I should, and so I did.

I worked at the factory five days. I was considered by the stepmother to be a good boy then, but when I quit everything changed. Hell popped from all sides. I got fired for smoking in the toilet, but I hated the work, anyway, and was glad to get kicked out. When I got home the fireworks started for sure. But I felt that I didn't have to work at that place, and didn't give a damn what anybody said about it either. The place was full of hoodlums, anyway. I figured that the "old lady" didn't have any business forcing me to work where I didn't want to, and I told her so, too. I lost the little respect that I had for her. I thought I knew everything that there was to know, and in that way I was too sure of myself in all respects. I rebelled at anyone at home giving me any advice about what I should do. I felt hard-boiled, and my association with the gang swelled my head. Anyway, all my stepmother wanted was my money and if I wouldn't get a job, I'd be kicked out. There was her greediness right there. She owned the building, and didn't need to be so impatient. She wasn't on the verge of starvation. She only wanted the money for her own culprits.

I tried to get a job, but work was scarce. Finally I went to the city hall, to a social worker, who has died since, and she sent me to a drug manufacturing company to work for twelve dollars a week. When I brought the news home, everything was rosy again. It was congenial work, but I worked with girls and we joked and fooled around too much, so at the end of the first week I got the "bounce."

After receiving the money, I thought to myself, why should I work hard, without any encouragement except to take all the money to the "old lady." If I was to be out of work, she would kick me out into the street, so I made up my mind to shift for myself, for I well knew that she had no love for me, and being prompted by twelve dollars in my pocket, I sallied forth. I went downtown and took in the Carpentier and Dempsey fight, and thence to West Madison Street. I was free again and didn't care about anything. I was like a colt kicking up its heels after being tied down for a long time and breaking the fence; I was free, with nobody to stop me. Feeling great, I spent my money right and left. I had a feeling of exhilaration. It was like taking a sip of wine and wanting more. Life was tempting and pulled me on until I was broke and down and out. But while the money lasted, I lived a gay life, leave me tell you—visiting all the movies, gambling, and eating in them hashhouses. It was a feeling of freedom that possessed me. I always thought it was a great thing to be able to eat in a hashhouse. I liked to see somebody watching me eating in one of them places. It made me feel that I was somebody, a kid eating in one of these places with no one to stop me. So whenever I had money I would take one of the first seats by the door, where people could see me, and put on a superior air. All in all, I thought I was somebody of consequence.

When my money ran out, I was down and out again. I began to look shabby and dirty, so I went to the Working Boys' Home[4] and told them my story. They took pity on me and took me in and told me I could live there, and they got me a job the next morning. I worked at this job just one week. I had the habit of going to poolrooms at night and staying quite late. That was contrary to the rules of the Home, so they bawled me out and I resented it. They bawled me out twice, and at the end of the week I drew my check, quit my job, and ran away from the Home.

I went immediately to the News Alley, and there met an old

[4] Located in Area B (see Map I, opposite p. 34).

pal that I had become acquainted with in St. Charles. I showed him the bank roll, and that strengthened our friendship considerably. So we started to blow it in. I was lord of all for a few days. We had our "wild women," went to movies, and had plenty to eat. We also shot crap, which is the term of the underworld vernacular, and in a few days the dough was gone. This little spurt of fortune and adventure had turned my head. Now I wanted a good time. I had tasted the life and found it sweet. But I was in a predicament, for I had no money, and you can't enjoy life without dough. My buddy, being an old "jack-roller," suggested "jack-rolling" as a way out of the delima. So we started out to "put the strong arm" on drunks. We sometimes stunned the drunks by "giving them the club" in a dark place near a lonely alley. It was bloody work, but necessity demanded it—we had to live.

As I'd walk along Madison Street there'd always be some man to stop me and coax me into having sex relations with him. My friend and I used this little scheme to entice men into a room to rob them. This very day a fellow stopped me and asked for a match. I accommodated him, and he started a conversation. He was about eight years my senior, and big and husky. He said he was a foreman in a machine shop, and when I said I was out of work, he promised to get a job for me at his shop. He invited me to have supper with him up in his room, which was built for light housekeeping. He was a kind guy, with a smile and a winning way, so I went up to have supper on his invitation. We ate, and then he edged up close to me and put his arm around me and told me how much I appealed to his passions. He put his hand on my leg and caressed me gently, while he talked softly to me.

I had to wait a few minutes for my buddy to come to help put the strong arm on this man. I couldn't do it alone. My buddy had followed us all the time and was only waiting for a chance to come to my rescue. Finally, he came and we sprang into the fellow with fury. He started to grab me and my buddy dealt him a heavy blow.

We found thirteen dollars in his pockets. Since he had tried to ensnare me I figured I was justified in relieving him of his thirteen bucks. Besides, was he not a low degenerate, and wouldn't he use the money only to harm himself further?[5]

I never gave a thought about the day of reckoning and the consequences for these seemed too far off. I was living in the present, literally leading a hand-to-mouth existence, and whatever wrong I did was only a part of the course of events. I needed food, and wanted a good time, but was too young to supply all my needs except by stealing. And why should I work when there were easier ways to make a living? Consequences? They didn't worry me when I was happy, with plenty of money and pleasure.

One day my partner didn't show up, and right then and there I lost all my nerve. I needed someone with me to steal. I was too cowardly to steal alone. A companion made me brave and gave me a sense of security. I couldn't to save my soul steal a dime alone.

After my partner left I decided to go to work, so I went to the City Hall to see Mr. M. H. Cone,[6] my parole officer, who had stood by me on many other similar occasions. He turned me over to his assistant, a very kindly woman, who got me a job in an engraving company for twelve dollars per week. Here I was, in rags and dirty, and went to the vice-president of the company. He bade me sit down. He was kind and gentle and gave me a heart-to-heart talk about making good, all of which impressed me not a little. Seeing the rags I had on, he called up a clothing store and instructed them to dress me up and charge the bill to him. Here was this big man taking pity on a little waif like me, and it gave me a new lease on life.

During all this time I had been only a waif, sleeping in vacant houses, in all-night movie shows, in poolrooms, alleys, missions, and flophouses. I was dirty, ragged, and carefree. I didn't care

---

[5] This is a very excellent example of rationalization.

[6] In regard to his contact with Stanley at this time, Mr. Cone states: "Miss Amelia McNaughton of the Central Howard Association took Stanley in charge. She secured a position for him as messenger in a large factory. His likable characteristics appealed to the vice-president of the concern, who took him into his own home, intending to adopt him as his own son, having no children of his own, had Stanley appreciated his opportunity. Here he soon wearied of wealth as 'too lonesome' in its enjoyment, and disappeared."

what happened to me; I was simply holding on to the thread of life.

After I got this job I was taken back to live with my married sister. I arranged to pay all my money to her, and she was to clothe and feed me in return. I was allowed to do as I pleased, so long as I paid my bill at the end of the week. But I had been so undernourished and had dissipated and exposed myself to so much that I was very weak. I grew weaker and weaker and could hardly go to work. I began to have spells of depression. I was sick and weary and weak. The doctor at work examined me and said that I needed rest and better food. He reported my case to the vice-president, and in a few days he asked me how I liked to live with my sister. I answered that it didn't make any difference where I lived. There seemed to be nothing in life for me. I was too young and weak to survive without somebody to soothe me and help me out of my depression. It would have changed matters if there had been.

So I went to live with the vice-president of the company. He was married but had no children. His wife was kind but particular. They played the part of the Good Samaritan, but I didn't take advantage of it. They planned to adopt me, and I would be the sole heir to this wealth and home. Also, I had an eternal berth in his established business. Perhaps I could be president sometime. My future looked rosy, but alas! the few flowers of my life bloom only to fade and wither. My hopes only mocked me in my struggles.

The surroundings in my new home and neighborhood took my breath away. My first day at the foster-home was like a sweet dream. The new luxury seemed to dazzle and blind me. My new father rode with me to work every morning and home in the evening. We had nice lunches together at noon. He talked nice to me, gave me spending money and good clothes, but I missed my old pals and the gay life we had lived. Here I did not have any boy chums, but had to spend my time playing the victrola. My foster-parents didn't have much life, but spent their time reading and playing a tame game of cards. They had lots of company of snobbish people, and they looked down on me. Even if they were nice, it was because of pity and charity. There was something missing. Eating at the table I was ill at ease. I couldn't do the things just right, and my foster-mother looked at my blunders through the corner of her eye. I compared everything with my sister's common fare and poor surroundings, and finally longed to go back to my friends and pals. Back home I wasn't dressed up all the time, and could play and romp and gamble and swear. But here I was not free to move and talk as I was in the habit of doing before. Everything was different—strange and stiff. I felt out of place—a city waif dependent upon charity. I had been in jail half a lifetime, but now I was suddenly placed in luxury after living in a dirty hovel. My adventurous spirit rebelled against this dry life and it soon won out. That is one of life's cynical jokes, how I felt. I said to myself, What's the use of having riches if you can't enjoy life?

Going down Canal Street one day on an errand, I saw a poor Italian fellow. He was not a bum but a refined foreigner who was broke and down and out. I could see by his expression that he was hungry but had too much pride to beg. I made my delivery, and on my way back I dropped a four-bit piece in front of him. He picked it up and offered it to me, but I told him to keep it as a reward for his honesty. He thanked me profusely and then introduced me to his friend, a young Italian-American lad. I took a leaning toward this lad merely on his carefree smile—a sort of fascinating smile. A smile that bespoke of adventure, and I, a youthful fool, believed in adventure. So we established an acquaintance, he for my money, and I for his experience in the world.

The turning-point in this part of my life occurred that same day. At noon as I was lounging in front of the building where I worked, a solicitor was introducing a punch board for prizes. I took to the novelty of the thing and bought one. The president appeared just at that time and warned me against gambling in any form and asked me to leave the punch board alone, which I did for the time being. As soon as he was out of sight, I ran after the man and took the whole board. I was popular with the office people, I suppose from pity, and soon got rid of the punches, which amounted to seventeen dollars and twenty cents. That afternoon the president gave me five dollars to buy an Easter present for his son. Then I had twenty-three dollars in my pocket, and as I rode to the Loop to buy the present I debated temptation and the right. *Temptation won without a struggle.* True, I hated to disappoint the vice-president, he had been good to me, but when I thought of living in his home and compared that with the fun I could have with so much money, my course was decided.

Going down to the poolroom in Canal Street, I found my pal, the "Dago." I suggested to him that we leave town immediately. Having had lots of experience on the "road" and seeing my money, he consented to go. He asked to take his chum along. I consented, and we were off. The change of events fairly dazed me. It takes only a minute to change one's whole life course. We took a train to Gary, Indiana, for we were bound to New York City. I was like an extravagant prince at Monte Carlo, with my body guards and valets who were always on duty as long as I had a nickel in my pocket. But in two or three days my money ran out and my pals ditched me, the dirty crooks, and I was left alone. I knew I was not experienced enough in the underworld to be an interesting pal to them. It hurt me terribly, but I made up my mind that I'd show them sometime. So with a grim determination I hopped an eastbound freight that evening and was off.

This was my first ride on a "blind," and it thrilled me through and through. I began to feel like a man of the world as I hobbed-nobbed with the crooks and bums who traveled the road. Already I had met all types of human wrecks. Some gave me warning to turn back to Chicago; these I laughed at. Others told me thrilling stories of their experiences and the future that was in store for me on the road. Others approached me and tried to get me to do immoral sex acts with them. I had already learned that a boy on the road was a constant victim of sex perverts. I yielded to them a few times but the act was nauseating to me, for I preferred to have relations with girls or to masturbate alone. I reached Niles, Michigan, after dark and had to get off the train because that was a division point. As I jumped off it seemed like I was lost. Darkness had dimmed my enthusiasm, and now I felt lonely and almost inclined to return to Chicago. As I stood by the tracks in the darkness danger seemed to be lurking everywhere.

I was hungry but didn't have a dime, so I found my way to the town. As I stood gazing into a bakery window an elderly man approached, and I determined to beg the price of a meal from him. I stopped him and asked for the necessary coin of the realm. I being short and frail, he gazed with amazement, when I told him I had tramped my way from Chicago. He was kind and led me to a restaurant, where we dined together. We chatted in a congenial way, and the old man warned me about the temptations of life. I told him about my past, and he fairly sobbed with pity and sympathy. After supper he told me to go to the Salvation Army, and maybe they would find a job for me. I thanked him kindly for the favors and went to the Salvation Army.

I reached the Salvation Army and a meeting was going on. I stepped inside. One of the workers, who had a face of agony, saw me come in and he led me up to the front row and handed me a songbook and a Bible. As the sombre ceremony was going on I was at the head of the bunch—more meek and humble than was usual for me. The captain of the place, noticing me so devout during the service, approached me when it was all over, and asked me what a little fellow like me was doing there. I said I bummed from Chicago, and that I didn't have a home. He shook his head in pity. I said I wanted to find some work. Immediately he inquired at some places and found a job in a restaurant and hotel. I was to receive my room and board at first. I thanked him and said that I'd repay him by attending the meeting every evening, which I did. I raised my voice higher than any bum who ever sang and prayed for a meal. But I got comfort out of the place, for everybody was kind and pitied me.

The owner of the restaurant and his wife took a liking to me. But Harry (the owner) was a Dutchman and had a furious temper that he could not control. Woe betide the individual who fell under it. He was a hard taskmaster, but he had many good points. He was generous and showed his generosity by buying me some new clothes before I done a day's work. His wife was a gentle woman, very kind, and she treated me like an angel. She was the first real woman I ever knew, and it was a pleasure to work for her. She had a little child, and it was fond of me from the the start. As I played and romped with the child day after day, there sprang up in me a feeling of sympathy and kindness that was new in my life. I became happy and contented.

I helped to take care of the child, washed dishes, swept the floor, ran errands, mopped, cleaned the house, and made up the beds in the hotel. I took an interest in my surroundings. But at the end of the fifth week, a tragedy occurred. I overslept three hours one morning and Harry raved when I went down. When his temper had subsided sufficiently to enable him to talk, he ordered me to wash dishes. I was so unstrung and nervous at the bawling out that I dropped a dish. Harry scowled at me and chased me from the kitchen and threw me into the alley. His wife protested in my behalf, but to no avail. My clothes were in my room upstairs, so I played safe by waiting until evening to get them, so Harry would be cooled down. At evening I walked in and Harry greeted me with a tolerating smile. I told him I had stood all I was going to, so he complied and gave me my clothes. He gave me some money, more than was coming to me, and told me to come back any time and I could have my same job back.

I strolled around town awhile and dropped into the town butcher-shop. I knew the owner, having gone in there many times for meat orders. I told him my trouble, and he asked me to go home with him that night. I agreed. He lived on a farm three miles from Niles, was married, and had two children. He said I could live on the farm with him. The farm was ill kept, the land not tilled, and the buildings were in general disorder. I was to straighten out the place the best I knew. I started out with optimism, but in one week I gave up the job. The farm was lonely and dull. There was no excitement and no pleasure. I compared it in my mind with dear old "Chi," the town of my birth, and also the origination of my hard luck of being born. Lonely, downhearted, and broke, I decided to go back to "Chi."

I walked back to Niles and caught a "blind," supposedly to Chicago. But I soon learned that it was not Chicago bound, but was going eastward. Why should I care? For after getting on the "blind," my spirit returned and I didn't care if I never saw Chicago again. I felt adventurous again. I had a fellow-traveler with me. He was a one-arm lad, about twenty-two years old, weak and frail, but he had an iron determination to do what he set out to do. He was begging for a living, and of course people pitied him because of his physical condition. He was bound for New York City and had been there many times, and he fired my imagination by telling me stories about the big buildings, the ocean, and the Statue of Liberty. I soon decided to go with him. He wanted to "make Kalamazoo," our next stop, and then we would be off.

We got off and my pal gave me a half-dollar for breakfast and candy and instructed me to wait for him at a certain place while he "made the town." That was the last time I ever saw him, for my plan was soon shattered. I didn't walk a block before I was accosted by a policeman who asked me where I was from and whither I was going. Being bewildered by the sudden turn of events, I could not give a clear answer, so was taken into custody. Jailhouse bound again.

The jail at Kalamazoo was sanitary. I was put in the juvenile quarters, in a big room all alone. This dampened my enthusiasm for the road quite a bit. After a long lonely wait, I was taken downstairs and questioned about my past record and asked if I would work. I said I would, so the next day they found a job for me, but could not find a home. Then they took me to a Catholic priest, who recommended that they send me back home to my sister. He gave the necessary fare, and I was put on a Chicago train, with four cents in my pocket, which was for carfare.

While on the train a man greeted me and started up a conversation. He was a wealthy manufacturer, and I could not make out his motive for being interested in me. He got all my past history and my present predicament, and then told me he would give me a job in his office and put me on my feet. He painted a rosy future for me. Still I was suspicious of his motive. People always have a selfish motive of some kind when they are so willing to help. But we carried on a pleasant conversation until we arrived in Chicago, where we took a taxicab to his office. I was fully convinced he was an official of the company when we reached the office, for everybody greeted him and took orders from him. After the clerks had gone he gave me some advice about making good and all that bunk. He promised to give me a job, and after I had showed good intentions, he would buy clothes for me. So he gave me five dollars and sent me home to my half-sister, requesting that I return the next day. So I left, but felt that there was an ulterior motive behind his generosity and made up my mind to say goodbye to him forever. And I did.

I went to my half-sister's home to live. I paid her five dollars, and then went out to get a job. This I could not find, so I was "given the gate" at the end of the week.

The first place I went to was West Madison Street, the haven of rest for bums, prostitutes, degenerates, and the rest of the scum of the earth, who gather there to drift on to some other place. "Floaters" is a good name for them. But this place held lures for me. The lures and the irresistible call drew me on like a magnet, and I was always helpless before them. I was like a canoe on a storm-swept sea, buffeted here and there, helpless and frail. I had about as much chance of controlling my desires to drift with the current of the underworld as the canoe had of braving the storm. But here I mingled with bums and derelicts like myself, and people did not stare at my rags and misery. Here I felt at home, for "misery loves company." So I drifted on with the rest of the human driftwood—carried on by the current of West Madison Street's exclusive "Four Hundred" or more.

While sitting in a hashhouse the second day after I left my half-sister's home, I met a little lad who was an escape from the Chicago and Cook County School for Boys. He had been sent to this school for running away from home, bumming away from school, and stealing from his foster-parents. His parents had died when he was seven years old, and he had been placed in a foster-home by a welfare agency. But he found the foster-home different from his own home and couldn't get used to his new parents, for they were snobbish and tried to force him into submission. Not feeling right there, he stole some money and ran away. He was now twelve years old and out shifting for himself. He

was afraid he'd be arrested and returned to the School, so I painted a rosy picture of adventure that we could have on the road.
I felt like an old timer after my trip to Michigan. He consented
to go, glad enough to get away from the police and his foster-parents. That afternoon we gathered a hatful of cigarette "buttses"
along the street, to have a good supply for our trip. We slept in
a flophouse that night, and the next morning went to the railroad
yard in Cicero, where we caught a west-bound freight. We didn't
care where it was going, just so it went somewhere. I was so excited that I would try anything. I wanted to explore the unknown
regions of adventure. Roy, my companion, was not as enthusi-
astic as I was, but he joined me in my songs of exhilaration as we
rambled along. Inwardly, I was a little timid, for I was not very
sure on the road yet. But Roy looked up to me as a lad of lots of
experience on the road. Of course I had exaggerated about my
road adventures to him. We rambled along, singing songs, smoking cigarette "buttses," and having a great time until the middle
of the afternoon. Being hungry, we got off at a small town to beg.
We separated. Roy went down one street and I went down another. I soon got a good meal from a grocer who was a good old
man and took pity on me. I then went back to the yards to wait
for Roy.

After a long wait I decided to leave without Roy, thinking
maybe he was picked up by the police and maybe they would be
after me if I didn't get out of town. I crawled into a box-car and
was soon on the move. In the car I met a man by the name of
Bill. Bill was a miner and was on his way to his home, in a little
town in Iowa. He greeted me and asked me where I was going. I
replied, "Wherever the freight will take me to." He was surprised
that anyone would be traveling with no definite destination. He
was a "small-town hick," but was a kind guy. After I had entertained him with my stories about adventure and Chicago, I "hit"
him for a cigarette in exchange. He gave me some cigar clippings
and loaned me his pipe, and I leaned back in the car and smoked
to my heart's content.

Bill pitied me so and took such a liking to me that he invited
me to go to his home and have a good dinner. I was prompted to

accept his invitation when he remarked that his wife was a good cook. At a small mining-town we got off the freight and went to Bill's home. We walked to a small cottage, where his wife, a woman much older than Bill, greeted us and prepared a banquet for us. I sure did enjoy that meal. I sure did like Bill and Mary, his wife. They were common people and were awed by my stories of adventure. Bill prepared a nice little cot for me, and said I could stay as long as I wanted to. Leave me tell you, I accepted his invitation, for here were kind people and a place to sleep and good things to eat.

I had a great time exploring the little town and sitting around the little grocery store, where the "hicks" whittled, smoked, and told yarns. One day, about two weeks later, we were all sitting on some long benches in front of the store. Bill, and some of the other miners, were drunk. There was a miners' strike on there, and Bill and another guy were arguing about the strike. Like a kid, I made some remarks on Bill's side. The other fellow flew at me and would have struck me, but Bill protected me and said in a drunken voice, "This kid is my friend, and anybody who lays a hand on him has to come to me and answer for it." That settled this episode, but the miners knew I was a stranger in town and accused me of being a spy. They threatened me, so I decided to leave town. Besides, the little town was becoming dry and dead. Bill wanted me to stay, saying he would protect me and care for me, but I had decided. Bill had pull with the railroad agent, so one day he put me on a "blind" and I was on my way back to "Chi." In a way, I hated to give up the free meals and room, for they were not to be found everywhere. In a few hours I was back in Chicago, and then to my old haunts at Madison and Halsted.

Necessity drove me to look for work, which I found in a restaurant on West Madison Street, near Halsted. I had to wash dishes from 7 A.M. until 9 P.M., with only a few hours of rest. It was hard work and poor pay, but I had to do it or beg (I was too proud to beg as a profession), borrow, or steal, and I choose the safest way, at first. I worked for four weeks at this place, and became sick. I was weak and had spells of nervousness and depression and long severe headaches. I got so weak that I had to be sent to the Cook County Hospital for a week. The doctor said I needed a rest, and that I was too young and frail to work such long hours. I was despondent and longed to die and get out of my misery. The doctor had given me a prescription, but I was too poor to have it filled—not having a cent in my pocket. Going back to Madison Street I found that my old job was taken, so I began to hang out at a poolroom with a bunch of crooks. These crooks were young boys like myself, fifteen and sixteen years old, but they were more wise to the world and tougher. There were four of us who hung around together. The other three had been in St. Charles School for Boys while I was there, and that strengthened our faith in each other. I was looked up to as the hero of the quartet because I had done fifty-six months in St. Charles, more than all the others put together. They naturally thought I was one who had a vast experience and was regarded as one might regard the big social hit of society.

These lads had been "jack-rolling" bums on West Madison Street and burglarizing homes on the North Side of the city. Knowing of my long record, they asked me to join them, so I fell in with them. We formed "The United Quartet Corporation," and started to "strong arm" "live ones" (drunks with money) and to burglarize homes.

My fellow-workers were fast guys and good pals. We were like brothers and would stick by each other through thick and thin. We cheered each other in our troubles and loaned each other dough. A mutual understanding developed, and nothing could break our confidence in each other. "Patty" was a short, sawed-off Irish lad—big, strong, and heavy. He had served two terms in St. Charles. "Maloney" was another Irish lad, big and strong, with a sunny disposition and a happy outlook on life. He had done one term in St. Charles and had already been in the County Jail. Tony was an Italian lad, fine-looking and daring. He had been arrested several times, served one term in St. Charles, and was now away from home because of a hard-boiled stepfather. We might have been young, but we sure did pull off our game in a slick way.

So we plied our trade with a howling success for two months.

Sometimes we made as much as two hundred dollars in a single day. But I had a weakness for gambling, so I was always broke. West Madison Street and vicinity was a rather dark section of the city, so it was easy to strong arm the "scofflaws." There were a lot of homosexuals and we played our game on them. We would let them approach one of us, usually me, because I was so little and they like little fellows, and then I'd follow him to his room or to a vacant house to do the act. My pals would follow us to our destination, and then we'd all rob him. We made that part of our regular business. Two or three times a week we would pull off a burglary on the North Side or on the South Side.

It was springtime and we would go out to Grant Park during the day and lounge around and plan our burglaries. We always planned very carefully, and each pal had to do a certain thing. It was our absolute rule that if any pal did shrink from his part in the deal he would be branded and put out of "The United Quartet Corporation." We had a common fund for overhead expenses. If a pal had to take a bum to dinner so he could find out if he was "ripe" (had dough) or if a pal had to rent a room to take a bum into, supposedly for homosexual purposes but really to rob him, the expenses came out of the funds.[7]

One day we were strolling along West Madison Street "taking in the sights," or, in other words, looking for "live ones." At the corner of Madison and Desplaines we saw a drunk who was talking volubly about how rich he was and that the suitcase he had in his hand was full of money. We were too wise to believe that, but we thought he might have a little money, so we would try. We tried to lure him into an alley to rob him, but he was sagacious even if he was drunk. He wanted to take me up to a room for an immoral purpose, but we decided that was too dangerous, so we let him go his way and then shadowed him.

[7] This is an interesting illustration of an organized delinquent gang. It not only functioned according to the code of the criminal world, but developed definite techniques which were adapted to the particular delinquency in which the group specialized. These techniques usually vary with different types of offenses. For example, the techniques employed in "jack-rolling" will be quite different from those used in burglary. It should be noted that these techniques are transmitted from one person to another or from one group to another, in much the same manner that any cultural element is disseminated through society.

He went on his aimless way for a long time, and we followed him, wherever he went. He finally went into a hotel and registered for a room. I saw his room number and then registered for a room on the same floor. Then we went up and worked our plans. It was not safe for all of us to go to his room, for that would arouse suspicion. One man could do the job and the others would stand by because they might be needed. But who would do the job? We always decided such things by a deck of cards. The cards were dealt, we drew, and it fell to my lot to do the deed. I was a little nervous inwardly, but did not dare to show it outwardly. A coward was not tolerated in our racket. Woe betide the one who shows it outwardly.

Putting on a bold front, I stepped into the hall and surveyed the field. Then I went to the drunk's door, my spinal nerves cold as ice. I tried the door and it was open, and that saved me a lot of work and nerve. The occupant was snoring, dead drunk, so the way was clear. I had a "sop" (blackjack) with me to take care of him if he woke up. I rifled the room, picked his pockets, and took the suitcase to our room. With great impatience we ripped it open, only to stare at a bachelor's wardrobe. That was quite a blow to our expectations, but we dragged everything out, and at the bottom our labor was rewarded by finding a twenty-dollar bill. With the thirteen dollars I had found on his person and the twenty-dollar bill, we had thirty-three dollars—eight dollars and twenty-five cents apiece. We debated what to do. Since the job would be found out and suspicion would be directed toward us, it was decided to separate for a day or two, then we would not be caught in a bunch. We divvied up the clothes. I got a pair of pants and some other small articles. Then we separated.

I got a room in a hotel on Halsted Street. The next evening while sitting in my room reading a novel, there was a loud rap on the door. Not being suspicious, I opened the door, and "a very well-known friend" greeted me with a gun in his hand. He was a policeman and ordered me to go down to the street with him, even without giving me time to get my money on the dresser. Who did I see on the street but the bum we had robbed the day before. He recognized his pants which I was wearing, and also he remotely recognized me from the day before. The policeman, being convinced that I was one of the guilty party, called the "patty wagon" and took me and the bum to the police station. Here the bum filed a complaint against me.

At the police station I was ordered to give the names of my partners. Of course I refused and said I didn't have any partners. For this remark I received a clout on the ear, and then a general beating and razzing. It was a terrible ordeal of razzing and cussing and making threats, but nothing could make me squawk on my partners. I would die first. My belief in the code was unbreakable. The code is considered by all criminals a standard to live up to, and it is an unpardonable sin to violate this code by squawking. Once a criminal violates it by turning against his partners in crime, he is branded as a rat by the underworld. One must learn to keep his mouth shut concerning other individuals when being questioned by the police or while doing time. A "rat" has been the cause of many a crook's downfall. Therefore he is the crook's worst enemy, not barring the police. I had learned when a child and in St. Charles to live up to this code. I regarded the "rat" as a snake in the grass. I was limp from the awful ordeal and filled with hatred. Seeing that I could not be forced to squawk, the guard threw me into a cell, with the parting remark, "Stay in there awhile, damn you, and you'll be glad to talk."

I lay in the dirty old cell for three or four days, harboring a peculiar revenge. I became sullen and finally became indifferent. There was no hope for me, so I just as well take things as they come, so I thought. Jail had ceased to hold any fears for me, for I was used to it. Inwardly, I felt like a hero who had won a battle single-handed. I thought I had done a great thing by stealing and standing up for my pals and therefore I was one of the going-to-be gunmen. I felt hard and began to wear a sneer on my face, and was always murmuring to myself, "To hell with the world, I should worry about a little thing like being in jail." My cell mates and the other prisoners called me the "baby bandit," and that set me up not a little.

So my trial came up in the Boys' Court. I was glad to be

brought to the Boys' Court because I thought if I was to go back to the "bandhouse" I'd rather have some new scenery. I was awed by the ceremony and inwardly scared. The judge asked if the complainant was in court. He was not; in my bewilderment I lost my head and pleaded guilty. That was a great mistake, because I would have gone free otherwise, because the complainant was not there. The judge deliberated a moment and then uttered the condemning words which branded me as a convict. My "rap" was one year in the Illinois State Reformatory and a fine of one dollar.[8]

I felt rather stuck up when the curious spectators in the courtroom stared in amazement to see such a little boy sent to Pontiac. Even the judge seemed to flush when he sentenced me, but he couldn't do anything else. I was really fifteen and a half years old, but gave my age as eighteen. In the "bullpen" the other prisoners asked me what my "rap" was. I told them, and one guy who had done time said, "A year wasn't so much, he could do that on his ear." But I wasn't so optimistic. In my fear I called my half-sister and pleaded for help. She said she couldn't do anything for me, and, besides, I got myself into trouble and I'd have to get myself out of it. Here I was, utterly without friends or relations or anyone else to help me bear up under the load. My sorrow soon changed to anger, and instead of crying, I said, "To hell with everything and everybody," and took up the new thread of life with a determination. If I was destined to be a criminal I'd just as well fall in line and get used to it.

I was handcuffed to another prisoner, thrown in line with a lot of other prisoners, and under heavy guard led out to the patrol wagon—amid the stares of curious spectators along the streets. Then to the County Jail. Speaking in plain words, it's the dirtiest hovel in Cook County—barring the Bridewell.

On entering the jail we were searched for articles not allowed there, took a bath, and were assigned to a cell. On entering my

[8] Quoting again from Mr. Cone's record: "Stanley was brought into the Boys' Court under an assumed age. Already he had been in St. Charles three times, tried in several foster homes and on farms, and could not get along in his own home, so the only course was to send him to the reformatory. With full knowledge of his age and criminal record, the judge gave him one year in Pontiac."

cell, I was greeted by two prisoners who were to be my cell buddies. Ernest was a first offender, charged with being a "hold-up"
man. Bill, the other buddy, was an old offender, going through
the machinery of becoming a habitual criminal, in and out of jail.
Ernest was seventeen, and Bill was twenty-one. The first thing
they asked me was, "What are you in for?" I said, "Jack-rolling." The hardened one (Bill) looked at me with a superior air
and said, "A hoodlum, eh? An ordinary sneak thief. Not willin'
to leave 'jack-rollin' to the niggers, eh? That's all they're good
for. Kid, 'jack-rollin's' not a white man's job." I could see that
he was disgusted with me, and I was too scared to say anything.
He was a braggart and conceited and hard-boiled, and related
his experience in the Bridewell and Pontiac. He described himself as a hero, and I believed him and was impressed and found
myself putting on airs. Ernest, the other cell buddy, was timid
and quiet, not hardened yet. He worried and complained against
everything. Circumstances had simply pulled him down into the
mire, and here he was struggling—pitiful sight to behold. He was
weak and cried, and was given the razz by Bill.

I stayed in the jail a week and enjoyed myself with Bill. I let
Bill run over me and show his superiority, and then he didn't razz
me like he did Ernest, "the kid," as Bill called him. Bill, being
an old timer and a notorious character, was prominent in our
block, so I thought I was traveling in fast society. I and he played
cards together in our cell, and I listened to his startling stories of
exploits. He showed me the plans for stealing he had worked out
while in jail and was going to use as soon as he'd get out again. He
was a "wise head" and well educated in the criminal line.

Finally, one morning I was awakened early and loaded into a
patrol wagon with seven other prisoners, and conveyed to the
Chicago and Alton Railway Station. We were on our way to
Pontiac.

As I said before, there were eight of us. Five were mere kids,
sixteen to eighteen years old, while the other two were twenty-
one and twenty-eight. We wiled our time away, smoking cigarettes and chewing tobacco continuously, for we had been told
that we couldn't have these luxuries in Pontiac. My mind was
dull, and I could not forget the long year that faced me.

We reached Pontiac and were herded into a waiting truck like so much livestock going to the market. As we turned into a main street the front of the institution glared out before me, and on its top floated an American flag, as if to give an air of respectability to the sordid hole. Arriving at the door of the institution, we were herded into the main office, and the clerk looked us over as if appraising us at our market value. He asked each of us our age, and hesitated when he came to me. I suppose he thought I was rather young, but I was taken in. We were then led to the vestibule, where we had a view of the whole institution, to wait for the guard who was to admit us. It was noontime, and the prisoners were coming from the shops to eat dinner. Being November, the day was hazy, and the gray uniforms of the prisoners struck me as the worst glaring scene I ever saw. The scene dazed me and I felt sick at heart; but I had more serious setbacks coming.

CHAPTER VIII

MINGLING IN HIGH SOCIETY[1]

The guard led me, along with the other prisoners, to the receiving and discharging department, where I was stripped of my civilization clothes and ordered to take a bath. Then I was given my prison uniform and led to the Bertillon Room, where my photographs and measurements were taken, and identification marks recorded. After having my hair shaved off, given a number for a name, and a large tablespoon to eat with, I was assigned to a cell.

The cell was bare, hard, and drab. As I sat on my bunk thinking, a great wave of feeling shook me, which I shall always remember, because of the great impression it made on me. There, for the first time in my life, I realized that I was a criminal. Before, I had been just a mischievous lad, a poor city waif, a petty thief, a habitual runaway; but now, as I sat in my cell of stone and iron, dressed in a gray uniform, with my head shaved, small skull cap, like all the other hardened criminals around me, some strange feeling came over me. Never before had I realized that I was a criminal.[2] I really became one as I sat there and brooded. At first I was almost afraid of myself, being like a stranger to my own self. It was hard for me to think of myself in my new surroundings. That night I tried to sleep, but instead I only tossed on my bunk, disturbed by my new life. Not one minute was I able to sleep.

When the whistle blew for breakfast the next morning I was heartsick and weak, but after visiting with my cell mate, who took prison life with a smile and as a matter of course, I felt better. He said, "You must as well get used to things here; you're

[1] This chapter is an account of Stanley's experiences in the Illinois State Reformatory at Pontiac, to which he was committed at the age of fifteen years. This institution receives commitments of youthful male offenders between the ages of sixteen and twenty-six.

[2] This is a vivid illustration of the type of situation in which the delinquent's conception of his rôle changes from that of a juvenile offender to that of an adult criminal.

a 'convict' now, and tears won't melt these iron bars." He was only seventeen, but older than me, and was in for one to ten years for burglaries. He delighted in telling about his exploits in crime, to impress me with his bravery and daring, and made me look up to him as a hero. Almost all young crooks like to tell about their accomplishments in crime. Older crooks are not so glib. They are hardened, and crime has lost its glamor and become a matter of business. Also, they have learned the dangers of talking too much and keep their mouths shut except to trusted friends. But Bill (my cell partner) talked all the time about himself and his crimes. I talked, too, and told wild stories of adventure, some true and some lies, for I couldn't let Bill outdo me just for lack of a few lies on my part.

I found Pontiac to be a very clean and sanitary prison, compared to the County Jail. But like St. Charles, the way of the transgressor of the prison rules was hard there. For even a minor infraction of the rules, a prisoner would be sent to the "screens" or "hole." That is, the solitary confinement. It is just a dark, barren cell. It has a toilet and bowl and a dark screen in front of it, so the prisoner cannot see out or have anything to eat or smoke pushed through to him. My God! it is solitary, all right. You just as well be confined in the bowels of the earth, beyond the reach of human beings. I cannot describe the horrors of loneliness and mental stagnation that I felt many times in the black, bottomless pit.

The food at the prison was bad, but the working conditions and recreation better than I had expected. We were allowed out in the yard almost every day, and we had many lively ball games, which helped to pass the dull hours away; for monotony and routine are the prisoners' worst enemies.

We lounged around for fifteen days without working. During that time I learned all about the place from the older criminals, getting on to the ropes and learning what was proper and what was improper, and how to get by. Being little and short, the prisoners called me "the midget." It was just like being petted and pitied, and I liked it, for that was the only consolation that I had, pity from the other prisoners and self-pity. At the end of fifteen days we were assigned to work.[3] I was asked what kind of work I was best fitted for. I said that I was an experienced laundryman, having worked in the laundry at St. Charles. I passed the test for schoolwork, and the school board decided that I had enough education, so I was assigned to work in the laundry, running a machine in the washroom.

For the first few days in the laundry, I sized up my fellow-prisoners. I had learned to keep my mouth shut until I got onto the ropes. The men in the laundry are mostly hardened criminals—ignorant and egotistic. Many were niggers, who were considered little better than beasts.

I got in well with the laundry bunch. They called me "the kid" and pitied me. Even the hardened criminals were kind to me and gave me tobacco and instructed me on how to get by in prison, and how to get by after I would get out.

The prisoner in charge of the mangle that I worked on was Billy,[4] a hardened criminal from Chicago. He was eight years my senior, and was in on a five to life sentence as a burglar and "stick-up" man. Billy took a great liking to me, mostly out of pity, and gave me instructions on how to get on in Pontiac, and how to get by with the police outside. He indelibly impressed two things upon my mind.[5] First, never to trust anybody with your affairs in crime. You never know when a partner will rat you if he gets into a close pinch and finds it an advantage to "sell his soul" to the police. Billy would ask me questions about my rap and my past experiences, but he would not talk much about himself. He was old and experienced, and was different from

[3] If the inmate has not completed the eighth grade he is required to attend school at least five half-days a week; otherwise he may work full time in one of the many "trade schools." The following types of employment are provided: masonry, tailoring, printing, shoe-making, carpentry, painting, tinsmithing, glazing, and work in the bakery and blacksmith shop.

[4] Billy was a notorious criminal character in Chicago. He was killed in an encounter with the police during the latter part of 1929.

[5] Stanley's contact with Billy illustrates the manner in which the code of the adult criminal world is transmitted to the young delinquent. Through such contacts the youthful offender not only becomes identified with the criminal world, but his wishes and ambitions become organized in terms of the values of the adult criminal group.

most of the glib-tongued young crooks that I had known in St. Charles. There, everybody wanted to impress you with their exploits; out here things were different. The older crooks were confident and set in their ways, more at home with crime, and had gotten over the glib-tongue stage of callow youth. I studied Billy every day and saw how different he was from the youthful crooks that I had known before. I finally learned that most of the older crooks there were like Billy, hard-faced and with self-assurance, and took crime as a matter of business. Well did I know that Billy could tell me any deeds of daring in a criminal line, but he was too clever a crook to talk about his exploits to other persons, especially to a young crook like me. From the few stories he told me about himself I knew he was a criminal of rare cunning and ability. He was a fine example of young manhood— tall, agile, brave, keen, and full of nerve. I could vision him "sticking-up" a man without flinching. I could see him in the midst of a robbery, with the police closing in on him, and with his pals frantic and unnerved, yet Billy would be cool and self-possessed. In fact, I thought he could face death without a quiver or qualm. I longed for some thrilling stories from his past experience, but confessions never passed between his steel jaws, and I came to respect and admire him for it. After all, he was a real crook and somewhat of a novelty to me until I got used to him.

Second, Billy chided me for petty stealing. His idea was to "do a big job or none at all." Of course, he considered that I was just a kid and wasn't old enough to "do a job" like him. He figured that the dangers and penalty were about the same whether you did a little job or a big one, so you just as well chose the best. Besides, he said that there was some satisfaction in doing a real man's job, and that it was easier to pay the penalty for a big haul. That sounded reasonable to me, so I thought if I ever pulled another job it would be a big one or none.

Billy was my buddy in the laundry all the time I was in Pontiac. He helped to make life easy for me and I owe him a lot, but I can never repay him. He died, and I know he died like a man.

At work or at play out in the yard, the prisoners would form into small groups and talk about the "outside." The outside that was so near, just over the wall, and yet so far away in time. They would talk about what they were going to do on release. Most of them planned vengeance and crime. They would pull off a big deal and then retire in luxury. Even while in prison, which they hated, they did not think about being arrested again. Consequences didn't concern them much. They thought only of getting by, and they were too egotistical to think that they would ever get caught again. It was only a "bum rap" that landed them in jail this time, and they would know better next time, so they thought. A few would talk about home and mother and going straight, but these were the younger crooks, and they usually got the razz from the older ones. The ones with tender feelings didn't chirp much when the hard guys were in the group, and they usually were there.

Prisoners are always interested in scandals of every kind. In reading the newspapers they always read all about crimes and then the sports section. If there's a big criminal case on, they read every line of it and then speculate on the possible outcome of the case. If the victim isn't wealthy, and if he has been brave and never ratted, the prisoners will be on his side.

Well, I got into these groups, for they were just what I liked. I was always interested in anything in the criminal line. It was fascinating. As a child I wanted to taste it and to dabble in it. I always read everything in the newspapers about crime. Every movie of a criminal sort or about adventure was fascinating. The "Smiling Jack" O'Brien case, the Gene Geary case, and the Church case, all fascinated me as a child, and I read all about them. When I was in the Chicago Parental School, I wondered what St. Charles was like. Then in St. Charles I thought it would be wonderful in Pontiac. My curiosity just pulled me on from one place to another. So I enjoyed these groups because the conversations were always about crimes and other things that were adventurous and appealed to my curiosity nature.

We always talked about the "old life" and how great it would be to get back in the old haunts, with the old bunch. Experiences with women always came in for their full share of consideration, for in prison a man's mind runs to the things he's most interested

in and the things he misses the most. These things are crimes and
sex things. We always talked and thought about them. I couldn't
get them off of my mind. Like all criminals, I wanted to get
ahead in crime. I was always planning new crimes and longing
for another chance to show my stuff. My mind ran in a gutter, and that gutter was crime. I always had been that way,
so in Pontiac I got what I always had wanted, and that made
life there more interesting. Crimes held lures and adventure
for me that nothing else did. There was nothing else open for
me. I couldn't think about anything else for thoughts about
crime always crowded out everything else, especially in jail,
where everybody is a criminal and always talks about his old life
of crime or the big haul he's going to pull off when he gets out.
Think about anything else? Bah! I couldn't, and besides I
didn't want to. Hungers for women in jail are awful. At night
on my bunk and the first thing in the morning a fellow's thoughts
drift to sex experiences. Sex stories that pass from one prisoner
to another, and they are many in jail, keep these hungers burning. Masturbation is about the only solution for these desires in
prison, and it is done by most prisoners. Here's where my day-
dreams helped to save my life. I could think about these forbidden pleasures in my dreams, and that was better than nothing.
I lived over a million times the wonderful sex experiences that I
had had before. These hungers are like the pangs of starvation
and hell. Masturbation didn't worry me. Why? Because it was
a necessity, just as food was a necessity.

So I listened with open ears to what was said in these groups of
prisoners. Often I stood awe-struck as tales of adventure in
crime were related, and I took it in with interest. Somehow I
wanted to go out and do the same thing myself. To myself I
thought I was somebody to be doing a year in Pontiac, but in
these groups of older prisoners I felt ashamed because I couldn't
tell tales of daring exploits about my crimes. I hadn't done anything of consequence. I compared myself with the older crooks
and saw how little and insignificant I was in a criminal line. But
deep in my heart I knew that I was only a kid and couldn't be
expected to have a reputation yet. I couldn't tell about my

charge, for it savored of petty thievery, and everybody looked
down on a petty thief in Pontiac. I felt humiliated in the extreme,
so only listened. Even the guards have contempt for the petty
thief. They were considered ignorant and cowardly. Nobody
had respect for you if you were in for petty stealing. The guard
in the laundry found out that I was in for petty stealing (I told
him that when I was still green), and they razzed me about it and
called me a sneak and accused me of all the stealing in the place.
He had contempt for me and would have liked to see me stay in
there for life. He looked up to Billy because he was an experienced criminal. The prisoners all had the idea that "if you can't
steal something big don't steal at all." So I kept quiet, happy
enough to listen to the thrilling stories of adventure. "Mikie"
O'Brien was one big hero in the place. He had done a lot of time
and was in for big stuff and besides, everbody had read about his
brother, Smiling Jack O'Brien, being hung for "picking off a
copper." He was certainly looked up to for that. I admired him.
I used to watch him all the time in the yard and in the mess hall.
I couldn't help it. Something about him caught my eye every
time I got close to him. That wasn't only true in my case, but for
everybody it was true, especially the younger crooks.

But I never really made any friends in Pontiac, being a petty
thief. Billy and many other prisoners liked me, but it was out of
pity for my youth and lack of experience in the world. So I didn't
make close friends out of them, for you don't make a close pal out
of a fellow that's so superior to you, even if he don't lord it over
you. And they looked down on my youth and little experience
and petty thieving and wouldn't trust me, and didn't want to
"spoil me." There was no mutual understanding, so to speak.

So I was forced out of confidential talks and humiliated to the
extreme by being looked down on for petty thieving. I learned
that pity and tears would not help me with the prison officials
and only made me look like a baby to the other prisoners. I made
up my mind to get used to prison life or die in the attempt, to get
along some way, and I'd never be a petty thief again. That was
the cause of all my worries in Pontiac. I'd do a real job or none,
the next time. But I couldn't help myself here this time. Once

you're marked in prison you're done for, and I had marks of petty thievery all over me. I was shunned, not trusted by my fellow-buddies. But I thought, I'm young and I've time to show my stuff, and I'll do it sometime.

So I became lonely and sad, and took to daydreaming and reading. I planned and dreamed about the big haul I'd pull if things didn't go right on parole. I read every book and magazine in the place, and this saved my mind from dying entirely. Prison life was monotonous, just like a machine. We ate, slept, and did our daily tasks without any variation. I cringed under the strict discipline, the monotony, and the humiliation of youth and lack of experience. It was made worse because most of the other prisoners took it so calmly, and that made me feel puny and cowardly. To the other prisoners, the hardened ones, prison life was just part of the day's work, a stepping-stone to freedom. It was a necessity, which they had learned to accept as part of their life's work. It was to be avoided, if possible, but when it came, it was to be borne bravely and without a whisper. So it impressed me.

As I turned over in my mind my past experiences and suffered agony in prison, I felt new feelings of revenge coming to the surface. I was like a dog kept in a cage and tormented by a vicious master. I had always been in a cage, and there had always been someone to torture me. For seven years I had been going out of one jail into another. Why? Because I was a victim of circumstances. Why couldn't I have had a kind mother, instead of a hell-cat of a stepmother; a father to teach me; a home full of comfort, where I'd gladly go instead of being in the shadow of fear of going home to eat supper. Why? Just because Fate had it in for me. As I brooded over this for days and weeks and months, life became poison and sour and full of hate and spite. In some of my moments of anguish I could have committed murder without a qualm. Like the other prisoners, I felt that I didn't get an even break, but I'd get even with somebody for the unfair play.

Prison guards delight in putting prisoners into the hole (solitary confinement). They pick out prisoners that they don't like and watch them closely to get something on them. When they break a rule, the guard writes out a misconduct slip and the "con" is sent to the hole to languish for a few days. No pleasure is it to be in the hole. It is dark, absolutely barren stone and iron, and stuffy. The odor is awful. No food or water do you get.

I happened to be in the hole on Christmas Day, on a "bum rap"—just hollering in my cell. I sat on the cement floor and brooded. I thought of my sister's home and of the warm fire and the Christmas tree they would have, and of the cheery little home lit up by tallow candles. Here I was shivering and lonely, starving in a damn dungeon. If ever any boy hated and longed for revenge, I did that day. It was a dirty trick, and all because the guard had it in for me. Why does the public blame a convict for killing a policeman or a prison guard? No man, I don't care who he is, is going to kill a fellow-being for nothing. There's always a reason, and most times that reason is harbored revenge and smoldered hate for some outrage, some low-down, cowardly trick, like the one they pulled on me that day and many other times.

My hatred for guards, like the other prisoners', was strong. Of course the guards are forced to be hard by the officials. Once he is lenient or even fair with the prisoners he is asked to resign or else be fired, to be replaced by an ex-boose fighter, who has a vicious disposition combined with a bad temper. Hatred against these guards is unquenchable once it is imbedded in a convict's mind. Antipathy is always in a "fish" (a new prisoner), and once the seed of hatred is planted it shall be nourished by injustices to him until it is full grown. Sometimes the guards are killed, and I think the prisoners are justified in slaying, instead of being run over and terrorized by punishment and severe beating. That is what makes prisoners worse instead of better. The idea of some ignorant, narrow-minded guard trying to reform prisoners is ridiculous and isn't fair to society and to the criminal. Society ought to rejuvenate Pontiac with some young blood for guards, somebody that is fair and not prejudiced against the criminal— unlearned farmers who only think of payment of justice, and they want interest with it besides. The way I feel about it was that not only me but all the prisoners were not getting a square deal, except the "rats," who would sell their souls for a piece of tough horse meat.

Anybody who rats on a prisoner in prison is the lowest, most contemptible sneak on two feet. Hence they are called "rats." Of course an allowance is given in some cases, but to make it your business to inform the "screw" (guard) about everything that is going on under the surface is not fair to prisoners. Because I feel that life is all a game, and hard enough for some, like myself. Also, the prisoner has a slim chance against the rest of the world, and it seems unfair for a rat to spoil even that little chance. It only makes life harder for the prisoner, and he will have to remain in prison just that much longer.

I believe that any game should be played according to the rules of the game. Violators of rules should be punished. Crime is a game, and therefore as a rat violates the rules or code by informing the "dicks" and the "screws," he should be punished when caught, just like other criminals are punished. I think everyone will agree with me in my feelings about these low rats. All prisoners who are worthy of the name will agree with me.

In the laundry there are rats, and in every department of the prison. They are like vultures preying upon rotten things— noiseless, seeking information about the prisoners' conduct, and sometimes framing a trumped-up charge against a prisoner because he has a grievance against him or wants to win a favor from the guard. A prisoner could serve five years and be a rat all that time, and nobody but him and the guard would know it. But woe betide said rat if he is exposed. He is branded and shunned by the good prisoners, and made miserable whenever they can make him miserable. When he is released there is always some one going out to get him. In a few words, anyone who rats commits the unpardonable sin. The worst sin of the criminal world, and often the penalty is death. These rats are composed of dope fiends, petty thieves, and other similar low characters.[6] A man with

---

[6] Material of this nature is indicative of the fact that the criminal world, like all social groups, has its own standards of conduct by which it seeks to regulate and control the behavior of its members. Like conventional society, the criminal group inflicts punishment upon those who violate its codes, and rewards those who conform. It is not surprising, therefore, that the "stool pigeon" or "rat" is an ob-

some manhood in him wouldn't stoop that low. The dirty, lousy, filthy vultures would knife a man when his back was turned. They are only born to be hanged. My feelings are always with the prisoners, for a sense of injustice by guards, hard work, bum food, monotony, and confinement would harden anybody, but consider the guards as bad as the rats. All of this is enough to make a thousand ministers of God turn our criminals. If a man does make good when he gets out, it's because he got better treatment than the other prisoners or else he had determination to make good in spite of his record, but the majority of prisoners lose that along with the rest of their virtues.

One beautiful day in October a runner came to get me, saying that I was going out. I said goodbye to the boys, and they wished me luck. I went to the receiving and discharging department for my suit of burlap. Oh, what a joy to get back into civilized clothes! The prisoner who was being released with me and I

---

ject of contempt from the standpoint of the criminal group. It is a significant fact, also, that within the criminal group there is a definite hierarchy of social groupings, ranging all the way from the petty thief to the gangster. The former belongs to the lowest group in the social scale and is looked upon with contempt in the criminal world.

Jack Black, who was a burglar for twenty-five years and published his autobiography under the title *You Can't Win*, gives the following description of the code and social castes of the criminal group: "The upperworld knows nothing about caste as compared with the underworld. Crookdom is the most provincial of small villages, the most rigid in its social gradations. Honors and opportunity are apportioned on the basis of code observance. There is no more caste in the heart of India than in an American penitentiary. A bank burglar assumes an air with a house burglar, a house burglar sneers at a pickpocket, a pickpocket calls a forger 'a short story writer,' and they all make common cause against the stool-pigeon, whatever caste he comes from. He jeopardizes the life and liberty of his own, which is the great unpardonable crime in the underworld code. He is the rattlesnake of the underworld, and they kill him on the 'safety-first' principle as swiftly and dispassionately as you would kill a copperhead. Respect for property in the underworld is as deep as it is in the upperworld. The fact that it is upperworld property which is involved makes no difference, for when property is transferred from the upperworld to the underworld it becomes sacred again.

"The burglar who shoots his partner for holding out a lady's watch goes up in the social scale of the underworld. Like the clubman who perjures himself to save a lady's reputation, he has done the right thing in the sight of his fellows. Each is a better gentleman according to the code" (*Harpers Magazine*, CLX (February, 1930), No. 957, 306–7).

went to the office to wait an hour for our final discharge. In that hour many thoughts ran through my dead mind. I compared the barren prison with the green grass "outside" and hoped that never again would I taste prison life. But I was completely alone. There was no one to help me. I hadn't seen a relative or a friend from the outside for a whole year. As I thought of my prospects I felt pessimistic, for circumstances had turned me back before.

CHAPTER IX

OUT, BUT AN OUTCAST[1]

We were conveyed to the depot in an automobile. My fellow-prisoner, who was released with me, commented on the glories of freedom, saying that he was going on the "straight and narrow" from then on. As we rode along, my thoughts took wings. Strange to say, I contemplated the beauties of the world, just after coming out of a hell-hole of misery and crime. Why did I think about such things? Because I was free again. The world had seemed to be working against me ever since I was born, and now I thought I was big and strong enough to fight the forces of fate that were against me. While the spirit of freedom possessed me, I resolved to make good, and show the world my good qualities.

We arrived at the depot and were given our fees for services rendered to the state. The sum was ten dollars. To me that money was handy, because it was to give me another start in life. Other prisoners regarded it as a farce, and used it to go out on a spree celebrating their release from jail. They would seek out their old haunts and houses of prostitution and satisfy the burning desires for drink and women which had hungered during their imprisonment. Terrible are these hungers in prison.

We had to wait a few minutes for the train, so we went across the street to have some "coffee and." It seemed strange to eat in

[1] In this chapter Stanley gives a description of the difficulties which he encountered during the first few months subsequent to his release from Pontiac. In the absence of any definite plan for his supervision, he was left entirely to his own devices. He returned to the home of his half-sister, toward whom he always had an attitude of affection. During the year of his incarceration in Pontiac, the half-sister had moved from the stock yards district into a community which had a relatively low rate of delinquency. Stanley's adjustment to this new situation was complicated by the fact that he soon became known in the neighborhood as an ex-convict. Despite a rather serious desire to make an adjustment, the antagonistic attitude of the neighbors, together with his own feelings of persecution and suspicion, soon induced him to leave his sister's home and neighborhood. In time he drifted back to West Madison Street and became involved again in burglary and "jack-rolling."

a restaurant again after eating the coarse prison fare, and what I mean, we ate with gusto. After eating, we bought cigars and cigarettes, luxuries which we had been deprived of for a year. We also bought a deck of cards to pass away the time on the train.

I seemed lost with my new freedom; it scarcely seemed real after being tied down so long, but I laughed and talked to the station-master. The train came along, and as it did so I experienced a great thrill. I was going back home. But what was home! I was like a man without a country. In reality, I didn't know what to do nor where to go. All my riches consisted in freedom, and I didn't know what to do with it. I had no home and didn't know what kind of work I liked—just a vague desire to make good. Red, my companion, and I played blackjack, chatted, and smoked.

There were four men playing rummy across the aisle, and Red and I, being tired of playing blackjack alone, asked them if we could break into their game. One hard guy with an eternal sneer on his face looked me over, and noting that I was a jailbird, said, "No!" in no uncertain terms. His sneering and superior attitude made me boil with resentment, but I could not retaliate.

The stares of the passengers on the train burned through me as if to read that I was an ex-convict, just out—a jailbird, to be feared and avoided. My feelings burned, but I philosophized. "I don't give a damn; I'll show them some day."

As we arrived at the station in Chicago, we jumped off the train before it stopped, so elated were we to get back to the "old home town," free again. We walked out on the street, and a sense of shame possessed me because of my heavy cowhide prison-made shoes and my burlap suit, while Red wore the latest style, and he didn't feel well with me, and thus soon excused himself from my company. I felt hurt and blue, so soon had the beautiful world changed for me. Even a fellow-prisoner could not stand my inferior position.

In my mood, I wandered instinctively back to my old stamping ground, West Madison Street. I walked down the "main stem" and took in the old familiar scenes that I had hungered for in prison. The feeling of contentment that possessed me told me full

well that I was home again. I thought of my childhood days when
I used to roam this very street, and of the many old friends I
knew there. The movie theaters, flophouses, the carefree human
derelicts, the other lures, all brought back my old feeling of freedom which had dimmed in jail. Walking along Madison Street
I bumped into many old friends, and they all asked me from
whence I came. I replied, rather proudly, "From Stir!" They all
wished me luck, and then hit me for the price of a "shot." I wanted to help them and felt drawn to them, but it was against my
principles to give them money for "shots." I took some of them
to a hashhouse for "coffee and," to celebrate my return, but I
wouldn't give them money.

The old sights seemed to entrance me all over again. The
crowds of bums hid me in my prison suit of burlap because I was
dressed little better than they were, so I was not noticed except
by my friends. After making the rounds of the old haunts and
meeting my old friends, I went to a dime movie but did not enjoy
it. I realized that if I stuck around Madison Street I'd lose my
money and get picked up again, so I fooled myself and went out
to my sister's home.

I was greeted with surprise, as they did not know that I was returning so soon. I was glad to be among my own people, and then
I resolved to get a job and make good, so I would have someone
to be proud of me. They invited me to eat supper, and at the table
we talked about my future. My brother-in-law said that all I had
to do was to get a job, work steady, and he would give me a home.
I agreed. That evening I entertained myself by playing the piano
and by helping my brother-in-law repair his Ford car. I was
deeply impressed by my brother-in-law's advice, and I seriously
thought well of myself.

The next morning I got a job at a big factory assembling electrical equipment, at thirty-three cents an hour. The work was
hard and monotonous and did not appeal to me. For two long
weeks I slaved, and the only thing that kept me from quitting was
what I thought my sister would think about it. If I was out of
work I could not pay my board and would have to go. I was doing
piecework, and had to put out sixty-eight cable-forms an hour.

The foreman and the inspector were continually nagging and pushing us to put out more and more pieces. I was new and young and couldn't keep up the necessary speed all day. The foreman picked me out especially and nagged me. He either disliked me or he thought I was green and lazy. I hated him and made up my mind that I wasn't going to be run over by a foreman. So one day I was waiting at the lavatory and picked up a newspaper and began to read it. The foreman saw it and reported me. He later said that I was laid off. I said, "Like hell, I'm laid off! You can go straight to hell. I have quit!" I felt bad about the affair. I wondered how the other boys could stand it. They must have been different from me. They stuck to their jobs, but I couldn't. The breaks seemed to be going against me again.

When I got home and told my sister that I had quit my job, she shook her head in a disappointed manner and told me that I was slipping again. I said, "I'll get a job somewhere where I won't be nagged and tied down so much." That evening my brother-in-law heard about me and bawled me out in an angry way. He said: "Jobs are scarce, and you'll either work or starve! Don't think I'm going to board you!" I changed my opinion of him right there, for I then learned that he wouldn't give me a break, even when I was in a pinch.

I went out to look for work, but it was scarce at the time. After a week of fruitless effort, I began to loaf around with the corner gang. These fellows were all working and doing well, but they had the habit of hanging around the corner and telling dirty stories about women. We took pride in telling about our exploits with such and such a girl, and tried to outdo each other in the number of women that we had conquered. We also had a little clubhouse where we played cards and shot dice and told stories. The fellows knew that I had done time, was an ex-convict, and they let it be known by making remarks about me when my back was turned. I overheard their remarks and they peeved me. Many times I got into brawls on that account. They often said, "Watch out for that jailbird, he has taking habits." Often when I would go into the clubhouse some fellow would say, "Hands on your pocketbooks, here comes the crook!" I tried to mix with them and spent my money lavishly. I was ignorant of the ways of boys on the outside of jail like these, and they looked upon me as a "dumb-bell" or "chump" that one could do anything with. What could I do? I couldn't fight the whole bunch at one time, and that was the only way one could fight them because they stood together against me. I had to grin and bear it, but in my heart I hated them and the whole world and began to be disgusted. I wanted to make good, but the tide was beginning to rise against me again.

The gang looked up to a leader, a dapper young fellow who was conceited and domineering. I hated him because he would show me up as a jailbird in the presence of the whole gang. I guess he thought I was disputing his rank, and therefore he was using my reputation as a target to abuse and show me up. We had many hot arguments over trivial things and only once came to blows, but we were parted before any damage was done. He gradually influenced the gang against me, and I was regarded as an outcast, an ex-convict, not worthy of their company. That hurt me terribly. My boy chums, who had liked me at first, were turned against me, and I was shunned by every boy on the street. They would resort to calling me names and rousing me to fury, but I was helpless before such a number.

I will give an example of how people looked down on me, even outside of the gang. One day I was standing on the corner near my sister's home, and I noticed a little child in the street, in the path of a rapidly approaching car. It looked as if the child would be killed. The mother, who was just coming out of a store, screamed, "Oh! my child will be killed!" Realizing that the child was in danger, I sprang into the street, picking up the child and carrying it to the sidewalk just in time to save it from the car. The mother took the child into her arms, kissing it, and then looked at me with a sneer on her face, and would not thank me for the kindness. She had recognized me and knew of my record.

Everybody looked down on me and distrusted me, and I grew disgusted with life. Here I was out of a job, practically without friends, and no one but my sister trusted me. I was just a person to be shunned. What could I do to wipe out the blot against me?

Nothing. My troubled spirit cried out for freedom. I wanted to go away, anywhere to get out of the misery I was in. I thought about West Madison and knew that there I would find at least human sympathy that would make life bearable again. As I was getting ready to leave, I thought of my sister's plight and how she stood by me. Her husband was not working, and if I got a job it would help her make both ends meet. Urged by a desire to stand by her, I sought work, but work was not easily to be found. In desperation I entered an employment agency and got a job for fifteen dollars a week, but I had to pay eighteen dollars for the position. I knew that that was robbery, but it was better than nothing. The work was at an ink and glue factory, in the stockroom, but I had to run errands when I was not busy in the stockroom. I didn't mind the work so much, but the place was filthy and unsanitary. The fumes were poisonous and sickening, but I stuck to the job like glue, determined to win the fight against the life I had led. Life was monotonous and deadening. Mentally I was dead. Life consisted only of long hours at work, no recreation, and poor pay. I tried to pay board and room and at the same time pay the employment agency on fifteen dollars a week. For weeks I thus plodded along, growing disgusted and tired of the drudgery and monotony of life in general. I was a slave for someone else, and life offered no chance or hope for anything better.

One day things suddenly changed in my favor. A young man about my age came to the stockroom to work. He appealed to me immediately. Something about his devil-may-care air and carefree smile struck me deeply. Something in me appealed to him, and soon there developed a close friendship. He was just the kind of friend I wanted. His ideas about life and his interests and desires were mine. He lived on the North Side, in a good home, but I lived in the stock yards. That made me terribly ashamed, but he didn't seem to mind it. He seemed to have everything that life could offer, while I had nothing. At lunch he would have sandwiches and cookies and other luxuries which I couldn't afford, but he shared with me, and that strengthened our friendship.

His adventurous spirit rhymed with mine. He talked about going on the road. I, being disgusted with the dull, drab existence that I was living, always responded that I was ready to go at his suggestion. The cold weather forced us to postpone our adventure for a few months. His stories of exploits on the road spiced of the very thing that I craved, and my hunger for that life grew until it gnawed like an empty stomach. He talked about beautiful California, the land of eternal springtime, so promising to a young man's fancy. His stories of adventures out there, although I believe they were exaggerated a bit, stimulated me and took away some of the distress of life for me. I became so happy that I forgot about being an ex-convict. What did I care if the fellows at home looked down on me or the people on the street stared at me? Here, at last, I had found a real chum, one whose spirit looked for freedom and longed for adventure.

Buddy (that was my chum's name) and I would go out every night to a show or dive and spend our money lavishly. He was crazy about girls (and I ran him a close second), and he led me into houses of ill-fame. I hesitated at first, never having done it before. But how could I say no to Buddy? Would he not call me a quitter, and was I not seeking adventure also? Was not life drab and monotonous? So I went in with Buddy without shame, paid my toll, and regarded what I did as just a regular business transaction. I didn't give a thought about life and never thought of its dangers. It was becoming interesting and adventurous. All I wanted was to satisfy my eternal craving for roaming, without a care on my mind.

But to get back to the girls, I will describe a house of ill-fame. First, you must know where they are located, and know the ropes, but we had no trouble, because Buddy was acquainted in thirty-five or forty of them. He took pride in knowing the ropes in every place, and impressed that fact on me, which made me admire him and feel ashamed of myself because he was so much wiser. After you know the ropes, all you need is two "bucks." Upon entering a house, one is confronted with a score of girls, all arrayed in scant clothing, displaying their charms to the men. Everything is enticing, arranged to appeal to the passions of the men, the music, the attire of the women, and the scented atmosphere. Buddy had a regular "broad" in each house, but I preferred changing off. We regarded these trips as adventures and went regularly two and three times a week. So I went on, my spirit of adventure holding me in its grasp.

One day Buddy asked me if I wanted to board and room with him. I said I'd like to but that my sister needed my assistance. He pushed me on by saying I could live with him for seven dollars a week, while at my sister's I had to pay ten dollars. The plan appealed to me, so one night I told my sister that I was going to leave. She protested. My brother-in-law became angry at the thought of losing the ten dollars a week and told me in no uncertain terms to get out of the house and not to come back any more. But I didn't care; I was going to a decent home, where I had a friend; and was not adventure in sight? So I took my scant wardrobe and boarded a street car to the North Side, where Buddy lived.

Gee! but it was a swell neighborhood to me. Green grass, trees, and the quiet pervading air soothed my aching soul. It was a haven of beauty and bliss compared with the drab and dirty stock yards from which I had just come. I arrived at Buddy's home and was greeted by his mother, a kindly and affectionate woman, who led me into a home which was furnished with taste, although not expensively. She, in a very kind and touching way, bade me lay my clothes in Buddy's room, for we were to live together. Right off I felt a new boy. Her kind and gentle voice and nice words, and the nice home, seemed to call up immediately something that had been hidden in me before. It was a deep sense of shame about my past life and also about the things that Buddy and I had done together. For it was I who accompanied him on his trips to houses of prostitution, and here he has such a good mother, who was trying to make a good man out of him. As I gazed into her kind eyes and accepted her generous hospitality I felt guilty of a great crime—a wolf in sheep's clothing.

She told me about her older sons, who were such good men, but Buddy, the youngest one, defying her, just because he was out after adventure, and he couldn't be stopped. Later I talked to Buddy and told him what a good mother he had and that we ought to be different, but he only laughed and said he knowed her better than I did.

CHAPTER X

HITTING THE ROAD

The very first night at Buddy's home he pulled me out to a poolroom, amid the protests of his mother. I didn't know how to shoot pool very good at that time, so I felt a little embarrassed when Buddy showed me how to hold the cue. He seemed to be wiser than me in almost everything, but I was determined to catch up with him as soon as possible. During the first month we made it a habit to go to poolrooms and houses of ill-fame regularly. Although we didn't steal, we did about everything else in the life of the underworld.

During this time I found that Buddy was a different boy from my first impressions of him. I came to see that he was a very selfish and egotistical lad. For example, he didn't have to pay board or room rent, so he put his money in the bank and then sponged off me all week. I began to feel that he was making a fool out of me, so my attitude toward him changed. However, I liked to hear his stories of adventure, and my soul seemed to cry out with impatience for the wide open spaces which he described.

One day Buddy told me that his brother worked in another ink establishment and that I could get a job for more money. I was glad to go, especially if I was to get more money. The next Monday I took the new job, but to my sorrow it paid only fourteen dollars a week. I felt more suspicious of Buddy then and wondered why he hadn't taken this job, since he thought it was so good. I saw it all very clearly after a little reflection. Buddy was trying to rise in the limelight, and my going would give him my old job, which was better than the one he had. He had framed me beyond doubt. I was angry, and told him I was through with him. He put up an oily line of gab, but I cut him short and left his home—going to Madison and Halsted streets to live.

Ever since I went to live with Buddy I had let him run over me, but I had secretly resented it. He often said that he was my boss, and that I was under obligation to him because he had taken me into his home to live. I didn't like that, although I endured it until he framed me in connection with the job. That was the climax, and for two weeks we didn't "rap" (talk) to each other. He felt very bad and came to my place of employment many times to make up. Finally, he planned a wild party at his home. There were to be ten couples, with lots of liquor, and Buddy invited me, so I felt friendly toward him and we began to "rap" again.

On the day of the party Buddy gave me twenty dollars with which to buy moonshine. I, feeling rather proud, went to West Madison Street and found an old friend with whom I had previously been engaged in "jack-rolling." I told him about the party, and invited him to go. He gladly accepted the invitation, and we put two gallons of "dago-red" and one gallon of moonshine into his car, and were off to the party. This lad was an old pal, but he considered himself somewhat above me, as he had been promoted to the beer racket from "jack-rolling," while I was doing time in Pontiac.

The party got off to a rip-roaring start, everyone taking a drink, and we were soon making merry—dancing, spooning, and singing. I didn't do much drinking; in fact, I never cared much for drinking, as my stomach wouldn't stand it. My girl and I spent most of our time out on the porch spooning. By midnight everyone was thoroughly intoxicated, and the relations were promiscuous and intimate. At four o'clock the party broke up. Buddy could not walk, so I put him to bed, and we sang him a farewell song and parted.

Joe (my Italian friend) and his girl and my girl and I went out driving from the party. Joe drove us to a black-and-tan joint on the West Side. He was a joint owner of the place, so felt at home and led us into a back room, where he ordered drinks. I refused to take liquor, saying I preferred ginger ale. Joe looked at me with a frown of disapproval, ashamed of my childish action. I answered his mental query by saying that I drank too much at the party and that my system would not stand so much. He sneered and said, "All right," and right there I knew that he had changed his opinion of me. I was a weakling in his sight. I knew he would never have anything more to do with me.

After chatting a few minutes, we all went upstairs to bed. At noon I got up, took my girl home, and then went to Buddy's home. He was still sleeping, but I awoke him, and we put the house in order so his mother would not be suspicious. Buddy knew his stuff, so he fixed up the house spick and span. We were back to our old relationship, and I was happy. I gave up my work at the ink company and got another job—at a wholesale grocery house.

My work at the wholesale grocery house consisted of labeling boxes of cheese, and it was humdrum and monotonous, but I had to do it to live and have the pleasures which were so enticing just at that time. I worked among negroes, and, being young and narrow-minded, I was greatly prejudiced against them. They were slovenly and ill-mannered, and it wasn't a day before I had a battle with one. He had the nerve to try to tell me what to do. I told him where to get off at, and added that I never had to take orders from a nigger before, and that I didn't intend to take them at the present time. He tore into me for calling him "nigger," and, although I do not wish to exaggerate my ability at fisticuffs, I would have defeated him easily had not a lot of other niggers come to his aid. Seeing my danger, I grabbed a heavy iron bar and held them at bay until they cooled down. That proved to them that I wasn't to be fooled with. I made up my mind not to let a nigger run over me, but I knew that I was in grave danger there, for they might attack me secretly and do me great injury. So I planned to leave as soon as the opportunity arrived.

Buddy got a new job, where he earned more money. He was planning to make a pleasure trip to Wisconsin as soon as he had sufficient funds. He told me that I could go if I had the dough, but of course I didn't have the money. At the end of one month he had saved one hundred dollars and was ready to make the trip. He and two boy chums and three girls left in a friend's car the next day. He couldn't do without girls. He bade me a fond fare-well, and they were off.

On my way to work the next morning I found out how much I missed Buddy. He was such a jolly little pal to have. He always had a smile, a smile that bespoke adventure and a happy-go-lucky spirit, and now he was gone. My only friend was gone, and I was all alone. I brooded over the good times we had had together and the pleasures we could have if he were only here. I became disgusted and cussed myself that I couldn't get the funds to go with him. I plodded along, staying at home alone after the day's work, because I didn't know what to do without Buddy. He was gone almost two weeks. One day I was working away scraping imported cheese, blue and despondent, when who did I see standing before me but Buddy! Gosh, what a relief for sore eyes was the sight of him! I grabbed his hand and shook it violently. He started to tell me about his trip. He was in trouble. He got in with a girl out at Johnstown and went too far, and her father had filed suit against him. Also the bunch he was with had burglarized a store and were seen in the act. The police had given chase, but the gang had escaped. In the mêlée Buddy had torn his new thirty-dollar suit, which he regretted very much. After telling a line about the "broads" at Johnstown, Buddy said he had to leave Chicago immediately, because if any of the gang got caught they might squawk on him and give the police his Chicago address. He asked me to go with him, and of course I was more than glad to get away from my monotonous work and the niggers.

Buddy stayed at a hotel that night, not wishing his mother to know that he was in the city. The next morning we met and planned our departure. In the afternoon we went up to Buddy's house, and Buddy waited in the alley for my signal. His mother was away, so we both went in, took a bath, put on old clothes, packed our good clothes, and hurried away. Buddy was anxious, but I was more so. My soul seemed to sense the coming of freedom that I craved. I wanted to roam, and to blazes with the world full of conventional shackles that tied me down to slavery. Why should I work with niggers when freedom was in reach? The thought of leaving tingled and thrilled every drop of blood in my body. My childish dreams were to be realized. Maybe I'd see California, the land of which I had dreamed many times. Like Alger's hero, I was going out to seek my fortune. Words could not express my joy.

We took a street car to the Union station, got information

about the train schedule, and then expressed our clothes to Omaha, Nebraska. We shipped them in the same package, collect, and Buddy kept the check. Then we boarded a Grand Avenue street car and went to the end of the line, where we got off, had a bite to eat, and got some sandwiches for the journey. It was still early, so we went into the inevitable poolroom and shot pool until train time. We were both highly excited and elated and talked—or rather, Buddy talked—about the promising future in store for us out West. I dreamed silently, and Buddy's talk was nothing but static that only interfered with the sweetness of my visions. My heart was light as a bubble; my troubles of the day before had vanished. Everybody and everything seemed to be different—friendly and buoyant.

Our train pulled out at 10:57 P.M. The night was very dark, and, being the first of April, was chilly, so we had to wear overcoats. We boarded the "blind"; that is, between the engine and the first car, which was supposed to bring us joy for evermore. Buddy and I got a thrill when the train started off, and when it picked up speed we were so overjoyed that we burst into song. As we sped along I inhaled deeply the crisp night air, and felt braced and invigorated. We smoked cigarettes, made plans for the future, and bade farewell to sorrow and trouble.

Before going farther I will explain the "blinds." As I said before, it is between the engine and the first coach. The road bums ride the blinds when they are in a hurry. It is very dirty; the cinders and smudge soon make one look like a black man. The experienced floater will ride the blind only on a passenger train, because there are usually empty box-cars on a freight train, and these are much cleaner, although not so speedy. In about an hour we reached Elgin, and there we got off, for we were tired. We went up to the Y.M.C.A. and asked for a room, which we got. We went right to bed and slept soundly till morning. At 8:00 A.M. we arose, dressed, and as we stepped into the hall Buddy asked me to help him put his coat on, which I did. He then took it right off and had the nerve to ask me to help him put it on again. He laughed proudly and said, "You're my valet on this trip and you'll do everything I tell you to do. I don't want you to be slow about your duties, either." I boiled with fury and resentment and told him to go to hell, and that I'd go my own way. I wasn't going to be anybody's slave; that I was out after freedom. The good Lord saved him from a pounding right then, because I could hardly hold myself. I left him there, and as I parted he shot back a haughty laugh and a parting word, saying, "I have the receipt for our clothes, and when I get to Omaha I'll sell yours and pocket the money." That was a challenge, and I took it up.

My one determination was to get to Omaha in record time, to spite that double-crossing rat. I ran to the yards and caught a freight train. In the same box-car that I got into was another human derelict. He was about forty years old. He greeted me in the hobo lingo, like this, "Hello, Buddy, where are you headin' for?" "Omaha," I replied. "That's just were I'm goin' to," he said. He started to chat in a very congenial way and laid his hand on my leg. Immediately I knew he was a moral pervert, looking for a victim. I knew his kind like a book and always resented their advances. He was short, massive, and strong, and could have overpowered me, but he was a coward. He noticed my resentment and withdrew to the other corner of the car. At the next stop I left the freight train because it was a local and too slow. I was eager to beat Buddy to Omaha. I waited at the depot and caught the Omaha Limited "on the fly." I got on top of the coal-heap, and the motion of the train rocked me to sleep. Occasionally I would be awakened by the shrieking of the train as it thundered on through the darkness. I had always liked trains, especially the engines, and here I was sitting behind this steel monster that panted and puffed, seeming to co-operate with me in my eager desire to beat Buddy to Omaha. How I was thrilled! It was a complete sense of freedom that I cannot describe in words. After an hour of such elation I fell into a deep slumber, which lasted until I was awakened in the roundhouse at Council Bluffs.

The "brakie" woke me up, dragged me off the coal-heap, and kicked me out. I regarded that as a natural proceeding and started to get my bearings. I found a lunchroom on Main Street, where I had breakfast, and as I paid my bill the mistress told me that she had roomers. I asked for a room. She asked me where I was from, and I said, "Chicago." Looking me over in a peculiar way, she said that I could have a room if I paid in advance. I did so, and she led me up to a room. It resembled the rest of the building, which was a dilapidated structure in crying need of repair. After sleeping in the "blind" and box-cars I wasn't so particular. I took a bath, cleaned and brushed my clothes, and inquired of the mistress the way to Omaha. She gave me the directions in her toothless way, for she was old and emaciated but wise in the ways of the world. She had seen better days, and now she was leading a sour existence, repenting the follies of her youth. She gave me advice about how to take care of myself in Omaha—telling me the evils and thieves, and warned me to keep a safe distance from them. I took her advice seriously—feeling that she was right. Following her directions, I boarded a car to Omaha, intending to get my clothes at the express office.

As I was riding on the car I thought of Buddy, wondering where he was. I wanted him to be with me, even if I was angered at him at Elgin. I stood ready to forgive him if I could find him. But Buddy was gone, and I was alone. Suddenly I felt blue, heartsick, and lonely. Memories of Buddy and our pleasures together filled my eyes with tears. I wanted to go home, back to West Madison Street, to find friends and sympathy that would soothe my feelings. But now the car had reached my destination and I got off, undecided whether to frame Buddy and get our clothes. It was playing him unfair, but I figured that he'd do the same thing by me, as he said he would. So I entered the express office and gave the clerk the details. He asked my name, and I gave Buddy's. My nerves tingled, because I knew the situation called for a good "line." After a rapid fire of questions, which I answered with clever ease, the clothes were delivered to me. He cautioned me about the dangers of lying, and then I gave him my rooming-house address and departed. I felt rather proud of my cleverness, after the episode, and figured that I could take care of myself from then on. Buddy would have done the same thing to me, so I felt no qualms on that score.

It was evening when I returned to my room at the rooming-house in Council Bluffs. At the supper table I was introduced to the other boarders, who were all common manual laborers—except two, who were would-be traveling salesmen.

After being introduced, they all seemed to distrust me, and cast suspicious glances at me and at each other. I resented these glances, and thought these people a bunch of narrow-minded galoots, ignorant of the ways of the world, while I classed myself as a clever young crook, superior to them, even though I was a young boy.

After supper the men gathered around a table to play cards. I, being lonely and desiring companionship, asked to join them. They thought I was too young. But one asked me if I had any money to lose, and after saying that I did, they gladly admitted me to their game of pitch. I soon found that they were sharks and could trim me easily, and I was so thrilled that I couldn't stop. At ten o'clock the game stopped, and I had lost five dollars and sixty cents. Having a few dollars left in my pocket, I offered to buy drinks for the bunch, and they were the kind that never refused. They thought I was a regular guy, although they knew I was only a kid. That episode gained me a lot of friends to talk with, and I didn't think myself the loser by any means. They bade me a cordial good-night, and we went to bed. The homesickness of the afternoon had gone, and I soon fell into a deep slumber.

The next morning I went out to look for a job. There was a depression at the time, and work was scarce. Being young, I didn't have much chance when many strong and skilled men were seeking work. Returning home, I contented myself by playing the piano.

The landlady had two daughters, and I sort of shined up to them. I made a favorable impression upon them, and we were soon going to movies together. Their names were Nellie and Ruth, and I favored the latter. She was just my age, sixteen, and had beautiful blond hair. Her features were finely molded, so unlike the coarse features of the stock-yards girls that I had known before, who were flabby and ill-mannered. I spent most of my time with Ruth, taking long walks with her up to the Bluffs. These trips we enjoyed greatly, and there sprang up a strong friendship and mutual understanding between us. I told her of the hard luck I had had in life, but I didn't tell her that I had done time. I told her my troubles simply because I had no one else to tell them to. She related her troubles, which were little things, and I soothed her as she soothed me.

Down in my heart there began to develop a great love for her because she was so sweet and innocent. But I was just a cheap crook who didn't deserve the kindness and love which she gave me, but then I concluded that I was not to blame. I could not help being a thief. Circumstances dragged me down. Ruth showed her love by doing nice little things for me, such as sewing on buttons, mending my clothes, making little tidbits or sweets which we ate on our walks to the Bluffs.

Life seemed just too sweet. I couldn't grasp the reality of it. Something seemed to be wrong. Certainly such peace could not last long for me. The sudden change from drabness to a world of blue skies seemed to jar me, so every day I fully expected to awaken from a dream and find myself in a prison cell, as I had done so many times in Pontiac.

About that time I experienced one of the greatest shocks of my life. One evening a large automobile stopped in front of the house, and a young man alighted. He entered the house and greeted everyone in a very familiar manner. As he was talking to Mrs. Rand, I overheard him ask for Ruth. My nerves chilled. I wondered who he was, and I soon found out. He was an old friend of Mrs. Rand's and had just returned from a three-month trip to California. Alas, he was Ruth's beau, and now he was back to claim her. I knew that there was an on-coming struggle for supremacy, so I naturally sized up my opponent. He was about twenty-two years old, good-looking, and had strong features that bespoke a strong character. I was only a gangling youth of less than seventeen years, while he was matured; but I was not to be torn away easily from Ruth.

Ruth evidently overheard Roy (that was my opponent's name) ask for her, for she came tripping into the room, delighted to see him. Then I had a sinking feeling at the pit of my stomach, because it looked as though she had strung me. They exchanged greetings and chatted about how much they had missed each other, and then Ruth led him to the kitchen, where she prepared a bite for him. I was restless, so I went to the kitchen, and, as an excuse, asked Ruth when supper would be ready. She replied, "At six o'clock," and looked at me in a very troubled way, as if to say that she was not at fault. After I went out she excused herself from Roy and came upstairs to me. She told me not to worry, for she was mine as long as I'd have her, but that she'd had to be cordial to Roy, as she didn't want to hurt his feelings. That was like Ruth. She wouldn't hurt anything, and I loved her for it. Assuring me that she would dispose of Roy in short order, she went back to the kitchen.

Just before supper Roy left the house in a very angry mood because Ruth had told him of her love for me. I thought the matter settled, but it was not, as I soon found out. After supper we gathered for our customary game of pitch. I became deeply engrossed in the game, but suddenly I felt some one grasping me by the collar of my coat. Turning askance I beheld Roy. He was intoxicated and was as mad as fury. As I slipped from his grasp, he flew at me with an oath, and right there I knew I was in for a bitter struggle. The fact that he was intoxicated was the only advantage in my favor. In a normal condition he could have whipped me in short order.

As he came at me, I side-stepped and gave him a blow on the cheek. He fell but was up in a second. We clinched, and then I realized how strong he was. As I felt his strong fingers around my neck, I fought desperately, more so because of the stake involved. Were we not struggling for Ruth? I knew that if I was humbled I'd be shunned as a weakling, incapable of holding my own among men. So I fought like a wildcat, and wrenched myself loose from his vicelike grasp. Avoiding that thereafter, we milled and struggled for about five minutes, until we were separated.

After that episode my relations with everyone at the rooming-house (except Ruth) was strained. Roy, as I said before, had many friends there, so all the sympathy was in his favor. They treated me rather chilly, and I thought it best to seek out a more friendly atmosphere. As I was making preparations to leave, a very dangerous thing happened to me. A girl was living at the rooming-house. She was well educated and refined. A man by the name of Dick, who also lived there, was sweet on her and tried to make love to her. He was only a day laborer, and she thought herself much superior to him and thus spurned his attentions.

One day Dick came to call on Susie, but she ran away from him and went to her room upstairs. He became very angry at her coldness and pursued her upstairs. She attempted to escape him and ran downstairs. While she was on the stairs he shot at her, the bullet striking her heel and knocking some leather off it. There was quite a commotion, and everybody was talking about it, including myself. Dick came down and asked what the trouble was, thus trying to get out of it in that way. I, like a fool, said I heard a shot. Dick turned on me angrily and said, "You're a liar, you sneaking little coyote, you never heard a shot. That was a tire that blew out." He gave me a slap on the jaw and stuck a gun in my rib and said, "You pack up and get out of here or you'll find yourself in the Missouri River." I was young, so this warning frightened me not a little, for I realized that I was in a tight place. I knew it was well for me to leave, so the next morning I packed up my clothes. I had no money, as I had not worked, so I decided to hit the road, riding box-cars again. The idea rather thrilled me, and I became anxious to leave.

I had a friend at the rooming-house, and he often talked about going to Chicago. So that morning at the breakfast table I described the wonders of Chicago to him. He was just like I was, ready to go at a moment's notice. He was twenty years old, short and heavily build, and had been raised on a farm. He had never been in a large city, and thought Chicago offered something for nothing, so he was anxious to get there. But before breakfast was over a big automobile drove up to the house, and two women and a man got out and walked into the house and inquired for me. I, being present, answered that I was the one they were seeking. The man was a detective from the express company, and he put the cuffs on me and bade me go with him. I got into the machine and we drove away.

As we were riding on to the city jail I looked back on the past and thought of the good times I had just had, and how I had felt that life had taken a turn for the better. I thought of Ruth, and I wondered how she would feel after hearing about me. And now I was about to enter the city jail, back to disgrace and oblivion. What was there really worth while in living? Why couldn't the world give me an even break just once? As the car pulled up in front of the jail, the officer ordered me to get out and led me to the jail, as the car sped away. I learned afterward that the women who were in the car were Buddy's aunt and cousin. They had found out in some way about the theft of Buddy's clothes and made a complaint against me. It was easy to find me, as I had given my address to the station-master. If arrested, I had intended to give up Buddy's clothes and tell the circumstances of the case.

The detectives led me to the desk sergeant, who questioned me about the clothes. I gave him a truthful account of the whole incident, because I knew that at most I could get only a short sentence. After the questioning, the turnkey put me in a long, lonely cell that was as filthy as the Black Hole of Calcutta. The cell was large enough for fifty men, but it was full of vermin, and the scum and stench was enough to sicken the dirtiest bum that ever walked West Madison Street. I walked up and down the cell, contemplating the future and wondering how much more of my life I would have to languish in jail. I gazed outside at the mild April day, and wished I were one of those free men who could go where they wished. But here I was, a criminal, an outcast, who must be locked up, not worthy of even a clean bed to sleep in. I sat down on the dirty old bed that was black with the filth from a thousand criminals and thought burning thoughts of the past, of fate, and of the cruel stepmother who was responsible for my predicament. My thoughts went back to West Madison Street, to my friends there, and I yearned to go back there and live there forevermore. Because there I was with friends, outcasts like myself, who wouldn't look upon me as an ex-convict. As I brooded over the probable fate that awaited me, I wept like a two-year-old wanting its mother. I felt alone, helpless, and stranded. I cussed myself for the thing that I had done. Why couldn't I keep going straight? I was in jail just because I was too stubborn to let Buddy have the best of me. But I had lost and I was to blame, so I brushed the tears away and gritted my teeth and prepared to take what was coming, as becomes a brave man of the underworld.

Late in the afternoon the turnkey opened the cell door and ordered me downstairs, where I faced the detective from the express company and the chief of police. They quizzed me about my past and my home. I told truthfully about everything except my incarceration at Pontiac. After prolonged questioning they agreed to free me if I left town immediately. I agreed, very much elated at this sudden turn of fortune, and ran out so fast that my feet could not keep step with my boundless joy.

I went to the rooming-house and found my friend who was going to leave with me. Before leaving I saw Ruth and bid her a rather prolonged farewell. She was very much upset about my going, and pleaded with me to stay with her. I was reluctant to go, but thought of the threat of the night before. She pleaded and protested, and I thought of our pleasures and wanted to tell the chief of police to go to blazes and I'd stay with Ruth. I soothed her by telling her that I would write, and that after getting a job in Chicago I would save money and come back and get her. She prepared a big lunch for me, against my protests, but inwardly I knew that I'd need the food before another dawn. We finally started off, and as I went out the door Ruth put some money in my hand. That was too much for me, so I laid it on the table, and we said goodbye, never again to see each other. It was heartrending for me, the saddest moment of my life, because she was the first girl I ever loved and had intimate relations with. My soul fairly ached with misery as I left her in the doorway. I walked blindly and with faltering steps out of the yard and down the street to the railroad yards. Here my friend and I were to catch a "blind" to Chicago. The words of one of my favorite melodies kept running through my mind and brought tears to my eyes.

CHAPTER XI

BACK TO MY PALS

As we sat on one of the rails of the rightaway I brooded over my miserable past and of what the future might hold in store for me. My heart was heavy, and I expected fate to pull another trick on me ere many days would pass. My life was always uncertain. I never knew what was going to happen to me. No plan did I ever have. Circumstances were the only plans I ever had. I was blue and my partner was no relief, for he was not sociable—more inclined to be glum and stolid. Besides, he was green, unexperienced in the world of men. He couldn't tell stories of adventure, and so he was not interesting, because I liked the adventurous spirit in men. The care-free, happy-go-lucky always appealed to me.

After an hour of quiet brooding I saw that our "through freight" was pulling out, so we hopped into an empty box-car. Once on the move I felt better. I looked forward to getting back to "dear old Chi," the town of my birth, and to the "main stem," the home of my pals and side-kicks.

In the same box-car with us were seven other floaters, ranging in years from sixteen to sixty years. They were all broke, but that is a minor matter to a bum who finds it rather easy to beg and steal food. As the train was rambling along, we talked about the next town and the chances to bum a feed. The bum's idea of begging was to go down the "main stem" and beg from the butchers and bakers, as well as from homes and passers-by. The conversations centered on bumming meals, daring exploits on the road, and moonshine, the floaters' old standby. I distributed the lunch which Ruth had prepared for me, and I felt sick as I thought of her past caress.

I got to talking with an old veteran of the road who had "rode the rods" for forty years, and I passed the time away smoking and listening to his yarns that were interesting, even to my rather sophisticated mind. I will always remember his parting word to me, which was, "My boy, you are very young, and if you've got a home, go back to it, and if you have none, then get a job and live a decent, upright life." He added that he regretted his misspent life and wished for another chance to make a man out of himself, but it was too late. Age had taken away the spirit of youth that is so necessary in rebuilding. That was good advice and rather struck me at the time, coming from an old veteran, but I was hard, full of nerve, and thought I knew it all. Also I never thought about the future or the day of reckoning. I lived life as it came along—taking things as a matter of course.

At the next town my partner and I went down to the "main stem," and he, being unwise to "stemming," I directed his course of attack—telling him to beg at every bakery and butcher shop, while I received his goods and hid them. I was in no mind to beg, and why should I stoop to such a task when I had someone who liked to do it and who was a howling success at it? When I saw that we had enough, we took our provisions and, following the directions of a fellow-floater, we entered the "jungle."[1] Here we found a couple of old kettles, and I built a fire and cooked an appetizing supper out of the wide variety of foodstuffs my partner had begged. Being ravenously hungry, we ate all of our provisions and then leaned back to smoke; nothing appeals to my imagination any stronger than an evening in the "jungle"—after a good supper, to lean back and smoke and tell stories of adventure and be free, out in the open spaces.

Not fifty yards away from us was a group of "bos" partaking of soup from a kettle—a typical scene to look upon in the "jungle." Although a little lonesome, I did not care to mingle with them, for I well knew some of the scum that travels the road would knife a man for the price of a "shot," and I instructed my companion always to be on the alert. But we were noticed by them, and one of their group—a big, bulky brute of a man— approached us, and I gave a warning signal to my partner. The

[1] Nels Anderson, author of *The Hobo*, gives the following definition of the "jungle": "On the outskirts of cities the homeless men have established social centers that they call 'jungles,' places where the hobos congregate to pass their leisure time outside the urban centers. The jungle is to the tramp what the camp ground is to the vagabond who travels by auto."

"bo" asked us—among other questions—if we had a red card (an I.W.W. membership card),[2] and I replied in the negative.

"Well, you'ed better fork over a buck apiece or I'll make it hot for you," growled the "bo," whose heavy visage and massive jaw indicated full well the fact that he had serious intentions. Not wishing to be defeated in the presence of my partner, I thought desperately for a way to escape. I rose to my feet, pretending to be searching in my pockets for a dollar, and, having a heavy stick in my hand with which I had stirred the fire, I struck him a heavy blow on the head. It stunned him sufficiently to give us a twenty-yard start ahead of him. He was enraged and pursued, but we easily outdistanced him. I was glad that was over and planned to hurry to Chicago. My partner, being a dumbbell in the ways of the road, took a lot of my time for I had to show him the ropes. I decided to ditch him when we got to Chicago, but not until then, because he could beg, and was thus my meal ticket.

After a long, hard grind we arrived in "Chi" and boarded a car to the "main stem." Gee, but I felt good to be back in the glaring light, the hurry and bustle, the gay places of amusement, and the crowds! To this day I cannot very well explain the hankering, only that since my childhood I had that irresistible impulse that I couldn't hold back to save my life. As we rode along on the street car, I pointed out, with much pride, the big buildings and industrial plants. My partner gazed with wonder and awe at the big city, it being the first time he had been in one. He wondered how I knew so much and did not get lost in such a big place. I was vain then and got a kick of pride out of introducing him to the city. He was fairly fascinated by the "human driftwood," the cheap places of amusement, peanut stands, and everything. After this novelty wore off, I decided to go out to West Madison Street to my old haunts. I was ashamed to go back to my sister's home. As we were walking along with the crowd I decided to ditch my partner, because I didn't want my friends to know that I was associating with a dumb-bell.

[2] "In every permanent camp (jungle) there is likely to be a permanent group that makes the camp its headquarters. Sometimes these groups are able to take possession and exploit the transient guests. The I.W.W. has at times been able to exclude everyone who did not carry the red card of that organization" (op. cit.).

I ditched him easily in the crowd, and then went directly to an old haunt—a poolroom formerly frequented by my old gang. There I found many of my friends, among whom was my partner in "jack-rolling" in the past. We exchanged greetings—delighted to see each other—and he asked me about my experiences on the road, which I related with some feeling of superiority. Tony (that was his name) was Italian, and was one year my junior—and was inclined to be timid, but not a coward by any means. His heart was warm, and he always looked up to me. I told him I was hungry, and he immediately invited me to have supper with him, and I accepted with alacrity. During supper we talked about making some easy dough, but I was fatigued after riding in box-cars, so we arranged to meet the next morning and work out our plans. On leaving, he gave me money for my room that night and for breakfast the next morning, and we bade each other a fond good-night.

I slept like a top that night, and the next morning I met Tony. We worked out a plan for "making drunks," which was crude, although it didn't seem so to us. After adopting our plan for that night, we played billiards and "made the old joints," where I met the old pals that I had not seen since going on the road. I was in my own world now, among friends, where I didn't feel blue and wasn't looked upon with suspicion by everybody. Best of all, I was happy—not a care on my mind, but making money, and I already had my mind made up how I was going to do that. I felt hard-boiled, experienced in the ways of the world. Stealing was easy; it was a necessity. Besides, I seemed to want to be tough. Prison held no fears for me. I felt that I was smart enough to get by without getting caught. Besides, I was used to prison. There was nothing for me to lose by going back there, for no one cared where I was or what became of me. So I wanted to bum and make my living in the easiest possible way. Then, too, I was helpless, being in the web of life of crime from which I could not escape—and were not all my friends here?

That night Tony and I embarked on our tour of the slums after "live ones" (bums with money), which were fairly plentiful in that district at that season. The drunks who had recently come in from the labor camps would usually have money. Their first stop after hitting the "main stem" was the blind-pig, where they would soon be drunk with moonshine. The "hustlers" ("jack-rollers") hung around in these joints and relieved the bums of their money while the latter were in a stupor. After becoming intoxicated the drunk is thrown out of the blind-pig by the bartender. He may either lie in the alley or roam the street; in either case he is an easy victim for "hustlers." Tony and I not only made the blind-pigs, but we toured the alleys, streets, and vacant houses as well.

This first night we were walking along the street and spied a drunk who appeared to be a "live one." We waited until he got near a dark spot, and then surrounded him. He was very drunk but was large and husky. My nerves were a little shaky at first, but throwing all caution to the wind I sprang at him—putting the strong arm on him and bringing him to the ground. An alley was close by, so we dragged him into it and proceeded to search him. He didn't have anything in his pockets but a gold watch and chain. The man was well dressed, so I figured that he must have money somewhere. Sure enough, we found a money belt, which I cut off. Making sure that no one saw us, we left the bum in the alley and went to my room. We were overjoyed to find ninety-six dollars in the money belt. The watch was worth ten dollars, so we were well satisfied for one night, so split evenly and went home.

It took me some time to regain the nerve necessary to attack drunks. I was like a baseball player who had been out of the game for a month without practice and then suddenly entered again. But I soon regained my old courage and lost my sympathy and feeling for everybody but Tony. He was a good partner in crime, as well as a good pal. We got along like brothers, because we understood each other. In plain words, we would be willing to go to hell for one another. He moved into my room, and we made it our official headquarters. There were "scarlet women" in the same rooming-house with us, and they spent much time at our room. All in all, we were well satisfied with life, and as long as plying our trade brought such handsome returns we did not suf

fer any qualms of conscience about our stealing. My cup of joy
was overflowing.

Tony and I continued to "make drunks" and to break into
apartments for about three months, and then his brother ran into
him on the street. Tony was bumming away from home, and this
brother ordered him to go home or he would swear out a warrant
for him. Tony had to go and that left me without a pal. I was
very lonely. I met many of my old friends and one of them,
knowing of my success of "making drunks" and that Tony had
left me, wanted to establish a partnership with me. Realizing
that I would have "cold feet" if I went out alone to steal, I considered this offer and sized him up for the job.

Jack (that was his name) was a well-built, swarthy Kentucky
lad of twenty-two years. I looked at his strong arms and shoulders with approval, and although he was not a polished city chap,
he knew the ropes around the West Side, so I agreed to take him
into partnership with me. We played billiards a while, and then
I took him to supper to sort of seal the bargain. I told Jack about
my room and invited him to take Tony's place there. After telling him about the conveniences, along with the women, he readily accepted, for he was an ardent admirer of the opposite sex.
Women were the cause of his downfall. He had had an illicit
affair with one, culminating in a tragedy, which made it necessary for him to leave Kentucky. And here he was, a human derelict at the age of twenty-two.

We went out for the first time the next night. I picked out a
"live bum" and we stalked along behind him until he approached
a dark street, and then, to try out Jack's ability, I told him to
strong arm the bum. Jack didn't hesitate, for at the designated
spot he did the trick which brought us the sum of thirteen dollars.
I was more than satisfied with Jack's ability and painted the
future rosy, as long as I had a partner like him.

We had a regular racket of "jack-rolling" and breaking into
homes, and made more money than we needed for legitimate expenses, but we got rid of most of it through Jack's acquaintance
at the newspaper alley. This alley was usually filled with a large
number of "newsies" and truck chauffeurs. I had been there

three years before, but Jack took me again and introduced me to his friends. I easily made friends, and it added another adventurous hangout to my list, to frequent in the future. It proved to be a good place to lose money, as there was a continuous crap game going on there, and Jack and I lost fourteen dollars the first night. Many a lad has lost his last hard-earned penny in that alley and then turned to stealing to keep up with the fascinating game. You'll steal or do anything to be a good guy in a crap game like that. You're too fascinated to worry about the losses. It's a lively contest, and you are out to win at any cost.

These games were run by a couple of Italian toughs and "pugs" from the West Side. It was a lucrative enterprise for them, for they got a rake-off of 10 per cent or more on every "pass." I gave them credit for their cleverness. One would think that a group could shake dice without someone getting a rake-off in that way, but not so in that alley. The Italian lads had a gang and guns to back them up, so they would not sanction a game in the alley without a rake-off to them. I saw them break up more than one game that didn't offer a rake-off to them. But even so, they were popular with the boys, because in the underworld a member is given credit if he gets away with anything, even though it is against one another.

Jack and I left the alley that night broke but confident that we would get a "live drunk" on the way home, which we did. The haul yielded thirty-three dollars, so we were on easy street again. After the usual roundabout course from the scene of the deed to my room Jack went to sleep, but I read and meditated. I thought of the news alley. I was always very much fascinated by any form of gambling, especially crap games. My thoughts wandered to Jack's friends and how well dressed they were. They apparently all had good rackets, for their appearance bespoke prosperity. I thought that I would in time, through Jack, come in close contact with these guys, and maybe they would take me in. I remembered that they were genial and quiet spoken and acted inconspicuous. Their very air of self-assurance seemed to fascinate me and draw me to them. They were to me on a higher scale of the underworld social ladder than a "jack-roller," and naturally I wanted to get in with them.

During breakfast the next morning I asked for further information from Jack about his well-dressed friends of the racket. He replied that they were "jack-rollers" at one time, but, having tired of it, took up burglarizing and sticking-up, and prospered by it. He added that each one had a "swell broad" on the string—keeping them in an apartment—and always had lots of dough in their "kick." Digesting the bit of news with my breakfast, I created the idea that "jack-rolling" was getting a little menial for me, so I asked Jack to give me an intimate knockdown to his friends, to see if we could break in to fast company.

Jack consented, so that night we went to the alley. The well-dressed guys were there. They were swell-looking guys and appealed to my fancy. Jack pulled the leader of the gang out of the crowd and started to introduce me to him. Jack said, "This is Red, my side kick, and we're out hustling live ones now, and he'd like to get better acquainted with you guys." Jerry (that was his name) was the leader and brains of the gang. He scrutinized me sharply and sneered and said, "Kid, you'd better go back home where you came from, because the racket I've got is hot, and a guy needs lots of nerve to hold up in it. You wouldn't do, anyway; you're too little and skinny and young. You'd better go out and get a little more education. You'd be a coward in my game; you're just a petty thief, and you can jack-roll drunks, but it takes nerve in my racket."

This angered me and filled me with resentment, for he had humiliated me to the extreme. He didn't know my ability, and here he was saying that I didn't have any nerve and couldn't steal. He even did not know that I had done time. He judged me by my size and my clothes, for I was not well dressed then. That wasn't fair, and I thought he ought to give me a chance before humiliating me in Jack's presence. I called Jack aside and suggested that we leave. He wanted to shoot craps. I consented because I wanted some way to pass the time away and to forget Jerry's insult, which troubled my mind.

It was daylight when we went home, so we didn't dare to attempt to rob a drunk. I was blue, very blue, and disgusted, and didn't want to go to my lonely room, so we went out to the park and spent the hot July day lounging around. I couldn't forget Jerry's insult. Of course he was superior to me, but he didn't need to lord it over or rub it in. I made up my mind, then and there, that I would get up in the racket and show him up. I'd get a racket of my own, and then I would sneer at him, and, besides, I could have good clothes and maybe a "swell broad" all my own. Maybe I was only a jack-roller and he a superior crook, but I was young. I'd get a little more experience and then show my stuff. I was just as brave as he was, for it takes nerve to be a petty thief or a "jack-roller."

Night came along and we made our regular tour. Business was poor, so we had to go to an old vacant building where bums would "flop" for the night. One time we had made a haul of one hundred and fifty dollars off a drunk who had found his way into this old building to sleep. Since that time we made it our last stop on our tour at night. This particular evening we went there and mounted the rickety steps, which squeaked under our weight. The building was old and dilapidated, having been razed by fire several years before. On the second floor we found six or seven men stretching out in fitful slumber. Jack and I searched them one by one for dough. Some offered no resistance. Some, however, would fight, and we had to give them a tip on the head with our "billy" or give them the strong arm to avoid noise that might attract the police.

Ordinarily, we didn't bother with small sums of money, but this night we were as flat as Aunt Jemima's pancake, so we took everything that resembled currency. After searching every man on the second floor we went to the third floor. Here we found one man. He heard us coming and asked what we wanted. I replied by asking for matches. As he gave the matches to me I "brushed" him off—finding that he was "ripe" and that his roll was heavy. As I returned the matches I grabbed his arms in a firm grasp. My hold was suddenly broken, and I was seized by the enraged German. He got a strangle hold on me, but Jack came to my assistance and broke him away. We both sprang upon him. As we were struggling I felt a razor almost to my stomach. Realizing the grave danger, I told Jack to hold him while I put the strangle hold on him—forcing him to drop the razor, which fell with a clatter below the window.

This man was large and husky, and fought like a demon. I finally put the "arm on him" and Jack relieved him of his dough, along with his watch and foreign coin. On releasing him, he sprang at me, yelling at the top of his voice. Knowing that we had to make a quick getaway before the police came, we started to maul him, "giving him the club," and soon "put him to sleep" —so we thought.

We walked out of the building and toward home. While walking along we inspected our loot, which consisted of about sixty dollars and the watch. Jack cautioned me that someone was following us, but looking back I could see no one, so told him that he had a pipe dream. But as we were turning the corner at Halsted Street I was jarred by a sudden hold of my collar. Turning, we faced a policeman and the guy we had just robbed. The police said to the Dutchman, "Are these the lads that robbed you?" Seeing his watch in my shirt pocket, he said, "Yes, there's my watch." We were caught. It was a dirty shame, after having fought such a battle. I thought we well earned our money in the struggle, because we had a close call with the razor.

It was indeed a surprise to Jack and me to be taken so unexpectedly. On the way to the station, I visualized the future prison bars and myself behind them. I thought myself to be lost to the world for about ten years. I imagined the torture and the drabness of prison and shuddered. No more could I roam but must be tied down to pay the penalty which society exacted. We arrived at the station—a very familiar place to me, as I had spent dozens of nights there since childhood. In front of the sergeant we stood while our victim made out the formal complaint against us. We were then searched for the money and the watch. My money I had hid in a seam of my coat so the officer could not find it. Becoming angry, he said, "By God, strip off all your clothes and I'll tear them to pieces to find that money!" While he responded to a call from the sergeant I started to put the money—

a "sawbuck" (a ten-dollar bill)—in my mouth, but being caught in the act, received a severe blow on the jaw by the "bull."

We were then put into a cell. It was not a cell, but a vermin-ridden hole in the wall. I took it rather philosophically for a while, having become hardened and used to such filthy holes. Jack also was brave and took it like a man. There were eleven men in the cell, which was built for four. We either stood up or sat on the dirty floor to eat our slice of sausage and slice of bread that we received once a day. We all drank from the same pail of water, like so many pigs at a swill-trough. The water was dirty and must have been diseased, for all the diseased crooks and dirty drunks slobbered in it. An open pail was used as a toilet. My feelings revolted against such filth. I finally became dejected and despondent. Life seemed to hold nothing but a prison cell and a bad reputation for me. I was getting lower and lower in the mire. Sadness and gloom settled down upon me like a heavy cloud, and I thought what an unfortunate creature I was. It was all because of a bad start in life and no opportunity. As I sat brooding, a fellow-prisoner in the next cell began to sing a very sad song. Prisoners always sing their songs sadly. As he sang in a beautiful tenor, I felt a tug at my heart and I cried like a baby. We asked for another song, and it was sadder than the first, and I couldn't stop crying. I felt like a lonely orphan boy, but the song and my crying soothed my heart, which was aching for sympathy and pity. Lying on the floor of the cell, I fell into a deep slumber, my eyes still damp with tears.

The next day was Sunday, and I was awakened by the songs of mission-workers in front of the cell. One of the group, an elderly man, seeing I was young, asked me to pray. I always got a kick out of shocking mission-workers by being hard-boiled and full of sin, so I told this one that he could bring me some cigarettes because I was down and out and past redemption and prayer wouldn't reach my sinful soul. Besides, I was a Catholic and my creed forbade me to listen to another creed. Then, too, I was going to the penitentiary, where religion would do me no good. I knew he was a grafter, anyway, for these mission-workers are in for graft, that's the way they make their dough. He finally gave me up as a hopeless case.

That same day we were taken to the identification bureau, where our finger-prints were taken, as well as other measurements. Despite my assumed name, the record of my commitment to Pontiac was found. The process of identification is like branding steers out in Arizona. Prisoners are herded and kicked and cuffed and razzed like brutes. This is called "showing the gold-fish" or the "third degree." It makes you harbor resentment and hate and make up your mind to get even. As I was being measured the "dick" asked me if I didn't pull off a stickup out at Fifty-ninth Street. When I truthfully replied in the negative, he said, "You're a damn liar! You're a jack-roller, aren't you? You'll roll bricks from now on out in the quarry at the band-house." I took this meekly, but inwardly I boiled with resentment at my helplessness to retaliate. I thought that one of these days I'd have to "plug" a "copper" because my feeling was so strong. After measurement, we were taken back to the station. The next morning, I woke up early, so glad was I that we were going to trial, and we would get out of that dirty hole. There were fourteen men in the cell with me now. We were packed in like sardines. The odor was awful. Many of them were drunks and threw up on the floor. It was a great relief to be led out of the cell and taken to the bull-pen at the court. Jack and I looked around and saw a drunk that we had robbed recently. I quaked with fear lest he should recognize us, which would mean more "raps" against us. We smoked and speculated on the possible outcome of our case. I was sure of commitment. One bum asked me how the weather was outside. I replied that I didn't know, and that the weather did not concern me, for I was on my way to prison for five years or more.

Finally, we were called to the bar, and the judge asked our victim if we were the ones who robbed him. He said, "Yes." He excitedly described the fight, and added that we not only robbed him, but broke two of his ribs by hitting him with a brick. We signed our waiver, pleading guilty. But I denied that we beat the victim and added that we went into the old building to sleep, and that the bum tried to kick us out and we resisted. I said we took the money out of necessity, for we were hungry and broke. The judge viewed the stolen money and eyed my Pontiac record. Then came the condemning words, "One year in the House of Correction, and one dollar and costs." The words fell with a thud on my ears. I was going to the Bridewell. I had heard tales of the horrors of the place, and my heart became heavy and laden. I reasoned that the sentence might have been worse. In fact, I had fully expected a five-year sentence because of my previous record, so I got some satisfaction in that.

An hour after the sentence was pronounced, we were herded into the bus with half a hundred other prisoners and shipped to the Bridewell. It was a beautiful July day. There had been a heavy rain the night before, and the grass and trees were green and lovely. Everything was bubbling with life and overjoyed, but it was only mockery to my broken spirit. The birds were singing, but not for me. I was out of tune with everything but the dejected faces of the other prisoners and the grim gray walls of the prison that appeared in view as we turned into the prison yard. As I looked upon the old prison where I was to spend the next year, my spirit seemed to leave me altogether.

CHAPTER XII

THE HOUSE OF "CORRUPTION"[1]

The load of prisoners were herded into a large barren room like so much livestock. The guards gave orders in a gruff and hard-boiled manner, as if to cower the new prisoners from the start. Going before the clerk I answered the usual questions regarding birth, age, and so on. I gave my age as nineteen (I was really seventeen) because I didn't want anybody to know that I was a mere kid. I remembered my experiences in Pontiac and made up my mind not to let that happen again. The clerk gave me the "once over" and assigned me to the tailor shop. Then I was ordered into a long line. At the end of the line a colored prisoner was "shaking down" new prisoners for forbidden articles. He "shook me down" in about ten seconds, as if that was his occupation on the outside. I thought, say, but I'll have to go some to keep up with the standard of prison efficiency here. After taking a hurried bath I felt refreshed and then received my prison uniform by a prisoner who asked me how much time I got. I replied, "Only one year." He said, "Only one year? Kid, you mean life. A year in this place is a lifetime. It's one hell of a dump to do time in. God! kid, you have my sympathy, and I wish you luck." After donning my uniform, I received a slip of paper, and on it was written my sentence and my prison or convict number.

With my name went the last vestige of civilization. As I thought of it I felt that I had lost something of value to me. I had the same feeling in Pontiac, but not so strong. Here I was only a common convict, without a friend and without a name, only a

[1] At the age of sixteen years and nine months, Stanley was committed to the Chicago House of Correction for a period of one year, on a charge of "jack-rolling." His experiences and contacts while incarcerated in this institution are described in the present chapter. This institution receives commitments of adult offenders, both male and female. Practically all commitments are for short periods of one year or less.

number to answer to. I was just like all the other derelicts cast upon the rocks by cruel circumstances. The institution was a dirty hole, even worse than the worst stories I had heard about it. We were led, in double line, to the yard, and then to the south cellhouse, which was old and dilapidated. The whole building was old and ugly. True, there were some flowers and grass, but the drabness of the walls and cellhouse seemed to snuff out Nature's effort to beautify that "Black Hole of Calcutta."

Once in the cellhouse I gazed around and noticed the actions of the other prisoners. They seemed to move around like slaves, forced to submission and held down by some brutal force. Misery and vengeance were written in every line of their faces. The prisoners here were different from the ones at Pontiac. At Pontiac they were mostly young men, just starting out in their criminal careers. They were more hopeful and determined and were looking forward to the future. But here, in this hole, the prisoners were mostly old men, only shadows of human wreckage, stooped and bent, looking into the graves that they had dug for themselves by their dissipations. Literally a cesspool of human derelicts, the dregs of the underworld. There were some young boys, like myself, scattered through the place.

After being led out to the mess hall for supper of beans and bread, I was thrown into a cell with a lot of other prisoners. I became sick and vomited. The awful odor of the mess hall, the sight of the other dirty prisoners eating like animals, would turn the stomach of the lowest bum that ever trod West Madison Street. A guard, seeing me in my agony, accused me of pulling off sob stuff and told me to straighten up or he'd bend me double. He grabbed me and kicked me into a cell, where I lay on my dirty bunk through the night. The air was dense and filled with that indescribable prison odor. The cell was made of old and crumbling brick. The dampness seeped through the bricks, and the cracks were filled with vermin and filth. The cell was barren except for the dirty bunk and the open toilet bucket in the corner.

The bell that meant lights out and bedtime rang. The closing of cell doors seemed an echo of my thoughts that I was in hell. Hell it was that night and whole year through. I stared through the bars into the shadows and thought of my past life, of my sister who had mothered me, my stepmother who was the cause of all my trouble, my pals in stealing, and our good times. I thought how sweet it would be to be working, to be free to go where I pleased, and to sleep in a nice bed. Then I thought of Council Bluffs and of Ruth. My emotions were already worked up, but when I thought of her my eyes filled with tears. They were silent, bitter tears of repentance. I shuddered to think of it. My spirit was crushed. The damned jail had stripped me of everything. I was a miserable creature, to be shunned and mocked by everyone.

I fell into a slumber, only to be awakened by vermin crawling all over my face and body. I had not removed my uniform, because I felt so sick, so got up and took it off, but sleep was not possible. So I waited and longed for morning to come to relieve my misery. As I waited, I felt the dreadful silence of the cellhouse. Only the occasional round of the guard broke the clammy, weird quietness of the dungeon. I felt hopeless and longed to die and escape the misery that faced me.

The next morning my cell partner greeted me, saying, "Well, you're my cell buddy, eh, kid?" I replied in the affirmative. I fixed my bunk and then washed my face in a trough with a half a hundred other prisoners. We were then led to our breakfast, which consisted of a plate of oatmeal, without milk or sugar, two slices of bread, and a tin of watery coffee. I couldn't eat but gave my portion to the prisoner next to me. It was all nauseating, and I was glad to get away from the dirty mess hall.

After breakfast I was led to the tailor shop to work. It was a big room, housing both the shoeshop and the tailor shop. The instructor or guard was old and rather stern. He looked me over, shook his head, and said, "I'll make a tailor out of you, boy." Then he assigned me to a sewing machine, to get instructions from another prisoner. We exchanged greetings, and after asking me my "rap" and how much time I had to do, he started to break me in. He told me about himself. He had done time in California, Missouri, Indiana, Michigan, Ohio, and was now serving a one-year sentence for burglary, and was also wanted in

Indiana for the same rap. He impressed me not a little, and I could see the hidden fire in his eyes, but he was calm outwardly and indifferent. I was just the opposite. In front of my machine was a window, and as I gazed out at the gray walls that stood between me and freedom and life, I could hardly subdue my emotions. But I soon got relief from Jim (my work partner), for he was carefree and gave me a chew of tobacco. Although I didn't like to chew, I did it to be sociable, and, besides, it helped to drown out my feelings. All day I watched Jim sewing shirts. He was a great relief, but still I worried and brooded, and when the whistle blew in the evening I could hardly walk. I was weak from lack of food, and, besides, I was sick of the miserable place.

That evening as I sat on the floor of my cell I got acquainted with Halfpint,[2] my cell buddy. He was an old man, about forty-five, with gray hair and hardened features. All in all, he looked like the usual hardened criminal that one sees in the cartoons of the morning newspaper. He was short and little, and well fitted for his racket, for he was a con man and blackmailer. *Something about him appealed to me from the start, and I soon felt a great relief from the heavy feeling I had had all night.* He had had a wide experience in crime, having done a one to ten sentence in Sing Sing, five years in San Quentin, one to ten in Joliet, three years in the Iowa State Penitentiary, four months in the Cook County Jail, three months in the New York City Jail, six months in the Cleveland Workhouse, and many short terms in the workhouses, police stations, and jails, and was now serving a year in the House of Correction. His life had been full of thrills and adventures. He had started out as a poor lad, working on a farm, but finding that monotonous and not suited to his ability, he had gone to New York City to seek his fortune. There he got in with bad company and started on his criminal career.

He had been in the House of Correction several months, so he gave me tips about the way to act there. He said, "Buddy, you've

---

[2] Stanley's contact with Halfpint is another excellent example of the manner in which the young delinquent assimilates the social values and philosophy of life of the experienced adult criminal. Through such contacts the young delinquent not only acquires new knowledge concerning criminal technique but acquires the code of the adult criminal group.

got a year to do, and a year in this joint is like doing ten years in stir. Keep your mouth shut and mind your own business. And whatever you do, don't be a rat; they're bumped off when they get out, and it's a dirty trick to rat on a fellow-prisoner, anyway. Don't antagonize the guards; hate them all you want to, but work them for your own good." I thanked him, and then he went on: "Kid, you're in here for a year for jack-rolling. This ought to teach you a lesson. Leave me tell you, the next time you pull anything off, pick out a racket where there's dough, so if you get caught it's worth doing time for, and if you get away, you're all set for the rest of your life. Now compare us here. We both got the same rap, one year in this hell-hole, but I pulled a ten-thou-sand-dollar deal, and you got less than a hundred dollars. Don't you get me? Besides, get into a respectable racket, so you can dress well and mingle in society. A jack-roller hain't got any chances, anywhere. Take it from me, kid, when I get out of here I'm going to pull off one big haul and then retire for the rest of my life."

He compared the House of Correction with the other institutions he had been in, and said that it was worse than the mexican prison, which is often considered the worst in North America. "Sing Sing—my God, kid, it's a playhouse alongside of this rat hole." But yet he didn't worry much about prison life, and I marveled at his indifference. To him jail was nothing more than a stepping-stone to freedom, and he figured he'd have better luck next time. The old prisoner does not worry about doing time unless it's a long sentence. You get hardened to it. It's just an item on the debit side of the criminal's ledger-book. The underworld insists on bravery. A coward is shunned, so a prison sentence must be borne bravely and without complaining.

Halfpint had a lot of education, and this, coupled with a glib tongue, gave him a great asset for his work. He used his smooth tongue to garner tobacco for us and to get out of hard work. He was the wisest prisoner I ever knew. I compared myself with him and saw the difference. He was a con man, who at one sweep of his hand could make enough dough to live on for the rest of his life, while I, a petty thief, could hardly steal enough to live on.

Then, too, he was able to dress well and was looked up to, and his racket was not very hard work. I could see that among criminals he was respected and a hero. I felt humiliated inwardly, and made up my mind to get a racket that would bring me good returns. Halfpint promised to help me in working out my plans, and I had a whole year to do it in.

I started in the humdrum, monotonous routine of prison life by making shirts in the tailor shop, and after the day's work, back to my cell. The monotony was terrible. The only diversions were reading and dreaming, but the former was scarce. Every night after I went to bed I would read awhile by the light that twinkled dimly in. After my eyes would grow tired I would lay on my bunk and dream. I dreamed of getting a racket of my own and having a "broad" on the string like Halfpint said he had. I visioned myself as a criminal superior with a big automobile, driving around town putting on airs. These dreams carried me away from my misery, and I would pass into slumber, to be awakened by the clanking of cell doors into the most miserable existence I ever had or ever will have. The horrors of that House of "Corruption" cannot be described. I can only say that when there I lost all respect for myself, felt degenerated and unhuman. I shall never fully recover from the influences of that old south cellhouse. I always will feel that it was an insult to put me there. It's an insult to put any human soul there. In my anguish I planned vengeance and hatred. Consequences? I didn't give a damn what happened to me. Hanging, life-imprisonment in Joliet—anything would be better than a year in that vermin-ridden, unsanitary, immoral, God-forsaken pit. It wasn't discipline that I hated and resented; I was used to that. But it was the utter low-downness, animal-like existence that it forced me down to. It not only deadened my mind but I became a physical wreck, weak, nervous, and finally developed rheumatism and pneumonia and had to be removed to the hospital, which I shall describe later on.

At the tailor shop I had to make two shirts a day. That was after I got on to the work, so I would hurry and then sit down and daydream. The guards would awaken me from my reverie and bring me back to the glaring reality of jail life, which was in utter contrast to my dreams. I thank God for these dreams, for in them I found the freedom that my dying soul ached for.

In the tailor shop were two pals that I had known in Pontiac. So we became friends immediately and helped each other out by exchanging reading materials, tobacco, and by giving each other warnings and inside tips about how to get by. It was a little mutual aid society, which is very necessary in prison. The prisoners have to band together for their own protection.

The population of the House of Correction is composed of the lowest kinds of human derelicts and wrecks. It is the melting-pot for the scum of the underworld. Once caught in its net, the prisoner is as helpless as the moth in the spider's web. There's something about it that deadens the mind, that poisons the soul and blights every feeble ambition except stealing. I know. I existed in its scum for a long year. In my cell I had a calender, and I marked off each day that dragged by. Imagine marking off three hundred and sixty-five days in hell. My only enjoyment consisted in a little reading, dreaming, tobacco, and my conversations with Halfpint. How he could describe the joys of living, which to him consisted of a good racket, a swell "broad," and a fine automobile.

On Sundays we were locked in our cells all day, except when we went to meals and to the church services. I would sit for hours watching the gay groups in automobiles driving down the boulevard enjoying life, free, while I could only watch and long for my day of release. Halfpint usually slept on Sunday. He said that was the only cure for the dreadful monotony of the Sabbath. I agreed with him, but I could never sleep. I could only gaze through the window and then walk up and down my cell and dream the long day away. I longed for Monday, so I could go to work and break the monotony. It was a sorrowful day for me when Halfpint was released. He was a good cell buddy, very sociable, and had a wide experience and could always drive away the prisoner's worst enemy—monotony.[3] As he bade me good-

---

[3] One of the most frequent complaints made by inmates in penal institutions is with reference to the monotonous character of the routine prison life.

bye, I felt heartsick and very lonely. I almost died of homesickness, or something like that, for several days. But my relief from this feeling came when I was transferred to the new cellhouse and was assigned to the deputy's office to be a "runner."

The new job gave me more freedom, and it was wonderful to be out of the tailor shop. Life cleared up a little, and I appreciated the lucky break. I was aware of my good job, so I made up my mind to keep my mouth shut and to mind my own business. I expected to be asked to rat on the other prisoners, for I had always known that a prisoner who had a politician's job like mine had to be a rat. So I made up my mind that I would not rat, but would pretend to the deputy that I was ratting, and in that way I could hold my job and not go against my fellow-prisoners. So I got by on that plan.

Jack, my old buddy in crime, was working in the deputy's office. But he was very different now from what he had been in the racket. He was now selfish, hard-boiled, and had turned rat. He was mixed up in a lot of graft—smuggling tobacco, letters, and other forbidden articles to prisoners. He was getting handsome returns for this graft. When I went to the deputy's offices, Jack was promoted to a clerk, and I got his old job and much of the graft that went with it. I was put in charge of the plug tobacco that was distributed to prisoners. Every Saturday I'd give each prisoner a small plug of tobacco, about one chew, which was his pay. Tobacco was money in that place, as it is in any prison, so tobacco talked. I could get anything with a plug of tobacco. I took good care of my friends by giving them large plugs. I also bought candy, cigarettes, and even got some money from prisoners for plugs. I'd go to the kitchen and give the cooks a few plugs and get a decent meal in return. I was a millionaire for once in my life and a very important person. Jack, being a clerk, thought he had the upper hand on me and ordered me to give him a big supply of tobacco each week. I told him that I couldn't spare so much as he wanted, so he threatened to rat to the deputy about my grafting. The dirty rat, he would rat on me, even after we had been pals, and even when he was grafting more than me. I turned against him and told him where to get off at and then carried on my grafting secretly. We remained strong enemies from then on. He was a double-crosser.

I always stood in constant fear of being sent to the x——, so I was very careful in my new job. The x—— was a hell-hole of hard work and rotten food. The guard in charge of the prisoners in the x—— was a big, husky individual called "Stoneface." On my errands I could hear his deep voice calling forth orders and threatening eternal damnation to the helpless victims that cringed under the tyranny. He seemed to delight in razzing the negroes and "junkers." Small wonder that the x—— hung over me like a dense cloud of fear all the time I was in the place.

It was often Stoneface's task to subdue hard-boiled and stubborn convicts. The victim would be called to the solitary cell, and there Stoneface would do his not too honorable duty. I was filled with hatred. A hatred that smoldered inwardly, like fire, against the barbarous place.

Niggers out there were no better than brutes. Here they were given the hardest work, the worst cells, and subjected to the most brutal punishment. Everybody, especially the guards, are prejudiced against them.

Junkers (dope fiends) are considered a low class by the guards and get treated like niggers. Upon arriving the junker is given the "cure" at the hospital, and when the doctor pronounces him cured, he is sent to the quarry to do hard work, for the guards are prejudiced against him like they are against the niggers. Imagine a physical wreck wielding a ten-pound sledge-hammer all day, amid cuffs and beatings, and with rotten food. I always felt that the junkers had tortures enough with their habit without this added pain. I have always felt that a man in any circumstance should have an even break. It don't make any difference about their race or religion or crime, they deserve fair treatment. I sympathized with the poor victims, because I was as bad off as they were and having my miseries too. So I loathed and despised the guards. It was all like a cruel driver beating a poor dumb horse that is in heavy harness and hitched to a heavy load. It so worried me and tormented me that I could not rest, and, besides, being a runner, I saw the entire working of the place.

Old drunks and dead beats drifted in and out of the prison regularly. Here they retired in their old age, going out and coming in, until death relieved them of their misery. One example was Joe, who worked in the office. He was sixty-eight years old, had been in the Bridewell, he told me, many, many times during the last twenty years. These old bums were confined in the south cellhouse, where I was for a while, the oldest and dirtiest hole of holes in prisons. I have worked on farms, and I have seen dirty pigpens, but they had nothing on these cells. The prisoners walk along the halls for diversion. I was hardened to the dark side of life. I firmly believed that no one was good enough to help me out if I wanted to go straight, so the best thing for me to do was to get a good racket, like Halfpint had said, make a big haul, then laugh and sneer at the world that had given me such an unfair break. This hole was a workhouse and designed for short terms and small fines, but here I was, with a whole year to do. That was unfair and a great injustice to me. I planned to pull off a pay-roll job at a firm where I had worked. I "had the stuff" on the place, knew just where the dough was kept, when it arrived, and everything. So I was all set for the day of release. I talked it over with two of my old trusted pals from Pontiac, and they fell in with my plan immediately. They happened to be in the House of Correction the same time I was.

As a boy in St. Charles I had gone crazy about Alger's books, and wanted to be one of his heroes and go out into the world and make a fortune honestly, but now, bah! I learned that that was a lot of poppycock. My only chance to make a fortune was to steal it, as Halfpint had said. I had tried to work, but only received a mere pittance. That seemed foolish when a whole fortune could be made by a gun and a little nerve. So I figured I'd make one big haul and then be sitting on top of the world. I kept my thoughts to myself, except to my two trusted pals, and turned them over and over in my mind until the plan was perfect.

Just before Christmas I was made a runner in the hospital, to take prisoners over for venereal examination each morning. On these trips I met every kind of prisoner, from the habitual drunkard to the millionaire bootlegger, and talked with them. Old men, past their prime, negroes in the last stages of venereal disease, young men and boys just starting out, all passed through my hands. Most of them were past any hope of redemption, and it all made life seem like a miserable spectacle to me.

The food in the place was not fit for human consumption. Recreation? Such a thing never entered the minds of the officials. Life was low-down, deadening, and degenerating. My physical condition grew worse, until I could scarcely walk. They called me a runner, but for a month I had been so weak that I couldn't run. Finally, I was taken to the hospital and ordered to bed. The doctor examined me and said I was undernourished and had rheumatism and would have to remain in bed for a period, and that would cure me. Cure me, hell! I didn't want to be cured. Death would be an escape from the misery of it all. I had no future, not a single hope. Seven months in this hole had sapped the last drop of vitality. When I entered the place I weighed 142 pounds, and now I had been reduced to 118. A mere skeleton. I had really starved because my stomach could not stand the food. The damp cells in the cellhouse had made my muscles and bones ache.

The hospital was just one large ward, where dope fiends getting the cure, drunks with delirium tremens, venereal patients, and many others kept the atmosphere tense with their screams of pain and anguish. I lay on my cot day after day, thinking only of the cold and bitter circumstances of life. How could anyone get ahead in such a world? Where was all the kindness and brotherly love that was supposed to exist? I was damn certain it wasn't here. Even the nurses administered to the needs of the prisoners in a purely professional way, seemingly afraid they would be defiled by contact with us low characters. Kindness would have been mockery in that joint anyway.

The awful cries of the dope fiends was driving me insane, so I asked to be removed to the cellhouse. The hospital being crowded, my request was granted (it wasn't out of any consideration to me). But I could scarcely walk. I reported at the office for work. The doctor was there, and he saw me and began to talk about my case to the deputy. They talked in a low voice, and I overheard the doctor say, "That lad is very low. He will kick in [die] before the end of the month." His prediction almost came true.

I went to work, but in three days I took flu and was carried to the hospital, where I remained a week. Then I went to work again, but the next day I took pneumonia and returned to the hospital, where all hope of my recovery was despaired of. My fever was high, but my spirit and ambition were zero. At first I wanted to die, but at the crisis point, strange to say, some of my old grit and determination returned. The thought of the disgrace of dying in that hell-hole came to my mind and with it came a hope to live. I fought, and was soon on the way to recovery, but only after a hard fight, in which all the odds were against me. The doctors were surprised at my change of attitude, for they said that during my fever I had prayed to die.

During my convalescence of three weeks I spent my time reading, dreaming, and studying my fellow-prisoners. They were mostly dope fiends and drunkards who had been knocked about in this strife-swept world. In every face I saw the story of tragedy. For tragedy always leaves its marks upon the countenance. In my case, I had spent my life going in and out of jails, and now I was old and hardened at seventeen, had lost all hope of regeneration. In fact, I could see nothing but crime and jail bars ahead. That was all I was educated for; it was all my mind could think about; it held lures and hopes which nothing else did. Besides, all my friends were criminals, and I could not escape them. Not one close friend did I have who was not a criminal, and with them I was as helpless as the canoe in the hurricane. I didn't know how to do anything but steal. Manual labor was my only other choice, and I thought I was above that, and, besides, it was monotonous and poor pay. I reasoned that Fate was against me, and always had been, and therefore I was justified to steal. Everyone, by the law of self-preservation, has a right to existence, and I was just struggling to live. But I didn't care much, for I harbored revenge and a deep-seated antipathy toward the law and the circumstances that had always been my enemy. I had seen young snobs my age who had luxury and who had never done any work, and was I not just as good as they were? Why should I be forced to a life of slavery and hard labor when others were free to be idle and have a good time in life? That was Halfpint's idea about it, and, besides, I was not a fool, to be kidded by the circumstances of life into manual labor and a life of slavery to fill the pockets of grafters and snobbish people. In crime I was independent, but in work I always had to slave for somebody else and turn my money over to the "old lady" or somebody else. Jail? Yes, that is a danger, but I would be more careful next time in pulling off my jobs. I knew more now than ever before.

Next to me in the hospital was Herbie, a junker, who was taking the cure. He found out that I was a runner when I was well, so naturally I was good for a cigarette occasionally. I ignored him at first, but having experienced suffering myself, I often slipped him a cigarette once in a while. He repaid me by telling me of his experiences in life, and how he started to "hit M" (morphine). Experiences were always interesting to me, especially those of the underworld characters, because they are the most adventurous. He told me that he had had a sweetheart and that he loved her as she loved him. (Here I had a tug at my heartstrings, because I thought of Ruth.) One day he found a "deck" of "M" tied in her handkerchief. Asking her what she was doing with it, she at first denied using it, but finally broke down and confessed. She said that after a series of operations she craved something, and went to a doctor who was a quack and he gave her treatments, which made her craving stronger. Then she began to use "M" regularly, until it was life itself to her. Herbie was broken-up about it, but his fondness for her held him to her. One day, out of curiosity, he took his first dose, while his girl was not around. One dose led to another until the habit was formed. The habit became so strong and it led him into association with low characters, and, besides, he was poor and finally began to steal to get money to buy "shots," for a junker will do anything to get a "shot." He went lower and lower, getting entangled in bad company and mixed up in a dope ring, until he lost interest in everything but morphine. Life is just that way, a lot of entanglements, that hold you in their grasp and carry you deeper and deeper, until you become indifferent and don't care. At first you take a taste, a sip, dabble a little, then you get into the ring or the gang, and then your hands are tied. The thrill, the lures lead you on and you can't think about results.

Herbie told me all about dope peddlers, dope rings, the terrible agony that one had when he couldn't get dope, the ways of obtaining and smuggling dope, and how it poisoned and deadened the mind. The story chilled me, especially as I looked into Herbie's bleached face, which looked like that of a man of forty, while he was only twenty-two. My lord, life is certainly hard for some of us!

When I was released from the hospital I was weak and skinny. I went to work again, but with more hope, for I was to be released in a month. Just four more weeks and I would be out again. My system could not stand the prison food, but one of my prison pals took pity on me and gave me some money when he was released, so I bought some milk every day. That helped me to build up my system.

Strolling about the prison yard on errands, I noticed that it was spring, and the grass was green and flowers were budding. A few birds were chirping as if mocking the gray walls that could not hold them back. It was spring for me, too, for my days there were few. Soon I would try my luck again against the fate that had held me in bondage all my life. But what would I do. I had no clothes and no money, and no one had visited me during the long year.

I tried to think of my future but more crimes and jail bars stared me in the face at every angle. There was no hope but in crime. All my friends were criminals and besides I was a criminal and nobody would trust me—only look down on me and shun me. Somehow I was different from anybody but criminals and I always felt drawn to crime. Circumstances had turned me back into jail every time before when I tried to make good. But now I had lost my ambition and didn't care for anything but crime. Was I not completely alone in the world except for my buddies in crime and did I not always feel pulled to them and to the adventures and luxuries that crime offered? I was educated in crime, and as the last days of my sentence dragged along I planned to be more careful next time and to get in a safe racket that paid more and make one or two big hauls and then retire for the rest of my life. The odds against me were too great to overcome as the past ten years of my life showed. My struggles were only mockery, so why try any more? I had spent nine months in this hole and now felt the injustice that it had been to me. I had been caged and tortured and not permitted to strike back and inwardly I felt hate and spite. My thought returned to Halfpint, and I longed for him to soothe my depressed spirit.

One day, while on an errand, I met Mr. M. H. Cone, my St. Charles parole officer, who had always stood by me in my runaway days. He promised to help me by getting clothes and a job for me. After he said goodbye a new hope kindled in my mind. Maybe fate would change in my favor.

The night before my release I lay in my bed thinking of the great tomorrow. Sleep was not possible; besides it would have been dull compared to the sweet reveries in which I lived that night. My mind could not grasp the meaning of the freedom that was so near. The next morning I was called to the office and given my clothes, and I stepped into the world outside, bidding farewell to that hole that had almost robbed me of life.

CHAPTER XIII

SUMMARY OF CASE AND SOCIAL TREATMENT

Although we began our study of Stanley's career in delinquency shortly before his commitment to the House of Correction, most of the material was secured at the time of his release from this institution. Upon the basis of the materials available at that time, certain interpretations of the case were made and a plan of treatment was devised. A brief statement of these interpretations, along with a description of the steps involved in the treatment of the case, is presented at this point.

We have in this case a youthful offender of average intelligence and normal physical condition whose career in delinquency began at the early age of six and a half years, in the form of truancy from home and petty stealing in the immediate vicinity of his home. The case presents a picture of the origin and gradual formation of a delinquent-behavior trend as it emerged in the process of interaction between the individual and the social and cultural situation in which he lived. Through his personal contacts with experienced delinquents in the underworld life of West Madison Street and in the various correctional institutions to which he was successively committed, Stanley's delinquent behavior became increasingly serious, and his wishes and ambitions became more clearly defined in terms of the social values of the adult criminal world. By the time of his release from the House of Correction, it was clear that he definitely identified himself with the adult criminal group.

In making our interpretations of the case, it was assumed, in the first place, that there was perhaps a direct relationship between the early experiences in delinquency and the prevailing activities and social values in Stanley's play group and neighborhood. His earliest contacts with older companions, outside of the home, were with boys who were engaged in petty stealing, shoplifting, and sex practices. Evidence secured from independent sources indicates the prevalence of these activities among the children throughout the entire neighborhood. Furthermore, the extremely high rate of criminality among the young men between seventeen and twenty-one years of age is indicative of a community spirit and background which would not only tolerate, but even foster, delinquent practices among the younger boys in the neighborhood (see p. 36).

The influence of the underworld life of the West Madison Street rooming-house district is also quite apparent in this case. While living in this district, in which there is a marked concentration of adult offenders, Stanley was brought into close contact with adult criminal groups. Through these contacts he acquired the technique of "jack-rolling." This is not at all surprising, since that form of stealing is particularly prevalent in the district, having become a more or less traditional aspect of the social life.

It was assumed, also, that certain elements in the family situation were clearly related to the onset of the delinquent career. For instance, it is probable that the intense antagonisms which developed after the father's marriage to the stepmother, not only led to a breakdown of parental control, but were largely responsible for Stanley's repeated truancy from home. Perhaps the persistence of this family conflict situation largely explains Stanley's failure to make an adjustment in his own home at the time of his parole from the various correctional institutions to which he was committed. Another important element in the family situation was the fact that the stepmother not only sanctioned but actually participated in Stanley's early stealing activities. This is especially significant as an indication of the attitudes and moral standards of the family group.

In the third place, the case-study revealed certain aspects of Stanley's personality which greatly complicated his adjustment to other persons. Among the more outstanding of these aspects of personality were his attitudes of persecution, suspicion, resistance to discipline and authority, self-justification, and a definite tendency to excuse his misconduct by means of self-pity, fatalism, and by placing the blame on other persons.

In the light of the foregoing interpretation of the case, it was decided to place Stanley in an entirely new social situation, and to initiate a plan of treatment adapted, as far as possible, to his particular attitudes and personality. The first step was to secure a foster-home in one of the non-delinquent communities of the city. Because of his egocentric personality, it was thought necessary to select a family in which the relationships were sympathetic and informal. It was considered extremely important, not only to avoid formal methods of control, but to guard against any behavior which might be construed by him as personal discrimination on the ground of his inferior social status and delinquent record. With such considerations in mind, Stanley was placed in the home of Mrs. Smith (fictitious), who had three children, the youngest of whom was only two years older than Stanley.

The second step in the process of treatment was in connection with the problem of vocational guidance. Here again our problem was greatly complicated by Stanley's personality difficulties. He was constantly in conflict with his employers and fellow-employees. Furthermore, at the time of his release from the House of Correction he was devoid of any specialized occupational training and definitely resistive to unskilled labor. During the first two years of the period of treatment, we placed him in a great variety of positions. We observed that his most favorable reactions occurred in positions which gave him a sense of superiority and in which he was not under the direct control of a person of superior rank. This observation, along with the fact that he was able to express himself vividly and convincingly, led to the assumption that he might make an adjustment in the field of salesmanship. A position in salesmanship was secured for him two years ago, and since that time he has made a fairly satisfactory adjustment in that field.

Another essential aspect of the treatment was to assist Stanley in making contacts with groups of young people of his age in the vicinity of his new home. The development of relationships in these conventional groups was a gradual process and entailed profound readjustment of his interests and philosophy of life. In time these new group contacts gradually supplanted his older relationships in the stock yard district.

During the first two years of the period of treatment, we had personal contact with Stanley at least once a week. Through these contacts it was possible to give him insight into his own mental processes, and to assist him in solving many problems which necessarily arose during the course of his adjustment to the new cultural world in which he was placed.

Many of the personal difficulties which Stanley encountered during his readjustment are disclosed in the final chapter of his own story:

"I cannot fully describe the feelings that I had as I stepped out of the House of Corruption. The day was radiant with sunshine, and everything seemed full of life and active. But I was in a quandary about what to do or where to go. A vagueness came over me as I had no plans for my future. Now that I had my freedom I didn't know how to use it. My shackles had loosened and no more would I have to languish within that hole of torture and misery. I shuddered to think of the poor creatures left behind those gray, dismal walls.

"The prison clerk had given me seven cents for carfare. Walking along the street to the street-car line, I studied the seven cents in my hand, and cynically and silently sneered at the city's benevolent generosity toward its forsaken wards. After a year of idleness and monotony in that stagnant cesspool I was now supposed to make good on seven cents. A fine start, I'll say, with not one word of advice from anyone. They just kick you out of the place, and to hell with you.[1]

"As I walked to the car and waited with a lot of other people, I felt humiliated inwardly. I was wearing the same old suit that I had on when I entered the place a year before. It had been crumpled into a ball for a year, and was now dirty, moldy, wrinkled, and much too small. The odor of the thing was awful. With that outfit and seven cents I was now supposed to make good. Immediately my old feeling of humiliation came back as I felt the stares of the other people burning through me. How could anybody feel any other way in an outfit like that and after a year in that sordid place?

[1] The city makes practically no provision for the after-care of persons released from this institution.

"I was more than grateful to board the street car and sit down so that I would at least be partially out of the range of burning stares. Once in the car I began to take stock of myself. Financially I was penniless. Physically I was broken and felt weak. Mentally I was confused and uncertain about the proper course. I hadn't heard from any of my relations and didn't care to see them. They only made matters worse. In my desperation I decided to drop in to see Mr. Shaw. He had talked to me a few weeks before and promised to help me if I would come to see him at the time of my release. I viewed this plan half-heartedly, because I didn't have much faith in anybody's ability to help a derelict like me. I couldn't think well of anybody and was in that way too suspicious. Yet I had to go somewhere for assistance. I felt helpless and had nothing but my feeble carcass to carry me along. I arrived at my destination and started to ring the bell, but hesitated because of fear of meeting anyone in my rags. Driven by necessity, I rang the bell and was admitted. Mr. Shaw greeted me pleasantly and warmly. I started to apologize for coming and for my rags, but he interrupted by saying, 'Forget it, sit down and make yourself comfortable.' He was very happy that I had come, and said that he would get a job and a new home for me. He already had a new set of clothes for me, which I put on immediately. That made me feel much more respectable. Mr. Shaw's friend came in, and we all sat around talking that entire afternoon. I got to telling about my experiences, and they showed great interest, and the day passed before I knew it. We all went out to dinner and spent the evening together. I got a great kick keeping them laughing about the funny experiences I had in prison.

"After Mr. Shaw found a temporary place for me to live and gave me some money, we said good-night. He asked me to have breakfast with them the next morning, and then we would talk over the plans for my future. As I sat in my room I thought of my future and felt that things might turn out all right after all. We met the next morning, and spent several hours together, talking about the kind of work for me to do and through Mr. Moore he got a new home for me. After noon that day I started to write this story of my life, and in the evening I went to my new home. . . . .

"The first impressions which my new home made upon my mind are still very vivid. Mrs. Smith, who I was to live with, was a very kind and good woman with a pleasing personality and intelligent. At that time I did not realize how much her sympathy and advice would determine my whole life in the future. After she showed me my room, which was furnished modestly and with a taste, we went downstairs to the living-room, where I was introduced to her son. Her son was of my age, and I was fond of him from the start. He was not the tough-guy type of boy from the stock yards. He was a gentleman, well-bred and refined.

"Later that evening I met Mrs. Smith's two daughters, who were also refined and somewhat older than me. They seemed to accept me and not look down on me. The home throughout was modestly furnished and had an atmosphere of warmth and kindness.

"When I went up to my room that night my mind was flooded with feelings and emotions. I compared myself with Mrs. Smith and her children, and saw the awful contrast. I, an ex-convict, an ordinary bum from West Madison Street, being introduced into a well-bred family. They took me at my face value and treated me as if I were an honest young man, ambitiously inclined. I sat on the bed and went over the events of the last two days. It quite bewildered me to think that I had been transferred so suddenly from the prison, with the scum of the earth as my companions, into this refined family. The whole thing seemed strange and beyond my comprehension. I scarcely knew how to get into an honest-to-goodness bed and sleep, after sleeping in a prison bunk for a year. Lying in the snow-white bed awake, I dreamed. I thought how out of place I was, a city waif in such surroundings. And yet my new companions were nice to me, and it gave me courage and hope. With this hope I pictured myself in a good job, with nice clothes and able to act like respectable people. With these pleasant thoughts on my mind, I fell into a contented slumber—the first one I had had in the whole year.

"The next morning I awoke surprised. I was in a new world. I thought it strange that prison bars did not face me as I stared about, gradually collecting my thoughts. I was free, yet it took me some time to get used to my new life. It was so nice to put on civilized clothing and to wash my face with soap other than the coarse, strong prison soap, and to dry my face on a snow-white towel.

"On my way to take my new job that morning, I felt quite set up and happy. The odds seemed to be in my favor, and I resolved to get ahead in the world that had always been so cruel to me. I contrasted my new situation with my life in prison. Now I was free. When I thought of the horrors of my prison experiences, it seemed like a nightmare. I had atoned for my crime in full. Every ounce of punishment had been meeded out; for one day in that hole was sufficient punishment for any crime. Imagine yourself an inmate in that institution from which I was just released, eating breakfast, dinner, supper at the same table throughout the year, seeing the same old faces and hearing the same old voices, mingling with derelicts, amid cuffs and beatings. And, finally, to tumble into the bunk which is ridden with vermin and to breathe, during the long night, the strong odor and stench of the cell. The memory of the place shook me with horror. It seemed that I had just awakened from a terrible nightmare.

"Mr. Shaw had arranged for me to take a position at a telegraph company, and my application was accepted. To tell the truth, I was tickled to death. I had a job, and I was to get paid for it. I thought it was wonderful, and I was filled with joy. When I got home that evening I called up Mr. Shaw and told him of my good fortune. He congratulated me and wished me luck, and also suggested that I go to see him often. Mrs. Smith was pleased to hear of my good fortune and spoke encouragingly to me. I went to bed that night in spirits that were rare. I felt like an heir who had come to his fortune. I had a swell home, a good job, clothes, and friends. Dame Fortune was indeed smiling on me broadly. The kindness of Mrs. Smith, her son, and daughters was like a sweet balm. I was a quivering deer that had just escaped from the clutches of a lion. . . . .

"The neighborhood in which I now lived was clean, orderly, and in utter contrast to back of the yards. The people here were nicely dressed, refined, and quiet. Back of the yards everything is dirty, grimy, and the air is filled with the repulsive odor from the stock yards. The streets are always filled with dirty children, swarming in the streets and alleys; the mothers are always weary with the drudgery of hard work and bearing children; the fathers come home in the evening, dressed in overalls, weary and grimy from a day of toil in the factory or yards—everything is unattractive and in a state of confusion. Everywhere are mothers screaming at miscreant children, young men shooting craps on the corner or in the alley. Everything is drab. There are no trees or grass, only old buildings and dirty alleys to gaze upon. I began to feel quite set up to think of the swell neighborhood in which I now lived. . . . .

"For a long time I did not know how to act with Mrs. Smith. I seemed awkward and crude compared to them. This worried me. I seemed like an intruder, an ex-convict who was crude and vulgar, living with refined people. I went to Mr. Shaw with my trouble, and he told me that I was young, but in time I would acquire more education and fit into the new situation. He always encouraged me and treated me as one of his own friends. We would go out to dinner together, and through him I met a lot of other people. He talked friendly to me about all of my troubles but never upbraided me or told me that I was in the wrong.

"Mrs. Smith was always congenial, but for a long time I felt out of place in her home. She never acted superior or snobbish, but seemed like a real mother, full of sympathy and understanding. It was hard for me to talk freely, because I didn't have much to talk about but crime and prisons. There were many times when I felt like telling Mrs. Smith that she was too good to associate with me. The closest I ever came to that was one evening when I came home blue and depressed about everything in life. As I felt that all the world was against me, and there was that awful pull back to my old life, and the thoughts that I was a low criminal and not fit to live with these good people, I made up my mind to tell Mrs. Smith that I was not fit to be in her home, and then leave the city and go back on the road. On reaching home, I chatted with Mrs. Smith and told her that they were far better than me and that I should leave. She did not reproach me but gave me some motherly advice on the foolishness of such a thought. I realized that she was right, yet, at the same time, I thought that she was something too pure for me to associate with. Me, a criminal, an ex-convict, who had just come out of the filth and corruption of the Bridewell. I broke down and blurted out just what I thought, telling her that her home was too refined for me to live in. Mrs. Smith stood erect and very calmly and seriously informed me that I was as good as anybody. She patted me gently on the shoulder and gave me a cheering word that worked wonders with my spirits. It impressed upon my mind that there were really some good people on this earth, and life was worth living with a kind woman like this. Mrs. Smith and her two daughters and son treated me as their equal. They chatted with me and never failed to greet me every morning and evening, but at every opportunity I eluded them by some simple excuse, because I felt that my manners were not up to standard and I was ashamed of my clothes. I envied the well-dressed boys wherever I went, and from this envy I grew disgusted with my appearance, knowing that I was unable to dress as well as they. I was always out of place, a misfit and strange and different from the gay young people my age, who always seemed light-hearted and full of pleasures. So a victim of periods of depression I became, and in these periods I wanted to go back to the old life of crime, where life ran more smoothly and with greater ease.

"At times when I would feel blue, I would often go to the West Side, to see my half-sisters and be with the gang that met in the poolroom. I compared this neighborhood of squalor and filth with the beauty where I was living and saw the difference and was disgusted to think that I felt drawn to the West Side. Yet my pals held lures over me. I felt close to them, yet I was beginning to think myself above them. And as I began to think of myself being above them, I began to break away from them. They noticed the change and told me I was getting snobbish and stuck-up, and that pleased me more than anything else.

"I got along well on my job for two months, until the break

came. Working with me was a Jewish lad who seemed to be over-ambitious, and he aspired to take over my job, at least he had unwarranted designs, and I resented it inwardly. Outwardly I tolerated him. One day a number of us boys planned a joke on the Jewish boy, whose name was Isadore, but we all had called him 'Issie.' One of the boys wrote out a forged order, stating that Issie was to take my place and I was to be demoted. Issie took the order and summoned all the dignity at his command, at the same time proudly flaunting the order and almost immediately took over his illegal position. Issie ordered us around like a monarch. We obeyed every command with alacrity, and, behind his back and out of hearing, roared with laughter. The joke did not last long, as the boss asked him what he was doing at my desk. Issie, not a little surprised, produced the forged order, and the boss scrutinized it rather severely. Then, sensing the joke, he too chuckled and roared in laughter. Issie felt humiliated and I felt ashamed of myself, for I thought that it was a dirty trick in a way, but still it was a joke. Issie argued with me about it and complained. I tried to patch it up, but it was useless. Issie was determined to get even. He punched me in the jaw when I wasn't looking, so I let him take some of my medicine, which produced a black eye and a split lip. The culmination of the joke resulted in my getting the 'bounce.'

"I did not worry much about my dismissal. I felt that I would very likely find another job that would perhaps be better and would pay me more money. Going out of the building with my pay check, I walked on air. I had money in my pockets and I was free, and that was all that was of any consequence to me. I went to the baseball game that afternoon and witnessed a well-played game full of thrills. Then I went home, but I did not say anything to Mrs. Smith about losing my position. I did not wish to disappoint her, so I kept it to myself for a few days until I managed to find another job.

"In the meantime I went to movie houses, baseball games, and idled my time away in general, and I had a great time. The sudden change of idleness from the daily routine at work gave me a new sense of freedom. Working for a living is similar to jail in one sense, and that is the monotony of working at something which is not interesting. I thought that I needed a few days' vacation anyhow after being locked up in hell for a year. The mere thought of the joint angered me, and with this thought I seemed to live over again the terrible horrors that I had lived during that year. It was very hard for me to even try to forget about the place. My memory of the House of 'Corruption' was like a monster coiling over me, ever reaching and groping out for me, and trying to crush my very being. By a supreme effort I would manage to partially put aside these thoughts and carry on.

"After being idle three days, I put myself to the yoke again, much against my will, but yet what else could I do? I had to earn a living some way. I cared not to steal, well knowing the inevitable result. I hated to work at something that was monotonous, but I knew no trade or skill, and the only work open for such people as myself was work of monotony. And besides I wanted to attain the goal for which I was striving, and that was to come up to the standard that Mrs. Smith and her family lived up to, so the only opening for me was to work and struggle as I might in order to reach that goal. My new position paid me five dollars a week more, and that was the only thing that interested me.

"The people working around me were irritable most of the time and possessed about as much personality and animation as the historical Sphinx. The firm I worked for was an electrical house, and they were always busy, so that there was plenty of work for me to do. My job was to check all orders before they were to be shipped. As the job paid me a salary sufficient for my needs, I kept a stiff upper lip and rebelled inwardly at the hard-boiled bosses whenever they had an inclination to bawl me out. I finally told Mrs. Smith about being dismissed from the telegraph company. Of course she was surprised, and so was I when she calmly and kindly inquired about my leaving the job. I related the details to her, and she pointed out my weaknesses and the way to prevent its happening again. I then told her of my new job, and that it paid me more money, and she was glad and cautioned me about falling again. I worked at this job for two months and during those two months I spent my time foolishly, hanging around at my sister's home, and then spending the evening gambling with the guys in the neighborhood.[2]

"I was always welcomed in their midst and it also was my undoing to a certain extent. The hangout for us was a confectionery store a block away from my sister's house, and after eating my supper and telling my sister I was going home, I would go to the store and meet the gang. We spent our time playing cards, shooting craps for money. As I was working and drawing a neat little salary, I happened to always have money to gamble with and mostly always lost. It was fascinating for me. I delighted to cast my luck with the goddess of chance, who almost continually frowned on me. At the end of every evening's pay I would have to borrow carfare to get home and to get to work the next morning. I was always coming home late, when the household was asleep. It was hard for me to get up in the morning to get to work. Mrs. Smith cautioned me in a kindly way about keeping late hours, and added that it was more of harm than benefit to me. I seriously thought it over, but when evening came, the irresistible call drew me into gambling and every night it was the same way. I was seldom to work on time in the morning, and I barely managed to do my work right.

"A week before Thanksgiving, inventory was to be taken on all stock, and we were all informed that we were to be laid off for one week. This I did not like as that meant one week without pay. So I foolishly thought that it would be better to quit and look for another job and not lose that week's pay. I did not realize that most every other firm was taking inventory at the same time, so naturally no hiring was done and I was out of a job again for a week. During this week I spent my time in the morning looking for a job, and in the afternoon I would go to the hangout and

[2] It is clear, from these statements, that Stanley's group relationships in the stock yard district continued to exercise considerable control over his behavior for a long period of time after he was placed in the home of Mrs. Smith. The influence of these earlier relationships did not begin to diminish until other interests and relationships were established in his new situation. We may assume that the gradual changes which are taking place in Stanley's conduct throughout this chapter reflect changes in his group relationships.

pass the time away over there, conversing with the gang or perhaps play cards and lose more of the money that I needed to live on. My instinct guided me on to disaster, and I was bound helpless hand and foot. My West Side associates and the games of chance drew me like a magnet. Whatever kind of resistance I put up was battered down. After much effort I found a job, working in a mail order house wrapping packages. It was a slave-driving job. The Christmas rush was on, and all over and everywhere it was busy. An avalanche of packages greeted me every morning and what I mean I had to work in order to keep up with the girl who checked the orders. I worked there two weeks until I got in a scrap with the girl who checked orders. She was always disagreeable, and I always thought that she had a perpetual crabby look on her face. We got in an argument about some packages, and she started to lecture me by calling me a 'dumb-bell simp' and a few other uncomplimentary names. I resented this most strongly. Above all things I hated to have a girl give me orders. I simply told her where to get off at. She cried and told the boss. The boss was very much put out about it, and after severely reprimanding me he 'gave me the air.' I didn't care. I was free. I could go wherever I wanted to, and besides I did not have to take abuse from anyone. I was free and could go wherever I pleased. No more did prison bars hold me.

"Mrs. Smith was alarmed when I told her of getting the bounce. She talked with me for an hour, telling me that it was wrong to go along in that way. She told me that she thought that it would be so much better if I would act more diplomatic and deal more conservatively in those situations. I felt ashamed of myself, and I thought that and knew that I was wrong. I made up my mind to change my ways. I wanted to break away from gambling. I wanted to find a job and work steady so that I would be able to look Mrs. Smith in the eye and say that I was worthy of her interest in me, and besides I needed clothes to look presentable, and the only way I could get them was to work and earn the money to buy them; but I was gambling my money away foolishly and I knew it. I always thought that by knowing one's weakness that half the battle was won, and I began a crusade against that weakness for gambling, but it was a desperate battle.

"I got a job in a printing-house, packing catalogue sheets just off the press. I was working nights then, and I did not have a chance to gamble, only to work, eat, and sleep. I got along very well and seemed to be satisfied with myself. The job paid me well, and I always had money in my pockets, and Mrs. Smith was glad that I was working steady again, and so was I.

"One Sunday when I had a holiday I stayed home. A young lady, who also roomed with Mrs. Smith, asked me if I wanted to work in a hospital where she worked, taking care of experimental animals by feeding them. I told her that I had a good job, but I said I would consider it if the position offered me more. The position did offer me more, and I finally decided to take the job. I started the next day, and I was quite taken aback. The surroundings were different. The people who worked around me were pleasing, considerate, and not crabby as they were at the other places where I worked. The work was interesting to me. And for once I enjoyed working. I had my meals at the hospital, and that was a great help to me, as it solved one of my problems of making both ends meet. The animal-room was in the laboratory, and I had the opportunity to glance around occasionally and watch technicians as they conducted experiments in chemistry, surgery, and bacteriology. No more was work monotonous. The day seemed to be over when I thought that it had scarcely started. For the first time I enjoyed going to work in the morning. There were girls who worked in the laboratory, and they were all polite and of pleasing personality, and I got along with them nicely. I compared myself with them and saw myself as a savage, uncouth and vulgar. It harrassed me to think of it.

"I wanted to be refined and know how to act when in contact with people who were intelligent and handled themselves with well-regulated ease. Not that the girls and the doctors regarded me as inferior or low in their eyes, because they did not. They considered me as one of them, and that made me take stock of myself.

"Mr. Shaw talked to me many times about getting more education. When I started to work at the hospital and associated with

well-trained people, I saw the value of more education.[3] I enrolled in evening-school classes, and began to complete my high-
school education. I liked the school. I was learning things and
doing things that I liked to do, and by going to school I solved my
greatest problem—gambling. Instead of going over to my sister's
to eat supper and then meeting the gang, I ate at the hospital,
after which I rode home on the street car with the girls. They
went my way, and we would chat and have a good time. I looked
back at my foolishness and compared the fun I was having now.
It was different. It filled me with new life. It made me feel like
somebody, instead of going home late at night tired after dissipat-
ing my time gambling. I now wanted to get new clothes and look
well and appear well in the eyes of the people I was meeting. I
began to see how negligently I dressed. I wanted to look neat
and business-like, like the doctors and the internes. More so, I
fell in love with one of the girls at the hospital. She swept me off
my feet the first time I saw her, and I began to dream dreams of
future happiness. Dreams I had not dreamed before. So I began
to take note of my personal appearance. I wanted to look well in
the eyes of the girl of my dreams. I saw the way other boys
dressed, and I ordered a suit of clothes of the latest style, also
shoes, shirts, and the classiest of ties. When I stood before the
mirror and looked at myself was one of the happiest moments of
my life. I really looked with favor upon myself and thought of
the good impression I could now make on the girl of my dreams.
Then I began to feel like a new man.

"In the morning going to work I would board the elevated train
which brought me to work. Sitting in the car, I would try to imi-
tate some big business men, by scanning the morning paper hur-
riedly but importantly and putting on an air of reserved dignity.
I felt like I was somebody and I wanted to act like one.[4] I rarely
visited my sister, and when I did, it was Sunday, and I would be

[3] Stanley's interest in securing more education began to develop while he was
working at the hospital and clearly reflects the influence of the new cultural situation to which he is gradually making an adjustment.

[4] This is one of the many incidents indicative of the influence of the new situation in bringing about a change in Stanley's conception of himself.

all dressed up. I would feel very proud to come up to my sister's house, and pay her a call. And why shouldn't I feel proud? I had a good job, good clothes, and I was going to school. My sister told me that I had changed, and that she thought that I would get somewhere in life. The gang I had associated with looked upon me with more respect, and I realized and knew what it was to feel independent and able to take care of oneself. The girls I knew in my sister's neighborhood no longer interested me. In my eyes now they were different. Not that I didn't respect them, but I began to see how different they were from the girls at the hospital and in my new neighborhood. I wanted to be what some persons call a gentleman.

"Mrs. Smith noticed the change in me, and she commended and praised me, and I felt highly honored. I was on the right road, and I knew it, and I inwardly was elated with myself. The world was losing its cruelness and seemed to have more kindness and love. I could look anyone in the eye squarely without cringing. No more did people stare, but now they look at me, and I can sense that I look presentable, and I feel at ease. The girl I liked so much liked me, and we often went out together. I spent many an enjoyable evening with her when I did not have to go to school. I began to see the real pleasure in living, and I was glad and thankful that I was out of the old rut.[5]

"I worked at the hospital four months, when one day I went down to the pharmacy to have a prescription filled for myself, as I had a cold. The man who filled my prescription was a friend of mine, and we always lambasted each other in a playful way whenever we got together. This day I asked him to fill my prescription and he did. After filling it, we talked a while and kidded each other. For some reason he got offended at something I said, and he began to lambast me in earnest. I resented this and fought back. It ended in me being forced out of the room. I nursed my

---

[5] Stanley's favorable reaction to his work at the hospital was suggestive of the kind of situation in which he might make a satisfactory vocational adjustment. He was not only in full charge of his own work but he had close contact with a professional group which gave him a distinct feeling of superiority. This situation was more suited to his dominant personality traits than any position which he had held prior to that time.

grievance until noon, when I challenged him out to settle our little difficulty on the roof, where no one would see us. Instead of going up on the roof, he hit me when my back was turned in the hall, in the presence of other employees. With my anger up, I fought until we were separated by someone, and I went up to the laboratory and the doctor called me in and told me that I was no longer needed. It was a great blow to me, as I valued my position very much and I hated to leave behind those pleasant people with whom I had worked. Most of all, and worst, what would my girl think of my acting like a savage? But I knew no other way to settle a grievance. I had always settled them by physical force and no other way. So instead of bidding my friends goodbye, I sneaked out of the hospital, humiliated, but satisfied that I had fought for my rights. Mrs. Smith was shocked when learning of it, as she thought that I was getting along nicely and that a better job was hard to find. I defended myself by saying that he started everything; but Mrs. Smith informed me that there were other ways to settle these things, by using diplomacy and tact. This opened up my eyes, but it was too late. I was through as far as the hospital was concerned.

"Mrs. Smith took it upon herself to go down to the hospital the next morning and to plead for my cause, but to no avail. My act of indiscretion was too large in the eyes of the doctor, and all hope was gone. So I had to take it philosophically, but it was hard. . . . .

"After leaving the hospital, I took a job in a department store. My job was to pack hats in the storeroom, and it was dirty and monotonous. I found it disagreeable and confined and quit after working a week. I went across the street and secured a job in another department store as an adjuster of complaints. This was a better job, because it was not so monotonous. I was always meeting different people and learning the many eccentricities that we humans have. I worked here four months and quit for another job where I would get more money. I immediately took a similar job in another department store. It was springtime, and I longed to do outside work, as I felt cooped up in the store.

"I got a job as a painter, but this proved to be a flop, so I only worked a few days. I was forced to find another job, which I did in a mail order house, dumping out the contents of mail bags. This job I also hated because it, too, had that jail like restriction, so I quit after a few days.

"In the meantime Mrs. Smith became greatly concerned about me, and talked to me in her usual kind and sympathetic way. She encouraged me, and pointed out the importance of regular habits of industry. I knew full well the wisdom of her advice, and I wanted to make good and gain her approval. I had learned to look up to her and wanted to measure up to her standards. I went out to get a job, determined to use more diplomacy and tact. I had several jobs in the next few months, but they were all monotonous and I didn't like them. . . . .

(Two years after release from House of Correction.) "Mr. Shaw had talked to me many times about salesmanship, saying that he felt that I was especially qualified for that type of work. Through his efforts I had an opportunity to try my skill in this field, and found it to be the most fascinating type of work I had ever done.

"I continued to keep company with the girl I had met at the hospital.[6] We spent much time together, and became much in love with each other. She encouraged me by saying that she didn't care what I had done, she was concerned about what I was going to become. That gave me courage and spirit. I spent all of my leisure time with her and other young people that she knew. I became interested in the activities of these young people and gradually broke entirely away from the people of the West Side. The new life became fascinating, and I became happy that I had escaped from a life of squalor and misery in the stock yards. . . . .

(Two and a half years after release from House of Correction.) "With my success in selling came a feeling of confidence in

[6] Perhaps Stanley's contact with this girl, whom he later married, was one of the most powerful factors in his rehabilitation.

my ability to get along in the business world.[7] Sometimes I feel despondent; having a criminal record is a heavy hardship to carry through life. There is always the danger of it becoming known. In my conversations I am always tempted to tell of some experience I had in prison, but I have to forego the pleasure, for it would reveal my record and injure my standing. Sometimes when I am out with young people I find myself almost telling of incidents about my prison experience and catch myself just in time. . . . .

(Four years after release from House of Correction.) "I am now settled in the warmth and congenial atmosphere of my own home with my wife and child. For once in my life I have something worth while to work for. I want my child to have all of the advantages that were denied me. Already I have taken out a life insurance policy for him, which will mature when he is old enough for college. My hopes and plans for the future are all tied up in him. I want him to have a college education and be a refined professional man. Nothing in the world could now take the place of my wife and child in my life, as they mean everything to me. . . . .

"In looking back over my past life and comparing it to my present one, it is hard to see myself as the incorrigible boy who would not stay put. I am not surprised that the various correctional institutions, in which I was to be reformed to meet the requirements of society and to emerge never to sin again, did not reform me. Society can force children into correctional institutions but it cannot force them to reform. In order to reform a boy you have to change his spirit, not break it, and only sympathetic treatment will do that.

"My reformation I attribute to the people I came in contact with after leaving the House of Correction and through whom I met the woman who is today my wife.

"Salesmanship is hard work, but I've learned to like it. It pays well and it puts a fellow on his mettle. You have to know how to

[7] Stanley has already demonstrated considerable ability in salesmanship. This seems to be one situation in which his personality traits are definite assets. He is able not only to dominate the situation and assume a superior rôle, but in this field he is permitted to work more or less independently of other persons.

meet different types of people in an easy and diplomatic way. I get a great kick out of putting over a deal on a customer, especially a stubborn customer. . . . .

"I have not gone over to the stock yards for almost two years. I want to forget the people over there. I am very glad that I escaped from that life, but feel sorry for the children who live there and have to go through the misery and hardship which were mine."

More than five years have elapsed since Stanley was released from the House of Correction. During this period there has not been a recurrence of any delinquent behavior. Furthermore, he has developed interests and a philosophy of life which are in keeping with the standards of conventional society. While it is impossible to analyze all the factors which have been instrumental in producing these modifications in his interests and conduct, it may be assumed that they were due, in large part, to changes in group relationships. In other words, his present behavior trends, interests, and philosophy of life have developed as a product of his participation in the life of conventional social groups.

DISCUSSION

By ERNEST W. BURGESS

The case of Stanley is, and is not, typical of juvenile delinquency in Chicago. No single case could be representative of all the many variations of personality, of the permutations of situations and the diversity of experiences of the hundreds of boys who year by year have entered the Cook County Juvenile Court.

WHY THIS CASE IS TYPICAL

There can, however, be no doubt that this case is typical, in the sense that it has aspects that are common to a statistically high proportion of cases. For example:

1. Stanley grew up in a delinquency area. In 1926, 85.4 per cent of all the boys arrested by the police came from homes in delinquency areas.[1]
2. He lived in a "broken home." Of all boys brought into Juvenile Court in the year Stanley was first committed, 36.1 per cent came from "broken homes."
3. He began his delinquent career even before he started to school. Authorities in this field agree on the large proportion among criminals of those who are early initiated into delinquency.
4. He had institutional experiences in rapid succession: the Detention Home, the Chicago Parental School, St. Charles Training School, the Illinois State Reformatory at Pontiac, the House of Correction, but the treatment at these correctional, reformatory, and penal institutions failed to check his delinquent career. Healy and Bronner found in an intensive study of 116 cases of male juvenile delinquents committed to the Parental School that 68 per cent failed to make good on their return to the community, and in a similar study of 158 boys who had been inmates of St. Charles 72 per cent continued in their delinquent career.[2] Of boys with experience in the Parental School 39 per cent like Stanley were later inmates of St. Charles.[3] Of the boys who failed to make good after leaving St. Charles, one-half were later committed either to the State Reformatory or the House of Correction, or like Stanley himself to both.
5. He was a "jack-roller," and his experiences are typical of the jack-roller.

[1] Delinquency areas are those having rates above the median rate in the series. See *Delinquency Areas*, p. 208.

[2] *Delinquents and Criminals, Their Making and Unmaking*, p. 251.

[3] *Ibid.*, pp 290–99.

A large proportion of all jack-rollers, as an examination of scores of cases of this type indicates, are "runaway" boys. Boys who run away from home in Chicago, as well as "runaway" boys from other cities drift naturally into West Madison Street. All invariably come into contact with homosexuals in the hobo group and among those who submit to their advances a large proportion, like Stanley, become jack-rollers, exploiters of homosexuals and of drunkards. Stanley in his personality traits appears to be a fairly representative jack-roller.

Judged by these external characteristics, the experiences of Stanley may be assumed to be roughly similar to those of a large proportion of other juvenile delinquents. If this assumption is proved correct, then an intensive study of this case and of other cases may enable the student of human behavior to probe beneath the surface of delinquent acts and to take a firm grasp upon the underlying motives of conduct.

The point is sure to be made, Why study one case so intensively? Why not make an extensive study of one thousand cases on the basis of which conclusions may be arrived at which will be backed up with mass data?

A sufficient answer, perhaps, is that such studies have been made. Indeed, the findings recently published by Mr. Shaw and his associates, *Delinquency Areas*, constitute one of the most telling of the statistical studies which have yet appeared in this field. But the fact remains as succinctly stated by William Healy with reference to his quantitative examination of his own data, "Statistics will never tell the whole story."[4]

This one autobiography of a delinquent career is a concrete and dramatic exemplification of what a case-study may reveal about the causes and treatment of delinquency that can never be arrived at by more formal techniques like statistics, which must depend very largely upon external data.

The case of Stanley appears also to be typical in a more real sense than can be verified by any statistical calculation. It is typical (i.e., belonging to the type) in the same way that every case is representative of its kind or species. This case is a member of the *criminal* species, and so of necessity must bear the impress of the characteristics and experiences of the criminal. It

[4] *The Individual Delinquent*, p. 130.

may not be the best specimen, perhaps only a good specimen or even a poor specimen. There can be no doubt that any case, good, bad, or indifferent, is a specimen of the species to which it belongs.

The individual person is more intrinsically a specimen of any group of which he is a member than is a plant or animal of its biological species. The plant or animal is a specimen of botanical or zoölogical species, because through heredity there is transmitted to it a uniform morphological and physiological pattern. The human being as a member of a social group is a specimen of it, not primarily, if at all, because of his physique and temperament but by reason of his participation in its purposes and activities. Through communication and interaction the person acquires the language, tradition, standards, and practices of his group. Therefore, the relation of the person to his group is organic and hence representative upon a cultural rather than upon a biological level.

This point is dramatically put by William Bolitho in referring to Mr. Shaw's study of neighborhood tradition as a factor in delinquency:

Mr. Shaw, and his patient investigators into the connection of area with juvenile delinquency, have shown conclusively the district tradition, which each new immigrant family into a slum area takes over with the occupancy of the house. This area tradition, as it were impregnated into the very houses themselves, like the patina of soot that has eaten into the stones, can only be compared with the tradition of a great old school, of an ancient regiment, even of a monastery. The place is stuffed with history and example, handed down by boy to boy, until the house wreckers come.[5]

This intimate relation of the person to his group and neighborhood makes each person not so much a replica of a pattern as an intrinsic part of an ongoing process. Hence the study of the experiences of one person at the same time reveals the life-activities of his group.

This is why the experiences of any individual person reflect group opinion; why habit in the individual is an expression of custom in society; and why mental conflict in the person may always be explained in terms of the conflict of divergent cultures.

[5] *Survey Graphic*, LXIII (February 1, 1930), 506.

In the career of Stanley it is strikingly evident how he absorbs and expresses the attitudes, philosophy of life, and standards of the criminal world. It is also apparent that his reformation is quite as much or more a matter of changing his social groups as of effecting a change of attitudes or purposes. Actually, of course, the shift in group identification and the permutation of attitudes takes place simultaneously.

In analyzing any case as a specimen of the other cases of its kind, it is desirable and perhaps necessary always to make comparisons with other cases, both those which are like and unlike it. The following generalizations are derived, not alone from this autobiography, but from other documents of similar and dissimilar experiences.

THE BOY'S OWN STORY

First, this document, and others like it, indicate the value for scientific purposes of materials in the first person. The "boy's own story," the narratives of parents, the verbatim family interview are objective data. Much of the material on personality now extant, including the case records of social agencies, is vitiated for full use for research purposes by the fact that they are subjective records, that is, translations by the visitor of the language, emotional expressions, and attitudes of the person interviewed. A great advance in the study of personality has been achieved by the development of the record in the first person.

Those who have read this life-history in manuscript have all been astounded at its vivid and dramatic style. There is, of course, ample convincing evidence in contemporary books and articles of the literary ability of several ex-convicts. So far as the writer can judge, Stanley's style is not markedly superior to the run of present and former delinquents and criminals. Because of the enforced leisure of confinement, convicts read quite as much as any other group in our population, with the possible exception of teachers, clergymen, and writers.[6] Besides it seems to be universally true that one can talk or write best upon the

---

[6] The report of the librarian of the Illinois State Penitentiary at Joliet gives an average of sixteen books per capita a year for the inmate population. See A. A. Bruce, A. J. Harno, E. W. Burgess, and J. Landesco, *The Workings of the Indeterminate Sentence Law and the Parole System in Illinois*, p. 160.

subjects with which he is most familiar. Every person, we have been told, has the ability to write at least one book, his autobiography.

Astonishment at the literary excellence of a personal document is often followed by skepticism of its authenticity. In the personal interview or in the narrative, how is it possible to check the validity and reliability of statements?

The formal procedure to establish the validity of a document is to check up on the significant points, particularly upon apparently dubious ones. In the case of Stanley there was the court record, the work record, and by good fortune the report by Dr. William Healy. Other points not confirmed by these official records were tested by independent inquiry. The net result was the substantiation of the objective facts as given by Stanley, but quite often widely different interpretations of these facts. Stanley, in telling the truth as it appears to him, unwittingly reveals what we want most to know, namely, his personality reactions and his own interpretation of his experiences.

How does it come about that Stanley and other hardened young criminals tell the truth frankly and freely? Parents, teachers, and officers of the law are in unanimous agreement that nearly all "bad" children and on occasion "good" children are liars because they have discovered them in falsehoods. The answer to this paradox seems to be found in the fact that the lie is a response to a specific stimulus. The adequate stimulus for the lie response appears to be the punishment situation. Physicians, psychiatrists, and sociologists, whose attitude is that of scientific research into the solution of personal problems, elicit, not falsehood, but truth. Dr. William Healy once reported that in his experience with thousands of cases of problem boys and girls he found only a negligible percentage of deception.

The best guaranty, perhaps, of the reliability of a document is the degree of spontaneity, freedom, and release which a person enjoys in writing or in telling his own story. That is the essential superiority of a life-history like Stanley's to the usual formal record obtained by asking a series of "cut-and-dried" questions. To the extent that a person tells his own story in his own way, so that the narrative takes on the character of a chronicle, a defense, a confession, or a self-analysis, to that extent it is revealing and definitely and clearly manifests its internal consistency. The more a man tells, as all criminal investigators know, the more he is certain to entangle himself in inconsistencies and contradictions, if he is attempting to deceive. The lie persisted in and elaborated builds up ultimately a huge structure of falsehoods that collapses of its own weight. On the other hand, a document like that of Stanley's shows more unity and consistency with increasing detail. It stands up under the test of internal coherence.

Granted that Stanley has told the truth about himself as he sees it, the reader will have still a further question, What were the facts as they are about Stanley's stepmother, about the Parental School, St. Charles, Pontiac, and the House of Correction, about the prostitute who "befriended" him, the boy companion with whom he broke? The absolute truth about these or other points cannot be secured by the life-history and probably cannot be obtained by any other known method. But in human affairs it is not the absolute truth about an event that concerns us but the way in which persons react to that event. So in the case of Stanley, it is his reaction to the events of his experience that interests us, because they give us the materials by which we can interpret his attitudes and values, his conduct and his personality.

The life-history of Stanley in a dramatic and challenging manner introduces the reader to an intimate understanding of the social factors which condition the beginnings and persistence of a criminal career. "Broken homes," "poverty," "bad housing," "bad companions," "destructive neighborhood influences," and other common-sense terms are quite inadequate to define the dynamic relationship between the personality of Stanley and his varied and stimulating experiences. His career is a series of acts in response to changing social situations; the discrimination of his stepmother against him in favor of her children; the freedom and release of exploration in a disorganized immigrant area; the patterns of stealing presented by the neighborhood tradition; the lures of West Madison Street; the repression of treatment in the correctional and reformatory institution; the fellowship and code of an oppressed group and the education in crime freely offered to him by his associates in these institutions; the thrill of adventures in crime; the easy money quickly obtained and spent; the dulness and monotony of the chances to reform offered him. These are factors common to the actual experiences of thousands of youthful bandits and gangsters.

PERSONALITY FORMATION

An intimate and revealing life-history like Stanley's permits penetration beneath the surface, not only of the social factors, but also of personality traits. In seeing Stanley as he sees himself and his career, the reader is enabled to define and to analyze the processes of personality formation and of the creation of the criminal rôle.

In examining several hundred life-histories and in studying many of them intensively, the writer concludes that the manner of writing the document reveals at least four different personality types. There is the person who writes a chronicle of his life, putting down in order the external events of his career without explanation, or with only conventional explanations. He might be called the Chronicler. Then there is the individual like Stanley who writes a justification of his whole career. He may be termed the Self-defender. There are others who reveal what hitherto he has sedulously concealed of the drama upon the stage of his own thoughts. The writer of this document may be called the Confessant. A fourth fairly discernible type is the person who in his life-history dissects his every act and motive. The denomination of Self-analyst may be applied to him.

The personality traits of Stanley, which taken together indicate the self-defender document, may be concretely inventoried as follows:

1. Early rise and persistence of a sense of injustice
2. Self-pity
3. Hypercritical of others
4. Always right; never takes blame but readily blames others
5. Readily makes friends and as easily breaks with them
6. Excessive interest in attention

7. Lacks insight into his own motives and those of others
8. Suspicious toward others without sufficient cause
9. Ideas of persecution.
10. Substitutes rationalization for insight
11. Builds up rational system of explanation
12. Absorbed in his own ideas and plans and relatively immune to suggestions from others
13. Resentment of correction and resistance to direction
14. Tendency to escape from unpleasant situations by the method of protest
15. Tendency to moralize
16. Speed of decision and strength of reaction

The foregoing traits are, it seems, the characteristic attributes of the personality pattern of the individual who is able even under adverse circumstances to maintain his ego against an unfriendly and even hostile social world. Indeed, it may well be that the development of this type of individualistic personality is the one way in which certain human beings are able to meet the failures and disappointments of life.

The study of life-history documents has led the writer to accept, at least tentatively, the hypothesis that the main outlines of the personality pattern are fixed in the early years of the child's social experience and are subject to only minor modifications in youth and manhood.

A brief analysis of these traits of Stanley will, perhaps, clarify this point. The early rise and persistence of *a sense of injustice* may be taken as the key trait of which the others are natural outcomes. A situation in which a sense of injustice arises is one in which the stepmother discriminates against him as a stepson in favor of her own children. Stanley and his brother and sister refused to accept this situation and persisted in running away. Stanley, in his struggle with his stepmother, is sustained by the feeling of his own worth and her unfairness. Toward himself he early manifests the *feeling of self-pity* which protects his ego under later adverse situations. Toward his stepmother he continues to be *hypercritical* in attitude; this develops into unsparing criticism of the institutions of which he is an inmate and of persons whom he dislikes. It follows that in his unequal struggle against Fate (to use his own term) he tends to take the position of being *always right*. In this document he is disposed never to take blame, but to blame others or Fate.

It is significant to note that he *readily makes friends and as readily breaks with them*. While other persons are necessary to his existence, he is not a good group member. He seems to adjust better with older persons, especially those whom he admires, than with those of his own age. He is too much an individualist to feel strongly the claims of loyalty and affection in friendship. He cannot "roll drunks" without a comrade, but the relationship is one of utility rather than of sentiment. He is not devoid of sympathy and sentiment, but they are stronger when closely personal than when directed to others. He shows *an excessive interest in attention* and develops ingenious techniques to secure it.

His *lack of insight into his own motives and those of others* is a characteristic trait of the self-centered person. This arises from the inability to look at one's self in a given situation with something of the detachment of the point of view of another person. Stanley has imagination, but he is not introspective, although he has his moments of introversion (pp. 63 and 103). The *suspicion of others* without adequate reason and *ideas of persecution* develop naturally from the tendency to substitute *rationalization for insight*. Consequently, the person builds up a *rational system of exploration*. Stanley's system is that of Fate and lucky and unlucky "breaks"; this is the philosophy, in general, of the underworld; it is a philosophy that steels the resistance of individuals against the untoward events of life. The *absorption* of the person *in his own ideas and plans* results in *relative immunity to suggestions from others*.

Stanley exhibits in an unusually accentuated degree the traits of *resentment of correction* and *resistance to direction* which characterize persons of strong "ego" feeling. Since he is unable to maintain his ego by holding jobs, he tends to substitute *the protest method of escape* from the humiliating situation of being fired.

Finally, two remaining traits complete the clinical picture of the egocentric personality. He has the inveterate tendency to conceive his behavior and the behavior of others around him in *moralistic terms* of right or wrong. His behavior is impulsive, being marked by *speed of decision and strength of reactions.*

Stanley, no more than anyone else, is neither to be praised nor blamed for his personality traits. They were formed for him before he gained conscious control of his destiny. The point to be grasped is that the formation of the personality pattern is a natural product of forces in the constitution of the individual and in his childhood situation. Once this conception of behavior is clearly understood, we will learn to accept people as they are and work with, rather than against, the basic set of their personality.

Mr. Shaw once made the comment that personalities of Stanley's type may be unadjusted or maladjusted but they are not disorganized; in fact, they are if anything too highly organized. The traits of the egocentric person are those of an overorganized personality, one that is so rigidly set that it finds difficulty in making the usual normal adjustments to other personalities or to changing situations.

PERMUTATIONS OF SOCIAL TYPE

In analyzing this and other life-histories, a basic distinction must be made between personality pattern and social type. So far we have been describing the personality pattern which may be defined as the sum and integration of those traits which characterize the typical reactions of one person toward other persons. The personality pattern, according to our tentative hypothesis, is formed in infancy and early childhood through a conjunction of constitutional and experiential factors and persists with some modification and elaboration as a relatively constant factor through later childhood, youth, and maturity. It is determined, it should be noted, in the interaction between persons, but not by imitation.

The term "social type" does not refer to the mechanisms of personality reactions but to attitudes, values, and philosophy of life derived from copies presented by society. The rôle which a person assumes and to which he is assigned by society creates the social type. With Stanley, becoming "a professional runaway," "a delinquent," "a criminal," was taking on a rôle. His acceptance of the criminal code and the orientation of his ambitions to succeed in a criminal career have to do with attitudes and values and are elements that enter into the creation of a social type.

The so-called permutations of personality are the abrupt and often revolutionary changes in social type, not in basic personality patterns. The transformation of Stanley from a criminal to a law-abiding citizen was a change in social type; his personality pattern remained the same. All similar conversions as from sinner to saint, radical to conservative, Democrat to Republican, dry to wet, or vice versa, are changes in social type, not in personality patterns. Our hypothesis is that personality patterns, since they are fixed in infancy and in early childhood, are likewise susceptible to reconditioning only in this same period. The conditioning of social types takes place in later experiences and may accordingly be reconditioned in youth and maturity.

EXPERIMENTING WITH A NEW TECHNIQUE OF TREATMENT

Ultimately the value of all scientific discoveries in human as well as in physical behavior must submit to the test of their significance for purposes of practical control. In the field of personality study there are many indications that hypotheses on the causes of behavior problems may perhaps best be tested through actual experiments in treatment.

The brilliant success of the treatment processes set into operation by Mr. Shaw cannot be attributed to the accidental favorable outcome of a single case. In fact, this is only one of a series studied and treated intensively and experimentally with equally striking results. Accordingly the analysis of the treatment that follows will be based upon my knowledge of Mr. Shaw's general procedure as well as upon the special methods employed in this case.

The first step in the course of treatment is the approach to the boy, not by sympathy, but by empathy. Through his life-history his counselor is enabled to see his life as the boy conceived it rather than as an adult might imagine it. Empathy means entering into the experience of another person by the human and democratic method of sharing experiences. In this and other ways rapport is established. Sympathy is the attempt through imagination to put one's self in another person's place with all the fallacies which are almost necessarily involved.

The telling or writing one's life-story is itself part of the treatment. The very act of pouring out one's experiences not only has a cathartic effect, particularly where tensions and inhibitions are released, but also gives the subject perspective upon his life. This gaining of perspective upon one's experience is the chief way in which persons achieve control over their impulses and motives and work out their destiny toward some challenging goal.

Mr. Shaw does not use the methods of the psychoanalyst, he is not dealing with the materials of the unconscious, but with the memories, wishes, plans, and ambitions of the conscious mind. Working with these, he devises an experimental plan of treatment that attempts to take into account the personality pattern, the attitudes, interests, talents, and plans of the boy himself.

But more than any other student of delinquency and problem behavior, Mr. Shaw pays attention to the powerful factors of group and neighborhood influence. He recognized, as had Dr. Healy earlier, that, although Stanley could not live in the emotional tension of his home, one of his chief needs was the response and intimate appreciation which only wholesome home life can give. It was a case for transplantation. The environment was to be changed so that the powerful influence of the social situation would work for, rather than against, reformation. Lodging was secured for Stanley in a home which provided not only sympathetic maternal interest but also intimate contact with higher cultural standards. There was naturally enough a period of conflict between the old neighborhood gang life and the new life opening up before him. The decisive influence in this time of indecision was undoubtedly the continued contact with Mr. Shaw, the daily influence of his landlady, and the new associations he was forming at work and at night school.

Interestingly enough, the personality traits which enabled

Stanley to break so completely with his criminal past and the gang were the chief obstacles to his vocational adjustment.

The treatment of obtaining employment where the employer would take a special interest in his employee's progress, which had worked well in other cases with similar personality patterns, failed with Stanley. His extreme resentment against correction and his deep-seated aversion to taking orders seemed to make all attempts at vocational placement futile. Mr. Shaw's final choice of the occupation of commercial salesman showed his ingenuity in adapting treatment to the traits of personality. As a salesman in the field, he took orders only from himself and was not liable to correction from others. His personality traits of attractive manners, his forcible and logical presentation of points, and his ability to make friends were positive assets in his new vocation.

The life-history of Stanley, taken in conjunction with the facts on the concentration of delinquency presented in *Delinquency Areas* and the analyses of boy gang life and organization in Thrasher's *The Gang*, provide a foundation for new modes of attack upon the problem of the delinquent and the criminal. Attention has largely been centered upon case work with the individual, but that is only a partial approach. An all-round program will require, in addition, research upon the social factors in delinquency and the development of techniques of group and community treatment. This volume is a notable pioneer contribution to that end.

To many readers the chief value of this document will not consist in its contribution to an understanding of the personality of Stanley and other delinquents or of the methods of treatment of similar cases. To them its far-reaching significance will inhere in the illumination it throws on the causation, under conditions of modern city life, of criminal careers and upon the social psychology of the new type of criminal youth.

To them this autobiography will point the way to a basic attack on the conditions of boy life in deteriorating neighborhoods in Chicago. They will become convinced that the problem of the gangster and the gunman will be to get back to first causes in the neighborhood where traditions teach delinquency and where crime is the most interesting play of children. They will demand a thoroughgoing program of community prevention in place of the present emphasis upon institutional correction, the futility of which is so clearly shown by this volume.

To the writer the permanent significance of the case of Stanley lies in its contribution to the fund of scientific knowledge. It represents a distinct advance in research both in method and in fundamental conceptions.

The contribution in method inheres in the perfecting of the technique of the boy's own story, specifically for the field of delinquency but generally applicable to all personality study. This and other documents secured by Mr. Shaw provide objective data to all students of personality because they present the person's own story uncolored by translation into the language of the investigator. While he offers his own interpretations, the materials stand on their own footing and may be interpreted variously by other students.

For the first time in the field of delinquency this volume provides adequate material for description and analysis from the standpoint of explanation in terms of the cultural factors in behavior. In penetrating beneath the external behavior of the delinquent boy it reveals the intimate interplay between his impulses and the effective stimuli of the environment. It shows how the cultural patterns, of his home, of his associates in the neighborhood, of the delinquent and criminal groups outside and especially inside correctional and penal institutions, define his wishes and attitudes and so control, almost in a deterministic fashion, his behavior. His account also discloses how certain changes in his social environment, by affording contact in an intimate and sympathetic way with the cultural patterns of normal society, redefine his impulses and direct his conduct into fields of socially approved behavior.

With materials available for a more adequate analysis of the rôle of cultural factors in conduct, the stage is set for fundamental studies in the interrelation and interaction of the constitutional and cultural factors in human behavior.

Finally, this study in conjunction with the study of *Delinquency Areas* points the way toward research into the processes of social treatment.

APPENDIX I

BRIEF SUMMARY OF CLINICAL FINDINGS

At various times during his career in delinquency, Stanley was referred to behavior clinics for examination. The first clinical study was made by Dr. William Healy·at the time that Stanley was seven years and ten months of age. A second examination was made when he was fourteen, and a third at the time of his release from the House of Correction.

DEVELOPMENTAL HISTORY

At the time of conception the father was in good health but drinking excessively. The mother was "sickly." The pregnancy was full-term and the delivery normal. Birth weight was six and a half pounds. Stanley was breast-fed and showed no nutritional difficulties. No convulsions. He walked at nine months, cut his first tooth at seven months, and began to talk about the fifteenth month. He had chickenpox at two and one-half years and measles at three.

PHYSICAL FINDINGS

At the age of seven years and ten months Stanley was described by the physical examiner as being "a slender, rather delicate appearing child, who seems to be stunted and undernourished." Weight fifty-six pounds and height three feet and three and one-half inches. Numerous carious teeth; heart sounds normal—no murmur, arrhythmia, or enlargement; lungs normal; muscular development fair; hearing and vision normal; slight general adenopathy; nutrition fair; urinalysis and Wassermann both negative.

At fourteen he was still retarded in his physical development. Examination at that time showed that he weighed ninety-one pounds and was four feet two inches tall; teeth very carious; reflexes normal; vision and hearing normal; heart sounds negative.

During the period between fourteen and eighteen Stanley's physical development was very rapid. At eighteen he weighed one hundred and fifty pounds, was five feet eight inches tall. His general physical condition was described as being "very good."

PSYCHOLOGICAL FINDINGS

When examined at the age of seven years and ten months Stanley was described by the psychologist as being "very bright, somewhat ahead of his age. The results of the test showed that his intelligence was above average. He seems on the whole to be a very nice boy. During the examination he talked freely. He has a winning smile."

At fourteen his intelligence quotient, as measured by the Stanford-Binet

Test, was 1.04. On Educational Tests he ranked low in arithmetic and high in history and literature. The psychological tests at the age of eighteen showed an intelligence quotient of 1.06.

The following is Dr. Healy's summary of findings at the time of the first examination:

Physical:	Fair general condition; numerous carious teeth.
Mental:	Intelligence above average. We should class him as having good ability and poor advantages, the latter because of much truancy.
Delinquency:	Consists in stealing, running away from home and truancy from school. Bad sex habits.
Causative Factors:	(*a*) bad neighborhood; (*b*) bad influences in family and poor parental control; (*c*) bad companions.

Outlook is good if constructive work is done in the case If he remains in the same neighborhood and family the boy will probably continue in the same way. He needs a complete change of environment. A foster-home would perhaps meet the needs in this case.

APPENDIX II

For the benefit of those who are interested in the method employed in securing Stanley's life-story, we are presenting here the original document which he wrote prior to his commitment to the House of Correction. As previously stated, the long life-history already presented is an elaboration of this short initial document (see chap. i, pp. 22–23).

WHY AND HOW I BECAME A CRIMINAL

As far back as I can remember, and with what my sister told me (the sister who mothered us for two years after mother died), our home wasn't anything to brag about, or any decent place for human beings to live in after my mother died.

My mother died when I was four years old. My father remarried in one year; that was when I was five. The woman he married had seven children, and a bad lot they were, and there were eight in our own family, making fifteen in all. We all tried to live together in five rooms. It wasn't long before trouble started. My stepmother started to raise hell. She favored her children in every way. She blamed us for everything that happened, and gave them the best of the food, if there was a best. My two oldest sisters left home because they couldn't stand the treatment. The stepmother done with us just what she pleased. We were well abused, and continuously. When our father would come home from work and we would try to complain, she (stepmother) would say we were lying and if he wanted to take the part of such kids, why she would leave him. Of course he didn't want her to go, although that would have been a godsend for our home. Well, he always took her part, or there was trouble. That's one thing I've always held against my father. He should have stood by his children against a woman like her. I learned later, and I know now, that he wasn't much better than she was. Well, she beat us at every meal. Most of the trouble started at mealtime because we would get mad when she served her children first and made us wait. We only had one and two meals a day.

Things went on, and my older brother ran away and was put in jail just for running away from home. That only left two at home. I lived on with her for a year, and I was six years, and I could not stand the situation any longer. She told me to go out and pick rags and bottles and bones and make a few cents, which she said would pay for my board. I was only six years old, and my brother was nine, so I used to accompany him on these junking expeditions. It kept on this way until I got sick of the life. I was seeing other boys of my age with good clothes, spending money, and I didn't see why I shouldn't have the clothes, and most of all, right treatment.

200

Well, by this time I hated my stepmother. I couldn't stand to be in the house with her. I wouldn't do anything she wanted me to do because of the way I felt about her. We told her to make her own children do some of the work, but of course they were too good to work. The thing that made me feel worse was that her and her kids came into our home and took charge of it, said it was theirs, and finally drove us out. Wouldn't nobody feel right if strangers would drive him out of his own home. It would be bad enough if they had been nice about it. We were the only ones that suffered from it. They lived there and never got into trouble. Nobody ever took them into court or accused them of being criminals, and the way I see it, they were worse than we were. That's how the germ of criminality began to grow in me, getting disgusted at them and wanting to run away.

One day after a quarrel with my stepmother I ran away. I roamed the street all day and lived on bananas that I slipped out of a grocery store owned by a friend of my father. I guess he just about owed them to me, because we traded there a good many years.

I slept several nights in the alley and under doorsteps. I got pretty cold and wet and hungry, but that wasn't quite as bad as being at home. I can stand bad treatment from strangers better than I can from people who pretend to be my friends. You don't expect strangers to do anything good to you, but you expect more of your own father or even stepmother. My best friends all through my life haven't been related to me, anyway. Some people say there's no place like home. Well, that was true in my case, but I don't mean it in the same way they do. Well, I begged and stole food for three or four days, and was picked up by the policeman. I told him I was away from home because I didn't like it there. He called the patrol wagon and took me to the station. I told the police sergeant the same thing about my trouble at home, but he sent me back home. I ran away the same day, and during the next six months, well, I got so bad, I mean I ran away so much, they had to put me some place where they thought they could make me behave and be a good boy. So they sent me to the Parental School for not going to school. I spent five months of my boyhood days there, and I saw boys frail as a flower maltreated to the extreme. But I was lucky, as I was the smallest boy in the institution or else I would get beat up too. I wasn't half as bad or as dangerous as they thought I was. My mind was too young and undeveloped to realize what these things in institutions would do to a boy. But I had a vague idea that when I got to be a man I would stop all of those brutal and narrow-minded officials at the head of those state and city institutions.

Well, to get to the point, I was sorry when my stepmother came to the school to take me back home, or the place I wanted to stay away from. I had come to like the place, at least more than I did the hole to which I was returning. You will not be surprised when I say that peace did not reign long at home, and in a few weeks I was back in the Detention Home. I was returned to my half-brothers' and half-sisters' home (it wasn't my home). I ran away again and was arrested for the charge of being a professional run-away. Well, to some young boys and to me at that time, before I really knew anything, that was something to be proud of. A fellow gets over that idea after he gets older and done a little thinking for himself.

Well, as a matter of course, being a professional runaway, I went to St. Charles School for Boys. A school, I now say, should be turned into an or-phans' home instead of being a breeding place for crime. I am making a rough estimate when I say 60 per cent of all boys turned out of that school are out in the same old path of former life. I know. I meet boys that I was acquainted with there. Here is the probable thing they'll say: "When did you get out?" And I'll ask him, "Are you working?" "Naw," is the answer. "There is a joint (meaning a place to rob) I'm going to make soon and that will put me on my feet, and then I'll go to Frisco." That's what most of them say, and I've met a lot of old St. Charles chums during the last few months.

Well, I did sixteen months the first time out at St. Charles, and I'll tell you that was like sixteen years. I got mighty lonesome. There wasn't anybody at home who cared to go to see me or cared much what happened to me. Out there they had officers as boys' captains, and other boy petty officers who had the drop on you. It gives them an advantage over you, and if they have any grudge against you, they can be mighty dirty.

Here is a outline of the way they treat you at St. Charles: For talking or whispering or sometimes for sneesing, you will get beat up with a strap or about anything that is handy. If you try to report it to the family officer, he'll say, "He's the captain of the cottage, he knows best." While downstairs the captain will be telling of his exploits on stealing, to the other boys, who sit around with their eyes bulging out and their mouths gaped open admiring him. Of course, the captain knows best. Well, you can bet he knows about as much about criminal exploits and what's the best way to pull off a stick-up or blow up a bank. These fellows when they get to telling stories of their ex-ploits forget what's truth. The little fellows from a country town get their ears full about the first night in that crime-breeding place.

How can a boy reform when he gets the germ of criminality in him? Jail cannot reform no man, woman, or child. They have to reform themselves. They can do it if they had a little will-power and a little encouragement from some friend. Jail will only scare a man a short time after he is released. Then the same confident feeling comes back to him when he gets with the old gang. The germ gets in his brain and commands, "Steal, steal." But will-power will save a man if he's got any will-power whatsoever. If a criminal goes back home and out from jail his mind is dead, and he is ignorant and his brain only functions one way. The germ of criminality will say, "Steal," and he steals. If he wants to reform himself, will-power will do it, with encouragement from a good helper, as I said before. Jail only makes him defy the police and the law. But sometimes a boy comes out of jail and he has a mother and a good father to influence him to go straight. But in most cases that I have known, he always meets up with his jail friends, and they guide him in the way that he goes. Friends good or bad make us do what we do. If they are bad, then we are bad; if they are good, then we are good. A fellow gets bad through bad associates. You may get away with everything from the police, but you will get caught sooner or later. A fellow sometimes dies escaping, but he dies a criminal.

In many cases stepmothers or stepfathers, in most instances, will lead the boy to ruin. Like in my case. She nagged me, beat me, insulted me, drove my sisters and brothers and me out of the home. Favored her children, and I became a runaway. She will repay some day, if not in this world, in the next.

Well, to go on: After I left St. Charles, I stayed home a little while. Home was just like it always was, and I was worse. It got so I had an instinct to run away just to get out of her (stepmother's) reach. A few weeks out of St. Charles, and I went back for running away, as usual. I spent twenty-two more months. Just think, forty-three months of my young life on account of a selfish, no good, and hell-bent woman! I sometimes wondered how my father got to marry that woman. Her children just thought they had it all over us children. If we touched one of her children, then we got it from her. Well, maybe they had as much right as we did, but we just couldn't live there together. But after I left St. Charles the second time I had a confident feeling that I could steal and get away with it. I didn't care much what happened to me; it looked like fate was against me. The police were always watching for me and expecting me to break loose. Nobody thought I amounted to anything. I was getting more nerve all the time. The germ was getting ready to hatch at the best opportunity. The St. Charles parole officer and a good friend of his tried to help me. They got work for me, visited me, and talked nice to me, but I met old friends from St. Charles, and I thought, What's the use of trying? As I said before, a fellow's friends make him. I got tired of being good, the germ of criminality was too strong. I didn't have any will-power. I wanted to bum and make my living by begging, or any easy way. I didn't see any reason for working if I didn't have to. Fate was against me, anyway.

I went to St. Charles the third time, doing eighteen months. These eighteen months, plus the other two times, is fifty-six months, and five months in the Parental School is sixty-one months; five years in jail before I was sixteen years old. That's what made me a criminal. Doing time for practically nothing at all. Just running away from a home where I couldn't live in peace. I was well educated in crime, was disgusted with life. I came out of St. Charles and got a job, but got disgusted and quit. It seemed like everybody on the street thought I was a criminal and crooked. If I asked for a job, they always looked at me as if to say, "You crook, what jail are you out of?" I believed the strangers on the street thought that I was either a moron or an ex-convict.

Well, a few weeks out of St. Charles and I met an old friend from St. Charles, and we made up our minds to steal. We would walk up beside a drunk, bump into him, jostle him around, and then pickpocket him. You see how I became a criminal, by turning to bad company when I was disgusted with life. These drunks were all bums. But they had money. In that year the railroad and coal strikes were on. Well, these bums would go out and scab, and that made us want to steal off of them all the more because they had so much more money, and we didn't like scabs. These bums would go out of town to work as a scab, and they'd come to Chicago every pay day. The first crack out of the box they would go to a moonshine house on West Madison Street, the bum district, and near the old-time red-light district. They would go in and drink and soon be drunk with the rot-gut they gave you for fifteen cents a glass. It's like paying fifteen cents to die. Anyway, the drunk would come out and we'd follow him until we'd see a dark place to stop him and nail him and take his money. But the professional jack-roller gets it easier by asking for matches and then putting the matches in the pocket where his money is, then relieving him of the money, and the bum wins the matches. That's a thing I learned from a fellow at St. Charles who was a professional pickpocket and "jack-roller." We couldn't go on without getting caught, so one night, my buddy and I were standing on the corner and a drunk was on the corner signifying that he had lots of money. We followed him to his hotel. He wrote his name, and we looked at the register for his name and room number, which we found. We registered for a room on the same floor; when he went up, we followed. We waited thirty minutes and I went to his room. He was sick and vomited on the floor, showing that Chicago moonshine kills a man. Well, I took the bum's traveling bag to our room and ripped it open. It didn't have any money in it, but I got caught by a policeman. I was taken to the Boy's Court and sent to the Pontiac Reformatory, and you are a real criminal when you leave there.

The Reformatory is located in Pontiac, Illinois. When a prisoner is delivered there by the sheriff, he is "shook down," or, in plain words, searched for what he has in his pockets. He must take all his clothes off and take a bath. His hair is clipped off and his finger prints taken, body measured, and body scars recorded. That is taken for future identification. He also has the honor of having his picture taken. After his prison clothes are donned he looks and begins to feel like a horned convict, with round cap and blue clothes. They are called "fish" by the officials and prisoners until they are there six months. After measurements are taken, you are assigned to a cell, given a big tablespoon to eat with and a big red handkerchief. When I got my head shaved, put on the skull cap and blue suit, and was assigned to a cell, I knew I was a criminal. I never thought of it so much before. Before, I was just a professional runaway; now I was a criminal. I sat in my cell and thought and thought. It was different from St. Charles and the Parental School, for I did not feel like a criminal in those places. I didn't know before what it was like to be a criminal. I really became a criminal there. I cannot get away from the idea. When I ask for work, it seems that people think that I am a criminal.

If you commit a breach of discipline you go to court. The court is comprised of the assistant superintendent and a captain. They try you. If you are guilty, you go to the screens or "the hole," as the prisoners call it. It is a cell with nothing in it but a toilet, bowl, and a big screen running down the corridor. The prisoner cannot see out or have anything to eat or smoke pushed in to him.

You get books twice a week, and some magazines. The books and magazines are what saved my life down there.

They look on a fellow with contempt down there if he's in for petty thieving. They used to kid me because I was only a "jack-roller." They said, "That's like taking a penny from a blind man or robbing milk from a baby, and a fellow ought to stay there for life for stealing from a poor man like a drunk." After a while I didn't tell them why I was sent there. They figured the sentence was all the same, whether you robbed a bank or picked the pockets of a beggar. Most of the fellows think they didn't get a square deal, and they're going out to get even. They always talk about the old life and what they're going to do when they get out. Some of them take it hard and get sadlike, and others are hardened to it and say they're on a twelve months' leave. Most of them feel inclined to go straight as soon as they leave, but jail doesn't make a fellow go straight—it's will-power and good friends.

Well, I was released from Pontiac. Of course I was glad to get out, but I was disgusted with life. I was a criminal. I didn't care much what happened. There was no place to go, and everybody knew I was a criminal and an ex-convict. I tried to get work, but people must have seen that I was a criminal. It seemed that I had made a mess of life. It would have been better if I had never been born. Yet I figured it wasn't all my fault. Like most boys who go wrong, I didn't have much of a home to start with. Boys get into bad company, and they listen to that company and don't care what anybody else says.

When I get blue, I want to go back to the old life. I know the old germ of criminality is still there. I would like to have some more education and learn a trade, but the odds are against me. With a criminal reputation and as an ex-convict, I couldn't do much. Besides, we have to have a laboring class—somebody has to do the dirty work. My father died while I was in St. Charles, and they wouldn't let me go to his funeral. That was a mean trick, and I'll never forget it. My stepmother is married again, the third time, and she is the same as before. If I ever get a chance to testify against her, I will stay on the witness stand as long as I can. She started me on the downward path.

PHOENIX BOOKS
in Sociology

PHOENIX BOOKS
in Political Science and Law

PHOENIX BOOKS
in History